MW01200774

Abdellatif Laâbi

IN PRAISE OF DEFEAT

Poems Selected by the Author

Translated from the French by
Donald Nicholson-Smith

archipelago books

Archipelago Books
232 3rd Street #A111
Brooklyn, NY 11215
www.archipelagobooks.org

Library of Congress Cataloging-in-Publication Data available upon request.

Distributed by Penguin Random House
www.penguinrandomhouse.com

Archipelago Books gratefully acknowledges the generous support from
Lannan Foundation, l'Institut Français, the National Endowment for the Arts,
the New York City Department of Cultural Affairs,
and the New York State Council on the Arts, a state agency.

PRINTED IN THE UNITED STATES OF AMERICA

IN PRAISE OF DEFEAT

TRANSLATOR'S ACKNOWLEDGMENTS

For invaluable help and advice of many kinds, I wish to thank Jocelyne Barque, Pierre Joris, Cathy Pozzo di Borgo, and Alyson Waters. I am much indebted, naturally, to Jill Schoolman and her team at Archipelago. As so often, I am irretrievably indebted to my fiercest editor, Mia Nadezhda Rublowska. And I owe a very special thanks to Abdellatif Laâbi for his cordial assistance, not to mention his considerable patience.

D. N.-S.

CONTENTS

ABDELLATIF LAÂBI : SO MANY BETWEENS!

I am not the sort of nomad
who seeks the well
that a resident has dug
I drink little water
and I walk
well away from the caravan
　　　　—Abdellatif Laâbi

In 1966 the great German-language poet Paul Celan, an exile living in
Paris, France, called his new book of poems, to come out the following
year, *Atemwende*, compounding the nouns for breath and change; that
same year, a young Moroccan poet by the name of Abdellatif Laâbi
(born in the city of Fez in 1942) called his newly founded magazine,
Souffles, meaning "Breath" in the plural. I translated Celan's title as
Breathturn, i.e. a turning of, a change of, the breath. Something –
poem, movement, event – that wants to bring real change, does, has
to, take the breath away in order to effect this change and in the same
movement, it – poem or event – gives new directions to one's (next)
breath – one's pneuma, the systole/diastole that is the one certain way
we know that we are alive. In Morocco, Laâbi and friends wanted and
needed to draw many free, new and unsettling breaths, *des souffles* – and
the magazine by that name indeed did just that and was immediately
and has remained until today the great North African avant-garde

poetry magazine of the period. In Paris, Mohamed Khair-Eddine showed me a copy just before I embarked for America in late 1967 and I realized immediately that if poetry in French was to be again of essential use it would need to be retooled there, in a Maghreb struggling to create itself as a new, independent and revolutionary society, far away from a Paris living on its pre-war modernisms. *Souffles* took one's breath away, heralding the changes being made in Maghrebian poetry while proposing changes that needed to be made in the life of the people – that is, it could not but be a politically revolutionary magazine too. The absolute seriousness of Laâbi and his friends concerning this need for change, for an *Atemwende* at every level did not escape the notice of the powers that be, and the magazine was eventually censored and in 1972 Laâbi was jailed, tortured and submitted to all the humiliations a dictatorship will submit its opponents to. Abdellatif survived, kept writing poems, letters, prose, essays, producing a continuous and courageous witnessing to his and this society's fate. In 1980 he was released and in 1985 he moved to Paris where he still lives most of the time, in that permanent exile that seems to be the lot of so many of the century's best poets and doers – a poet, from Greek "poesis" to make, to do, is or should be, and in Laâbi's case is, indeed, a doer, an activist. In recent years he has been able to return and live part of the time in Morocco, though this is not without its dangers, as some painful misadventures two years ago prove.

* * *

Abdellatif Laâbi is without a doubt the major francophone voice in Moroccan poetry today. It may – and does, especially for some of the arabophone poets of the Maghreb & the Mashreq – bring up the question of why should a Moroccan author write in the colonial language after his country's independence? The most forceful way I have heard this question answered is by the Algerian poet and novelist Kateb Yacine who, when asked by journalists after Algeria gained its independence in 1962 following an eight-year war, if he would now write in Arabic, responded: "We won the war. We'll keep French as the spoils of war." Kateb went on to say that for a Maghrebian to write in Arabic would simply be to submit to an earlier, if more acculturated colonial domination, given that the autochthonous cultures are Berber with their own languages (Tamazight) and writing (Tifinak). Be that as it may, the multilingualism of the Maghreb has made for a very rich, multilayered tapestry of writing and, as I have shown elsewhere, it is exactly in those ex-colonies or ex-protectorates that an enriched French has made for a poetry more impressive than the relatively pale "metropolitan" version. Abdellatif Laâbi's language is proof of this.

He writes with a quiet, unassuming elegance that holds and hides the violence any act of creation proposes. Every creation is of course a breaking apart, a making of fragments – making *is* breaking – something Laâbi states *ab initio* in his poem *Forgotten Creation*: "In the beginning was the cry / and already discord." And this poem – as does most of his vast oeuvre – follows the movements of this cry, tracing its starts and stops, circling its essential enigma, descrying all the false mysteries

and hopes and fantasies it gives rise to, despite itself. Creating itself, the poem learns that "where nothing is born / nothing changes," and that eternity is but "an impenetrable jar / no magic will open." But the poem, Laâbi insists, will get us inside this act of imaginative creation. It is exactly the processual nature of his poetics, demanding a close listening to both inside and outside worlds, and the will and courage to follow changing meanders as the outside historical situation and the personal ecology of the poet's world evolve, at times clash, but always inform – taking careful account of both the "in" and the "'form" the word proposes – his work.

If the one constant in Laâbi's life has been writing – in the early prison volume *Beneath the Gag, the Poem* he framed it thus: "Write, write, never stop" – it is however also clear that there has been an evolution throughout his writing career. The earlier work shows all the outward projective force and explosive power the discovery of revolutionary possibilities immediately succeeded by the experience of injustice, jail and torture under a profoundly flawed and paranoid political system entails. The drive, jaggedness, mutilated syntax, dissociative, near-surreal, and explosive verse associating a sharply analyzed exterior world and an internal turmoil and questioning can remind the reader of some of the writings of the American Beat poets: this is indeed a Maghrebi "Howl." It is interesting to note, as Laâbi did on the occasion of a meeting earlier this year, that at that time he and the *Souffles* writers were unaware of the American poetry scene, and thus of the Beats and other "protest poetry" which they were to

discover only some time later. They were however knowledgeable about avant-garde traditions in European and especially French poetry from Rimbaud on through the surrealists, and, given their political readings, of some of the Russian avant-garde and of poets such as Pablo Neruda and Nazim Hikmet.

If over the years Laâbi has also produced a range of prose works – from novels, memoirs, tales, and essays, to plays and several volumes of interviews – poetry has clearly been the guiding light of his work. It is in following the changes the decades brought about in his poetics, that we can trace Laâbi's development, which has morphed from the early work described above to a quieter, lyrical voice – quieter, but in no way less searching, less demanding, less questing. The volumes of the last ten years may look deceptively simple at the level of their lyric line and language at quick glance (though the multi- or at least double-cultured metaphors remain often stunningly potent), but don't pre-judge: this is in no way a self-satisfied *Altenstil*; this is, rather, the calm, easy-breathing simplicity of achieved yet always again questioned wisdom, after a life of struggle. Maybe one should think about Laâbi's achievement here as Blakean, at the level of both *poesis* and lived life: it is the clarity of an innocence regained, with much exertion, after having gone through all the experience a human can take. It is the achieving of alchemical gold after many decades of labor in the double pelican of life and writing.

My own attraction to Laâbi's work over the years has been rooted in my fascination for what I've come to call "betweeness," that state of

exile (voluntary or not), of one's de facto multilingual (and thus non-linear) space in a post-colonial situation (and I'd argue that we all are post-colonials to some extent). Here is how he defined this space of betweenness some twenty years ago:

> I truly feel myself located on this hinge of being between life and death…, between a sun that is dying and another one whose rising has been confiscated, between two planets, two humanities that turn their backs to each other, between the feminine part in myself and my status as a male (which however has no desire to change gender), between two cultures that don't stop misapprehending each other, two languages that speak themselves so continuously in my mouth that they make me stammer, between the madness of hope and despair's just returns, between a country of origin that dribbles away and another country, an adopted one, that isn't able to firm itself, between a "natural" tendency toward meditation and an irrepressible need for action, between belonging and non-belonging, nomadism and sedentariness…So many betweens!

And Laâbi, in his life and in his work, has shown us the elegance and graciousness it takes to accomplish this task. What it takes to reside in this betweenness is negative capability, i.e. (in Keats's words) "when a man is capable of being in uncertainties, mysteries, doubts, without any irritable reaching after fact and reason." For Laâbi that means, for

example, to see the question of "identity" as something that is "more of a project than something acquired at birth." Culturally and ideologically this is of great importance in his world – where the culture given at birth is a knot of religion and politics that cannot be untangled – and in which "identitarism is one of the oldest and most insidious forms of integrism," which makes "voluntary servitude the price of belonging."

What makes this path in between so many in-betweens walkable, livable? How does this manifold doubleness not end up simply becoming a permissive fog in which one gets lost, voluntarily or involuntarily – or act outside the view of the world? Laâbi has been clear that his essential battle has been the one he fights against the hiatus between discourse and praxis, between thought and action, between the work – including that of *poesis*, of poetry – and the man. As he puts it: "For me ethics is the basis of politics as much as of literature or thinking." It is this struggle, what he calls his "solitary-solidary struggle," deeply committed, deeply political, yet situated outside any ideological system, a struggle toward the construction of an ethics able to equal the complexities of our world, that has been his compass.

The rest is poetry.

Pierre Joris

from

LE RÈGNE DE BARBARIE

THE REIGN OF BARBARISM

(1965-1967)

ŒIL DE TALISMAN

meurt tout
cerveau rapiécé le long des cryptes

                        meurt

meurt
      logos des cités
raison meurt
            broyée dans les rides
sans le secours des mains
meurt cerveau de grisaille

              meurt
proche la nuit où tant de chapelets

                    s'égrènent
pour le retour de l'aurore
que disent les sphinx

                quand impossible le retour
eux-mêmes ont vieilli
lassés de leur alliance

           avec le vent

maintenant
je cherche à ma tribu

           un langage

TALISMAN'S EYE

everything dies
patched-up brain down in crypts

                                       dies

    logos of cities

                                       dies

reason dies

           crushed by wrinkles
with no help from hands
brain with its gray cells

                     dies
night approaches with so much telling

                             of rosaries

for the break of a new day
as the sphinxes say

                 when none is possible
they themselves having grown old
weary of their alliance

                  with the wind

now
I seek a language

               for my tribe

qui ne soit pas un alliage
viennent à mes phalanges
                    les cyclones d'arganiers

collier de guêpes
                    à ma gorge de terre
c'est mon atroce lucidité
comme un miroir
                    rouillé de souvenirs
où vient cogner l'Histoire

maintenant je sais de quel pouvoir je suis investi
des peuples parcourent ma langue
quand nuit de flammes
                    édifie le silence
à coups de pilon
                    j'invente des berceuses

c'est mon atroce lucidité
qui ébouriffe ma voix
                    au rythme des caravanes
c'est mon atroce lucidité

that is not a hybrid
let cyclones of argan trees

                come join my fingers

collar of wasps

            around my throat of clay
my awful lucidity
like a mirror

            rusty with memories
that are the butt of History

now I know what power inhabits me
peoples run through my language
while flaming night

               constructs silence
with hammer blows

            I compose lullabies

my awful lucidity
that ruffles my voice

            to the caravans' cadence
my awful lucidity

qui me taille un âge
                    à la dimension du désert

maintenant
            j'ai besoin de dégueuler
                                des strates de narcotiques
et fumée de fumier
                    mots de raison pâles comme une tisane
je jette ces livres où j'ai appris l'orgueil

me voilà ici
            présent là
velu de nuit
            hérissé de guêpes
avec cette fragrance de muscles
comme une ossature de chameau
prêt à bondir sur la route
                    en un jappement

regardez donc si mes seins
                            ne bourgeonnent de maléfices
mais qu'on me laisse quelques veinules

that carves me out an era
                as wide as the desert

now
            I need to vomit up
                            layers of narcotics
and steaming manure
                        words of reason pale as herb tea
and throw away books that taught me pride

here I am
            present
night-hairy
            bristling with wasps
with that perfume of the muscles
that camel's boniness
ready to bound down the road
                            yelping

look and see if my breasts
                        are not bursting with maledictions
but leave me a few blood vessels

seulement quelques nerfs
     rien qu'un doigt
et je retracerai sur mon parchemin
une nouvelle cosmogonie
      dans l'harmonie totale de ses éléments

entendez le choc des idiomes
      dans ma bouche
la soif des naissances
entendez le clapotis des sueurs
       sous mes aisselles
la course des biceps
poussée de ma faune intérieure
       bonds de cavernes
plume ensanglantée
     ma tête sur chaque muraille
la chevauchée de mon souffle
éjectant des planètes
     dans ses éruptions

me voilà
   torrentiel à mon déluge
me labourant les angles

just a few nerves
                        nothing but a finger
and I shall outline on my parchment
a new cosmogony
                        its elements in perfect harmony

hear the clash of languages
                        in my mouth
the thirst for new births
hear the swish of sweat
                        at my underarms
the ripple of my biceps
driven by my inner fauna
                        springing from caves
pen bloodied
                  my head against every wall
my breath at the gallop
spewing planets
                  in its eruptions

here I am
            torrential in full flood
working my crannies

les cratères oubliés à mon incandescence
moi Atlas
        zébré de soleil
                à peuplades diurnes
récoltant dans mes chutes et mes gorges
l'écume piaffante d'un devenir
demandez aux vautours le goût de mon venin
callosité de serres
           ma grille de malédictions
proférateur je suis
          édifiant à l'insoumission
                   un royaume

ne me cherchez pas dans vos archives
effrayés par mes dénonciations
                je ne suis pas de la nature de l'écrit
cherchez-moi plutôt dans vos entrailles
lorsqu'une cavale de vers
           distord vos tripes
cherchez-moi dans l'urine des fièvres
dans le paludisme des ruelles
là
   dans la boue des cataractes
écrasez mes noms interdits

craters overlooked in my incandescence
I Atlas
      striped by the sun
                    of diurnal tribes
gathering up in my descents and ravines
the impatient foam of a future
ask the vultures what my venom tastes like
ruggedness of my grip
                    iron grid of my maledictions
accuser I am
           building a kingdom
                    of insubordination

do not seek me in your archives
fearful of my censure
           writing is not in my nature
look for me rather in your innards
when a host of worms
           distorts your gut
look for me in the urine of fever
in the malaria of the backstreets
and there
        in the mud of cataracts
erase my forbidden names

marchez sur les sorts que j'irradie
mais à mon cri
cassez des cruches de miel
égorgez des taureaux noirs sur les seuils des mosquées
nourrissez mille et mille mendiants
alors je viendrai
                    vous cracher dans la bouche
crever vos tumeurs
                    expulser vos maux ataviques
encore je vous préfère
                    en la droiture de vos socs
mes frères aux mains rugueuses
mes frères au sommeil de racines

venu
        jeté bas
                    par-dessus bord
étranger à la course des planètes
entre ciel et néant
surgi
        d'une chiquenaude
                    au début de la parole
je n'ai pas connu la pesanteur
                    la mathématique des révolutions

                    stamp out the spells that I cast
but at my call
break jars of honey
slit the throats of black bulls at mosque doors
feed beggars by the thousands
then I shall come
                    to spit in your mouth
destroy your tumors
                    rid you of your ancient ills
I still prefer you
                    in the straightness of your plowshares
my brothers with your rough hands
my brothers who sleep like roots

come
        tossed down
                    overboard
stranger to the course of planets
between sky and void
sprung forth
            in the blink of an eye
                        at the birth of speech
I know nothing of weightiness
                    or the mathematics of revolutions

arabe
      berbère
            homme plus encore
avec cependant cette marque
                  cette voix
                        indéfectibles

venu de vos lendemains
                fossoyeur de ruines
que ne prendrai-je sur moi
                  les erreurs de la nuit
et sans bride
           résonner les heurtoirs
pour que chaque seuil
               me tende ses logarithmes

oui
    je sommeille
depuis les salines de la montagne
une oreille suspendue à la roue du temps
je laisse pousser des bras
                pour mûrir un réveil
je ris oui je ris dans mon rêve
regardez mes paupières

Arab
    Berber
        above all human
but with this indestructible voice
            this mark

come from your tomorrows
           gravedigger of ruins
not to take upon myself
          the errors of the night
but unrestrainedly
        to hammer with doorknockers
until every doorway
      offers up its logarithms

yes
    I slumber
in mountain salt mines
an ear hearkening to the wheel of time
I let new arms grow
         to enhance an awakening
I laugh yes I laugh in my dream
look at my eyelids

que les caravaniers inséminent de germes
et mon œil terrifiant
                    précis
                              comme un sablier

seeded by caravaneers
and my terrifying eye

              accurate

                     as a sandglass

from

SOUS LE BÂILLON, LE POÈME

BENEATH THE GAG, THE POEM

(1972-1980)

CHRONIQUE DE LA CITADELLE D'EXIL

Écrire, écrire, ne jamais cesser. Cette nuit et toutes les nuits à venir. Quand je suis enfin face à moi-même et que je dois déposer mes bilans. Plus d'uniforme. Je ne suis plus l'arpenteur égaré d'un espace calculé pour la promenade réglementaire. Je n'obéis plus à la misère des ordres. Mon numéro reste derrière la porte. J'ai fini de boire, manger, uriner, déféquer. J'ai fini de parler pour appeler les choses par leurs noms usés. Je fume d'interminables cigarettes dont la fumée ressort des poumons en éclats de chaînes, en volutes âcres de rejets. La nuit carcérale a englouti les lumières artificielles du jour. Des étoiles échevelées peuplent la voûte des visions.

Écrire.
Quand je m'arrête, ma voix devient toute drôle. Comme si des notes inconnues s'accrochaient à ses cordes, poussées par des tempêtes étranges, venues de toutes les zones où la vie et la mort se regardent et s'épient, deux fauves aux couleurs inédites, chacun tapi, prêt à bondir, lacérer, anéantir le principe qui fonde l'autre.

Écrire.
Je ne peux plus vivre qu'en m'arrachant de moi-même, qu'en arrachant de moi-même mes points de rupture et de suture, là où je sens davantage la déchirure, la collision, là où je me fragmente pour revivre dans d'incalculables ailleurs : terre, racines, arbres d'intensité, effervescence grenue à la face du soleil.

CHRONICLE OF THE CITADEL OF EXILE

Write, write, never stop. Tonight and all the nights to come.
When I am at last face to face with myself. And must take stock. No
more uniform. No longer distractedly pacing a measured area for
the regulation exercise period. No more obeying wretched orders.
My number still on the other side of the door. When I am done
with drinking, eating, urinating, defecating. Done with talking, with
calling things by their worn-out names. I light endless cigarettes
whose smoke emerges from my lungs in broken chains, bitter swirls
of rejection. Prison night has gobbled up the artificial light of the
day. Ragged stars populate the vault of my visions.

Write.
When I stop, my voice begins to sound very peculiar. As though
unknown notes were clinging to its cords, driven by strange storms
from all those zones where life and death watch and spy on one
another, two oddly hued wild animals, each crouched ready to spring,
ready to slash and destroy the other's essential nature.

Write.
I can live now only by wrenching myself away from myself, by
wrenching away from myself my points of rupture and suture, those
places where I most acutely feel splits and junctures, where I cut
myself into pieces so as to return to life in unfathomable elsewheres:
earth, roots, trees of intensity, granular effervescence under the sun.

Écrire.
Quand l'indifférence s'évanouit. Quand tout me parle. Quand ma mémoire devient houleuse et que ses flots viennent se fracasser contre les rivages de mes yeux.

Je déchire l'amnésie, surgis armé et moissonneur implacable dans ce qui m'arrive, dans ce qui m'est arrivé.

Doucement mon émoi. Doucement ma détresse de ce qui fuit. Doucement ma fureur d'être.

Écrire.
Quand il m'est impossible de seulement penser à toi. Et que ma main n'en peut plus de brûler à ton absence là, ton souffle régulier ou haletant, l'odeur de tes cheveux, l'infini de ton épaule, ce silence où je devine coulant tout doucement en moi chaque variation de ta sensibilité. Tu déplaces une main, tu croises ou décroises les jambes, tes paupières cillent, et je sais l'exact frisson qui te traverse, le moment où cette lumière t'incommode, l'instant où tes narines frémissent à la fragrance qui vient de naître, l'image, oui l'image filante qui a brouillé tes iris. Tant de bonheur, est-ce possible ? Tu as la chair de poule seulement au bras gauche et tu plonges de nouveau dans cette vague mutuelle qui nous berce.

Mais doucement ma tendresse. Doucement ma fringale de certitude. Doucement mon rêve destructeur d'aphasie.

Write.
When indifference vanishes. When everything speaks to me. When my memory gets choppy and its waves break against the shores of my eyes.

I tear amnesia apart, rise up as an armed and implacable reaper of what is happening to me, of what has happened to me.

Gently my emotions. Gently my distress over what is disappearing. Gently my wild urge to live.

Write.
When it is impossible for me to even think of you. And my hand can no longer abide the burning from your absence. Impossible to think of your regular or panting breath, the smell of your hair, the infinity of your shoulder, that silence in which I feel every change in your sensations running gently through me. You move a hand, you cross or uncross your legs, your eyelids flutter, and I am aware of the precise sensation affecting you, the moment the light bothers you, the instant your nostrils quiver at a nascent perfume or an image, a fleeting image, confuses your irises. So much happiness – is it possible? You have goosebumps on your left arm only and you plunge once again into the mutual wave that cradles us.

But gently my tenderness. Gently my hankering for certainty. Gently my aphasia-destroying dream.

Écrire, écrire, ne jamais cesser.

Dix ans. C'est quoi dans l'équation d'une vie ? C'était une aube, au creux de ta chaleur. Quand t'étais-tu endormie ? Quand suis-je rentré ? Puis la sonnette s'est affolée. Ils défonçaient la porte à coups de poing. Nous avions su tout de suite. J'ai bondi hors du lit, me suis mis à la fenêtre, ai écarté précautionneusement le rideau. La voiture noire était en bas, dans la rue. Phares éteints. Une Fiat 125. Plus de doute. Puis nous avons entamé les préparatifs, comme pour un long voyage. La sonnette s'affolait. Ils défonçaient la porte à coups de poing.

Écrire.

Impossible de faire autrement. J'ai réfléchi à m'en trouer la cervelle sur ce besoin qui m'a investi. Depuis si longtemps. Et qui fait que la réalité qui se présente à moi est toujours fonction d'une autre, à venir. Qui fait que le présent est un projet permanent, le lieu où j'accumule la matière, les matériaux d'un édifice dont je ne connais encore rien, que je ne peux qu'appréhender comme la pulsation d'un nouvel organe qui s'est logé en moi, grossit à faire mal et petit à petit organise sa fonction. Comment dire cet espionnage vigilant et maniaque du réel ? Et son arène, c'est le vaste théâtre de nos luttes, de nos douleurs, du génocide et des résurrections, de toute vitalité qui ploie sous le joug du silence, de tous les cris clandestins, de toutes les mémoires décapitées.

Write, write, never stop.

Ten years. What does that mean in the estimation of a life? It was a dawn, curled up in your warmth. When did you fall asleep? When did I come in? Then the bell rang wildly. They were battering the door down with their fists. We knew right away. I leapt out of bed, went to the window, and cautiously drew back the curtain. The black car was down in the street. Headlights off. A Fiat 125. No more doubt possible. Then we began making our preparations, as if packing for a long trip. The bell was ringing wildly. They were battering the door down with their fists.

Write.

Impossible to do otherwise. I have racked my brains about this need which has taken me over. For such a long time now. And which means that the reality before me is always dependent on another reality, yet to come. Which means that the present is a permanent project, the place where I store the matter, the materials for an edifice that I still know nothing of, that I can apprehend only as the pulse of a new organ that has taken up residence in me, swelling painfully and gradually assuming its role. How to describe this vigilant, obsessive surveillance of the real? And its arena, the vast theater of our struggles, of our sufferings, of genocide and resurrections, of all the vitality bowed under the yoke of silence, all the smothered screams, all the beheaded memories.

J'ai réfléchi à m'en trouer la cervelle sur ce besoin qui m'a investi. Mais doucement ma lucidité. Doucement ma hargne contre les ténèbres de l'indicible.

Écrire.
Ce matin glacial de janvier. Premier jour d'exil. J'étais couché sur un banc, pieds et mains ligotés. Un chiffon me couvrait entièrement le visage. L'eau coulait, traversait le linge, se versait dans le nez. Impossible d'en boire.

– Verse par petites quantités, disait quelqu'un à un autre.

– Et toi, maintiens-lui la tête bien collée au banc, chuchotait la même voix.

– Verse encore, encore un peu, s'acharnait la voix.

– Ça suffit maintenant, concluait la voix.

On aurait dit une démonstration autour d'une table de dissection. « Conscience professionnelle », souci du travail « propre » et bien fait. Je ne les voyais pas. J'entendais des voix à distances inégales, le bruit des souliers raclant le sol. Des mains visqueuses aplatissaient ma tête contre le banc. J'étouffais lentement. Je pensais au rythme de

I have racked my brains about this need which has taken me over. But gently my lucidity. Gently my bile against the shadows of the indescribable.

Write.
That freezing January morning. First day of exile. I was laid on a bench, feet and hands tied. A rag completely covered my face. Water was running, penetrating the cloth, pouring up my nose. Impossible to swallow it.

"Pour it in little by little," said someone to someone else.

"You, hold his head tightly against the bench," whispered the same voice.

"Pour some more, a little more," urged the voice.

"That's enough now," concluded the voice.

It sounded like a demonstration over a dissecting table. Professionalism. Concern that the work be "clean" and well executed.

I could not see them. I heard their voices at various distances, the sound of their shoes scraping the floor. Sticky hands pressed my head flat against the bench. I was slowly suffocating. I was thinking

la résistance et de la mort pressentie. Mais quelle image, quel éclair d'idée de ce foisonnement pourraient rendre l'ampleur de ce moment où la ligne de vie se distendait, s'amincissait comme une corde à linge tirée violemment par les deux bouts et qui arrive au point où les fils commencent à craquer un à un ?

Écrire, ne pas s'arrêter.
À chaque page triompher de ce malaise, de ce sentiment d'inanité qui me paralyse par à-coups. Peut-on écrire, seulement écrire pour ébranler la férule de l'état de siège, lorsque chaque rue est devenue un traquenard, lorsque les réduits de la torture affichent complet, lorsqu'un peuple entier se vide quotidiennement de son sang, lorsqu'un pays est mis aux enchères, découpé en petits et gros lots de lupanars, de bases de meurtre, de chairs-graisse à machines, de mains esclaves. Et que dire que l'homme-de-la-rue, que le moindre adolescent jeté sur le trottoir du chômage et de l'errance ne connaissent et reconnaissent comme la face livide du malheur familier : attente, matraque, mépris, balles, haine solidifiée.

Mais doucement affres du doute. Doucement ma nausée. Doucement mon volcan irrédentiste.

Écrire.
Cette nuit devant moi, neuve de son silence, des mots qui germent, s'ordonnent et qui viendront entrelacer mon souffle, l'agencer en voix. Il fait bon fumer.

of the rhythms of resistance and of death in prospect. But what image, what flash of an idea of distension could render the extent of a moment when the line of life is stretched thin as a clothesline pulled violently from both ends until its fibers begin to snap one by one?

Write, do not stop.
How, on every page, to vanquish this distress, this feeling of futility that keeps jolting and paralyzing me? Can writing, simply writing, shake the rule of a state of siege, when every street has become a death trap, when the torture chambers have no vacancies, when an entire people is losing blood every day, when a country is on auction, divided up into lots large and small, brothels, murder sites, machine-greasing flesh, hands of slaves. And what can one say about the fact that the man in the street – even the merest out-of-work youth thrown onto that street as a vagrant – knows and recognizes what is in fact the leaden face of everyday misery: waiting police batons, contempt, bullets, hate materialized.

But gently my abyss of doubt. Gently my loathing. Gently my volcano of irredentism.

Write.
The night before me, new in its silence, words germinating, getting into order, ready to intermingle with my breath and generate a voice. It feels good to smoke.

Un train siffle dans le lointain. S'approche. Essaim de lucioles invisibles. Chaleur dans les compartiments. Le bar bondé de consommateurs. Voyageurs somnolents aux rêves cahotés, plus ou moins érotiques.

Un autre train s'en détache, roule dans la plaine andalouse, me restitue Grenade. Nous deux à Grenade. Tout était émerveillement : s'accouder à un zinc pour prendre un petit verre de jerez, se donner la main, épeler le nom des rues, regarder travailler les artisans calligraphes, dépositaires de l'héritage de l'Alhambra, demander son chemin à des passants avec lesquels le dialogue même le plus élémentaire vous transmet un frisson de fraternité, dormir, se réveiller au même degré d'intensité. Grenade où il était déchirant de s'aimer.

Un train siffle dans le lointain. S'approche. Me traverse de part en part. Se détache du tunnel de mon corps. Et de nouveau le silence que trouble si peu l'aboiement timide d'un chien probablement dérangé dans son assoupissement.

Écrire.
Au jour le jour l'étau. Prisonnier ! Qu'est-ce à dire ? Une cellule tout ce qu'il y a de plus cellule : 2,30 mètres x 1,30 mètre environ. Cubage dans les normes paraît-il. Murs blanchis à la chaux, oh si chichement. Une ampoule suintant la misère de ses 25 watts

A train whistles in the distance. Draws closer. Swarm of invisible fireflies. Heat in the compartments. Bar packed with customers. Passengers drowsy, jolted from their dreams, more or less erotic.

Another train emerges, running across the Andalusian plain, restoring Granada to me. The two of us in Granada. Everything was a wonder: leaning on a bar with little glasses of sherry, holding hands, spelling out street names, watching the professional scribes at work, embodiment of the Alhambra's heritage, asking the way of passers-by with whom even the most trivial exchange of words gave us a frisson of fraternity, sleeping, awakening in just as intense a state. Granada, where it was heart-wrenching to be in love.

A train whistles in the distance. Draws closer. Runs right through me. Emerges from the tunnel of my body. And once again the silence, scarcely broken by the barking of a dog probably disturbed in his slumber.

Write.
Day after day the vise. Prisoner! What does that mean? A cell, the most cell-like of cells: roughly 2.3 meters by 1.3 meters. Cubic volume seemingly standard. Walls whitewashed, but oh so stingily. A lightbulb exuding the poverty of its 25 watts

encastrée dans le mur, mise hors d'atteinte par un verre dépoli massif, un w.-c. à la turque surmonté d'un robinet en cuivre, la petite fenêtre réglementaire avec les non moins réglementaires barreaux d'épaisseur respectable et, grand luxe, une petite étagère où le « pensionnaire » pourra ranger ses affaires. Devant vous, la porte grise avec son judas lui-même aveuglé par un système ingénieux de plaque métallique à glissière, à son tour perfectionné par un autre système de blocage constitué d'un fil de fer qui passe dans un anneau au milieu de la plaque et l'immobilise à la base. Vous avez enfin une plate-forme en maçonnerie enduite de ciment qui prend pompeusement la moitié de l'espace et reçoit la paillasse. C'est là que le pensionnaire trône, dort, fait ses cauchemars et parfois, au bout d'un dédale de raisonnements obscurs et d'hallucinations, décide de se suicider. Nous sommes bien sûr à la « Maison centrale », le joyau de la chaîne des pénitenciers du Pays du soleil.

Écrire.
Au jour le jour l'étau. Au jour le jour sa négation. Le ciel irréel et muet s'anime d'une foule de nuages alertes, reproduit la geste terrestre. Le soleil bondit par-dessus les murailles, renverse la grisaille et rassure sur l'imminence du printemps. L'air circule gonflé à bloc d'inextricables messages. Des oiseaux irrépressibles étalent leurs offrandes de couleurs, construisent, se reproduisent, apprennent à voler, braquent sur les yeux des miroirs flamboyants où se reflète la marche de la vie. Le rêve s'étoffe, devient vision organique de ce que

set into the wall and made inaccessible by thick frosted glass, a Turkish WC surmounted by a copper faucet, the regulation little window with its likewise regulation bars of respectable thickness and (luxury!) a small shelf on which the "guest" may place his belongings. Facing you, the gray door with its spy hole ingeniously occluded by a sliding metal plate itself enhanced by a blocking system consisting of a wire passing through a ring in the middle of the plate and holding it in place at the bottom. A final feature is a cement-covered stone platform, arrogantly taking up half the floor space, on which is laid a palliasse. This is where the guest sits, sleeps, endures his nightmares and sometimes, after making his way through a labyrinth of hazy reasoning and hallucination, decides to kill himself. Here we are, without a doubt, in the "Maison Centrale," jewel of the penitentiary network of the Land of the Sun.

Write.
Day after day the vise. Day after day its denial. The unreal and mute sky enlivened by a host of brisk clouds reflecting the movement of the earth. The sun leaps over the walls, reversing the grayness and announcing the imminence of spring. The air circulates chockfull of undecipherable messages. Irrepressible birds display their colorful plumage, build their nests, breed, learn to fly, serve our eyes as flashing mirrors reflecting life on the march. The dream bulks up, becoming an organic vision of whatever lucidity

la lucidité dévoile. Le futur n'a rien d'incertain, il irradie, sature le présent de sa matérialité.

Au jour le jour, ce prodige qui consiste à vivre, se transformer, mieux aimer, espérer plus fort, connaître le bonheur, abolir la solitude, battre au rythme cardiaque du monde, au cœur même de la citadelle érigée pour la mort lente, la dégradation, la soumission grégaire, le cynisme, la tristesse sauvage, l'exil humain. Alors il faudra bien, de cercle en cercle, réunir les fragments éparpillés, il faudra bien partir à cette nouvelle conquête de ses propres actes.

Écrire, écrire, ne jamais cesser.

L'itinéraire de notre transformation. De nous deux, qui a converti l'autre aux exigences d'amour ? Comment démêler dans ce patrimoine indivis les éblouissantes offrandes que tu m'as portées, les dons fougueux que j'ai mis entre tes mains ? Qu'est-ce qui fonde l'amour, le transfigure sans cesse ? Et qu'est-ce qui le rend tragique, muraille d'aveuglement et d'égoïsme ? Qu'est-ce qui le brise lorsqu'il se déroule comme tous les ruisseaux inconscients de l'existence et qu'est-ce qui le ressuscite des cendres et vieilles peaux d'hommes et de femmes anciens ?

Il y a tant de zones à régénérer en l'homme, tant de fenêtres à ouvrir en son cœur, tant de facultés à libérer de la caverne d'hibernation.

reveals. The future contains nothing uncertain: it irradiates and saturates the present with its materiality.

Day after day, the miracle that consists in living, transforming oneself, loving better, hoping more strongly, feeling happiness, abolishing solitude, keeping time with the cardiac rhythm of the world at the very center of a citadel dedicated to slow death, degradation, herd-like submission, cynicism, brutal sadness, human exile. And so we have to circle and circle around, bringing the scattered fragments back together; we really must set about reconquering our own acts.

Write, write, never stop.

The route followed by our transformation. Of the two of us, who was it who converted the other to the demands of love? How can we distinguish within this indivisible heritage of ours between the dazzling gifts you laid before me and the fiery gifts with which I endowed you? What is it that grounds love, and transfigures it unceasingly? And what turns it tragic, changes it into a wall of blindness and egotism? What interrupts it as it flows free like all the unconscious streams of existence, and what revives it amid the cinders and wrinkles of old men and women?

So many aspects of man call for regeneration, so many windows in his heart need opening, so many of his faculties must be freed from

Le plus difficile est bien de ne pas créer de nouvelles illusions au moment même où on détruit les anciennes. Car l'amour est un continent fragile, qui ne fait qu'émerger, un continent qu'éclaire son propre soleil et sur lequel nous ne faisons que débarquer. Et si nous connaissons bien le périple qui nous y a conduits, nous avons tant à explorer, et bien d'autres périples nous attendent.

Écrire.
Est-ce l'épreuve seule qui a fait de nous ce que nous sommes devenus, dans notre rapport l'un à l'autre, dans nos rapports aux autres ? Il a fallu nous connaître, nous faire mal, errer de piétinements en balbutiements, nous taire et nous isoler faute de comprendre, triompher allègrement lorsqu'un rayon de lumière venait nous révéler une nouvelle acception de la tendresse, épauler notre désarroi, nous ouvrir la voie pour une étape inédite. Puis nous nous sommes mis à parler à mesure que le monde autour de nous devenait plus réel, à mesure que la poésie nous humanisait, à mesure que notre peuple par ses luttes et ses sacrifices nous octroyait une patrie vivable, à mesure de notre propre réveil au don. Tout ce périple, au bout duquel nous avons découvert que nos mains se ressemblaient terriblement, où nous avons découvert la fraternité.

Écrire.
De nouveau cette nuit incommensurable. Un avion surgit brusquement dans le silence. Son vrombissement éclate comme des

the cavern of hibernation. The hardest thing, to be sure, is to avoid creating new illusions while destroying the old. For love is a fragile continent, one that is only now emerging, illuminated by its own sun, upon which we have only just made landfall. And even if we are well acquainted with the crooked path that has led us here, we have so much yet to discover, and many more twists and turns lie before us.

Write.
Was it our trials alone that made us what we have become in our relationship with each other and in our relationships with others? We had to get to know each other, hurt each other, lurch from stumbles to stutterings, fall silent and cut out ourselves off in incomprehension, yet briskly prevail when a ray of light taught us a new meaning of tenderness, supported us in distress, or opened the door to a fresh chapter. Then we started to talk as the world around us became more real, as poetry made us more human, as our people by virtue of its struggles and sacrifices provided us with a livable nation, and as we ourselves awoke to the meaning of commitment. Thanks to this whole long journey, at whose end we found that our hands were extraordinarily similar, we discovered fraternity.

Write.
Once again the incommensurable night. An airplane suddenly breaks the silence. Its reverberation explodes like wild aerial organ

orgues aériennes détraquées. Il doit s'apprêter à atterrir. Pourquoi est-ce si poignant ? Et mon corps comme une caisse de résonance qui fourmille de partout.

Tu vois, un rien déclenche en moi ta présence, ce qui ne peut être simple souvenir mais vécu vibratoire qui me secoue sur mon grabat, me serre la gorge, me fait déposer le stylo, allumer machinalement une cigarette et m'éloigne dans cet espace croisé qui défie le temps et où nous marchons côte à côte, comblés.

Écrire.
Dois-je l'avouer. Je n'ai qu'une relative confiance en les mots, quand bien même je les tourne et les retourne dans tous les sens, les prononce à haute voix pour vérifier si le timbre n'en est pas fêlé, s'il ne s'est pas glissé dans le nombre quelques unités de mauvais aloi. Et quand je les enfile et ordonne, je dois me relire et me relire pour m'assurer encore que ce que j'ai écrit n'est ni ésotérique ni étranger à ce qui est recevable comme le fonds commun de nos peines et espérances. Écrire est une telle responsabilité. Et du moment que je l'assume (oh oui je l'assume), il n'est pas possible de biaiser, de se contenter de l'à-peu-près. Il faut pouvoir défendre chaque mot, chaque phrase, et si possible n'avoir rien à défendre, faire en sorte qu'ils s'adressent et s'imposent à la sensibilité de chacun comme ce crépitement familier de la pluie indispensable à la terre, comme ces fleurs innombrables et souvent étranges sans lesquelles le printemps avorte.

music. It must be preparing to land. Why is this so poignant? Like a sounding-board, my whole body quivers.

As you see, anything at all triggers your presence in me, a presence which is certainly no simple memory but rather an actual vibration that shakes me on my palliasse, grabs me by the throat, causes me to put my pen down and mechanically light a cigarette, and conveys me into an intersected space that defies time, where we walk side by side, completely content.

Write.
I might as well admit it. My faith in words is only relative, even if I hold them up and examine them from every angle, and read them aloud to make sure that their tone is true and that inferior elements have not crept in among them. And when I string them together and organize them I am obliged to re-read and re-read until I am satisfied that what I have written is neither esoteric nor unacceptable with respect to our common fund of torments and hopes. Writing is such a great responsibility. And from the moment that I shoulder it (and, oh yes, I do), there can be no cutting corners, no making do with the more-or-less. You must be able to defend every word, every sentence, and if possible have nothing to defend by ensuring that they address and impress themselves upon the feelings of every reader as easily as the familiar pattering of the rain that is so essential to the earth or as the countless and often strange flowers without which there would be no spring.

Mais doucement mon intransigeance. Doucement démon rationnel de la poésie.

Écrire, écrire, ne jamais cesser. Cette nuit et toutes les nuits à venir. Encore une nuit où je ne peux qu'écrire, me heurter à ce silence qui me nargue dans son idiome d'exil. Je me tends entièrement pour explorer cette voix de la nuit carcérale.

J'écoute, et peu à peu j'en perçois l'harmonie, j'en parcours l'étendue, reçois comme en contrepoint ses échos sanglants. Je traque le silence, lui arrache la puissante rumeur contre laquelle ses digues cèdent de plus en plus, s'effondrent en un fracas qui m'éblouit et s'éparpillent dans la nuit.

Le pays vient à moi, chant aérien surgi du fond de l'histoire, forge d'incandescence et de sueurs, de muscles huilés battant l'enclume de la matière rebelle, semailles, moissons, pain et olives noires partagés, écume de thé brûlant dont on se passe le verre de main en main, trompes, musettes et tambours soulevant les ruelles en processions bariolées, rires et trémoussements d'enfants ivres de musiques et de parfums, chevilles rouges de femmes juchées sur des tables rondes, battant la mesure avec les pieds, les seins vibrant en mûres grenades de fraîcheur, frénésie de crotales, musiciens déconnectés égorgeant ostensiblement des violons surchauffés, électrocutant les tambourins, éventrant des luths dodus flambant de toutes leurs incrustations. Long silence puis le pays revient à moi,

But gently my intransigence. Gently oh rational demon of poetry.

Write, write, never stop. Tonight and all the nights to come. Another night when I can do nothing but write, confront this silence that provokes me with its idiom of exile. I brace myself to the full to explore the voice of the prison night.

I listen, and little by little I perceive that voice's harmony, assess its depth, receive as if in counterpoint its blood-soaked echoes. I track the silence down, detaching it from the potent murmur against which its dykes slowly give way until they collapse with a boom that stuns me and their fragments are scattered in the night.

The country comes to me, an airborne chant from the depths of history, a forge rife with incandescence and sweat, oiled muscles hammering the anvil of recalcitrant matter, seedtimes, harvests, bread and black olives shared, frothy scalding tea in glasses passed from hand to hand, horns, pipes and drums enlivening motley backstreet processions, laughter of turbulent children drunk with music and scents, red ankles of women perched at round tables keeping time with tapping feet, their breasts shaking like ripe pomegranates of freshness, frenzied castanets, unharmonized musicians shamelessly torturing overheated violins, electrocuting tambourines, and disemboweling chubby lutes emblazoned with a surfeit of decoration. A long silence, then the country comes back

la face ravagée, méconnaissable. Cris ici ou là, d'une rixe, d'un viol, d'un meurtre. Cris d'enfants aux yeux hagards fouettés pour apprendre et se taire. Cris de deuils et de pleureuses se lacérant les joues, s'arrachant les cheveux, battant le sol de leurs foulards, se tapant les cuisses et se cognant la tête contre les murs. Cris de nourrissons abandonnés dans les baraques des bidonvilles, dans la pénombre de tous les manques. Cris chauffés à blanc de malnutrition et de fièvres. Cris de femmes battues à mort par des mâles saouls et désespérés. Gémissements et râles de ces femmes terrorisées, embrassant les pieds de leur agresseur pour demander pitié, pour l'amour de Dieu, pour les enfants, pour les misères partagées. Cris de Mars portés par le vent de haine des insurgés, écoliers mitraillés en plein soleil des fausses indépendances, blindés dinosauriens contre de tout petits rêves pressentis dans la germination des jours, la marée du soleil, le sourire des hommes. Cris de mes camarades sous le perchoir, la pau de ara, la magnéto. Cris quand le cri devient espéranto de résistance, mélopée épique du drame humain et de l'espérance. Oh mes doux camarades, ma chair hallucinée, mon cœur gros d'amour à n'en plus pouvoir, vos yeux inoubliables de promesses, notre tendresse irrépressible.

Écrire.
À mi-chemin, debout, au fil de l'étau et des blessures, j'écris.
Passent les ans
        galopent

to me, its face ravaged, unrecognizable. Cries here and there, from a brawl, a rape, a murder. Cries of stricken-eyed children whipped to teach them to be quiet. Cries of mourning, of weepers scratching their cheeks, tearing their hair, swatting at the ground with their scarves, slapping their thighs, and knocking their heads against walls. Cries of infants abandoned in shantytowns in the shadow of every kind of deprivation. Cries from the white heat of undernourishment and fever. Cries of women beaten to death by drunk and desperate males. Groans and croaks of terrorized women kissing the feet of their aggressors and pleading for mercy in the name of God and for the sake of the children and the woes they all share. Martial cries raised by the gale of hate of insurgents, schoolchildren machine-gunned in the blazing sunshine of false independences, dinosaurian armored vehicles deployed against tiny dreams conceived in the burgeoning passage of days, the tide of the sun, the smile of men. Cries from my comrades hanging from the macaw's perch – the *pau de arara* – or subjected to the magneto. Cries when the cry becomes the esperanto of resistance, the epic recitative of human drama and hope. Oh my sweet comrades, my delusional flesh, my heart filled to breaking with love, your eyes unforgettable in their promise, our irrepressible tenderness.

Write.
Halfway there, on my feet despite the vise and the injuries, I write.
The years pass
     at a gallop

Les aiguilles sécateurs fauchent les cadrans
broient la main du cyclope
                    avachi sur son trône
Mon peuple marche
et j'existe
            rebelle

                    Maison centrale de Kénitra, janvier 1976

The hands like shears section the clock face
and crush the hand of the cyclops

                                                   gone to flab upon his throne

My people are on the march
and I exist

          rebel

                                    Kenitra Prison, January 1976

À MON FILS YACINE

Mon fils aimé
j'ai reçu ta lettre
Tu me parles déjà comme une grande personne
tu insistes sur tes efforts à l'école
et je sens ta passion de comprendre
de chasser l'obscurité, la laideur
de pénétrer les secrets du grand livre de la vie
Tu es sûr de toi-même
et sans le faire exprès
tu me comptes tes richesses
tu me rassures sur ta force
comme si tu disais : « Ne t'en fais pas pour moi
regarde-moi marcher
regarde où vont mes pas
l'horizon, l'immense horizon là-bas
il n'a pas de secrets pour moi »
Et je t'imagine
ton beau front bien haut
et bien droit
j'imagine ta grande fierté

Mon fils aimé
j'ai reçu ta lettre

TO MY SON YACINE

My darling son
I have received your letter
You already talk to me like a grown-up
you say how hard you try at school
and I feel your passion to understand
to chase away the shadows, the ugliness
to pierce the secrets of the great book of life
You are sure of yourself
And though not deliberately
you list your riches for me
you reassure me on your strengths
as if you were saying "don't worry about me
see me walk
see where my steps lead
the horizon, the vast horizon over there
has no secrets for me"
And I picture you
your fine brow
so high and straight
I picture your great pride

My darling son
I have received your letter

Tu me dis :
« Je pense à toi
et je te donne ma vie »
sans soupçonner
ce que tu me fais en disant cela
mon cœur fou
ma tête dans les étoiles
et par ce mot de toi
je n'ai plus peine à croire
que la grande Fête arrivera
celle où des enfants comme toi
devenus hommes
marcheront à pas de géant
loin de la misère des bidonvilles
loin de la faim, de l'ignorance et des tristesses

Mon fils aimé
j'ai reçu ta lettre
Tu as écrit toi-même l'adresse
tu l'as écrite avec assurance
tu t'es dit, si je mets ça
papa recevra ma lettre
et j'aurai peut-être une réponse
et tu as commencé à imaginer la prison
une grande maison où les gens sont enfermés

You say
"I think of you
and I give my life to you"
without an inkling
of what you do to me in saying that
my crazy heart
my eyes on the stars
and through this word from you
it is no longer hard for me to believe
that the great Feast will come
when children like you
now men
will walk with giant steps
far from the poverty of the shantytowns
far from hunger, ignorance and sadness

My darling son
I have received your letter
You wrote the address yourself
wrote it with confidence
you thought to yourself, if I put this
Papa will get my letter
and perhaps I'll have a reply
and you started to imagine the prison
a big house where people are locked up

combien et pourquoi ?
mais alors ils ne peuvent pas voir la mer
la forêt
ils ne peuvent pas travailler
pour que leurs enfants puissent avoir à manger
Tu imagines quelque chose de méchant
de pas beau
quelque chose qui n'a pas de sens
et qui fait qu'on devient triste
ou très en colère
Tu penses encore
ceux qui ont fait les prisons
sont certainement fous
et tant et tant d'autres choses
Oui mon fils aimé
c'est comme ça qu'on commence à réfléchir
à comprendre les hommes
à aimer la vie
à détester les tyrans
et c'est comme ça
que je t'aime
que j'aime penser à toi
du fond de ma prison

how many and why?
but then they can't see the sea
the forest
they can't work
to get their children enough to eat
You imagine something mean
something ugly
something that makes no sense
and makes you feel sad
or very angry
You think too
that those who made prisons
are certainly mad
and so very many other things
Yes my darling son
that is how one begins to think
to understand humans
to love life
to detest tyrants
and that is how
I love you
how I love to think of you
from the depths of my prison

QUATRE ANS

Cela fera bientôt quatre ans
on m'arracha à toi
        à mes camarades
                à mon peuple
on me ligota
        bâillonna
           banda les yeux
on interdit mes poèmes
             mon nom
on m'exila dans un îlot
de béton et de rouille
on apposa un numéro
sur le dos de mon absence
on m'interdit
les livres que j'aime
          les nouvelles
             la musique
et pour te voir
un quart d'heure par semaine
à travers deux grilles séparées par un couloir
ils étaient encore là
buvant le sang de nos paroles
un chronomètre
à la place du cerveau

FOUR YEARS

Four years soon now since
I was snatched from you
                    from my comrades
                                from my people
they tied me up
                gagged me
                        blindfolded me
they banned my poems
                        my name
they exiled me to an island
of concrete and rust
they placed a number
on the back of my absence
they deprived me of
the books I love
                of news
                        of music
and let me see you
fifteen minutes a week
through two sets of bars separated by an alley
and they were always there
drinking the blood of our words
with a timer
instead of a brain

MORT MIENNE

À trente-trois ans
voilà que je pense moi aussi
à la mort
Ce n'est pas de la mort en majuscules
qu'il s'agit
mais tout simplement de la mienne
qui peut survenir un jour ou l'autre
et avec l'expérience de laquelle
il faut que je règle quelques comptes
Ce ne sont pas des idées noires
ou « l'effroi métaphysique » qui m'empoignent
non
c'est tout à fait réaliste
lorsqu'on a encore des années à tirer en prison
et que l'on est jour et nuit
à la merci de ses tortionnaires

Mort mienne
je te veux douce comme ces rêves heureux
où malgré tous les obstacles
je parviens au bout du dédale
à saisir et caresser la main de ma bien-aimée
à recomposer la couleur de ses yeux

DEATH OF MINE

At thirty-three
here I am also thinking
of death
It is not death in capitals
that I mean
but quite simply my own
which may occur any day
and with the experience of which
I need to clear some things up
These are not black thoughts
or "metaphysical fright" overtaking me
no
but quite realistic thoughts
when you still have years of prison ahead
and you are night and day
at the mercy of your torturers

Death of mine
I want you as sweet as those sweet dreams
in which despite all the obstacles
I reach the end of the labyrinth
and take and caress the hand of my beloved
retrieve the color of her eyes

à sentir le pétale d'une larme
se former sur le flambeau de sa pupille
Douce je te veux
une seule image
résumant toutes les splendeurs de l'assaut humain
toutes les promesses que tiendra la vie
Je te veux
en un frémissement d'aurore
forêt de mains couvrant la planète
et des rires chauds et des tambours en furie
et des flûtes abolissant les vieilles vieilles solitudes

Tu pourras alors me taper sur l'épaule
mort mienne
et je te suivrai sans réticence
Je ne laisserai derrière moi
ni trésor caché
ni biens immobiliers
mais quelques paroles
pour l'avènement de l'homme
et cette tendresse miraculeuse
qui me permet
mort mienne
de défier ton regard mécanique
et de m'endormir paisiblement

feel the petal of a tear
gathering at the flame of her pupil
Sweet I want you
a single image
summing up all the splendor of the human venture
all the promise that life holds out
I want you
as a tremor of dawn
a forest of hands covering the planet
and warm laughter and furious drums
and flutes abolishing old old solitudes

Then you can tap me on the shoulder
death of mine
and I'll follow you without hesitation
I shall leave behind me
neither hidden treasure
nor real property
just a few words
for the advent of man
and the miraculous tenderness
that lets me
death of mine
defy your mechanical gaze
and fall peacefully asleep

en sachant que mes rêves
ne tomberont pas en poussière
comme mon écorce matérielle
mais fleuriront sur les sentiers
que les hommes empruntent
pour échanger des soleils
en se donnant l'accolade
et pour lutter

knowing that my dreams
will not go to dust
like my physical shell
but will flower by the pathways
humans take
to change suns
as they embrace
and to struggle

TU PARLES OU ON TE TUE*

« Tu parles ou on te tue »
Ils t'ont tuée Évelyne
Tu n'avais pas parlé

En trois phrases ordinaires
sans coryphée
                sans chœur
sans théâtre ni spectateurs
sans l'intervention des dieux ou leur absence
la voilà
        la tragédie
« Tu parles ou on te tue »
Ils t'ont tuée Évelyne
Tu n'avais pas parlé

Qui
où
pourquoi
qui es-tu
        en quoi cela nous concerne-t-il
et pourquoi ta mort

---

* À la mémoire d'Evelyne, sœur d'Abraham Serfaty, décédée en octobre 1974, à la suite des tortures qu'elle avait subies lors de son arrestation un an auparavant.

TALK OR BE KILLED[*]

"Talk or be killed"
They killed you Évelyne
You did not talk

In three plain sentences
with no lead voice
                    no choir
neither theater nor audience
no intervention of the gods or of their absence
this is
        the tragedy
"Talk or be killed"
They killed you Évelyne
You did not talk

Who
where
why
who you are
                    how does that concern us
and why can your death

[*] In memory of Évelyne, sister of Abraham Serfaty, who died in October 1974 from the effects of the torture inflicted upon her after her arrest one year earlier.

ne peut pas rester anonyme
ne peut pas être le sujet
d'une oraison en famille
qu'on enterre
dans le même caveau d'oubli
après les pleurs
                    les couronnes
                              les accolades désespérées ?
Non, non
regarde
je prends ce chalumeau
je le règle sur la flamme courte et bleue
et je vais tailler froidement
une croix lancinante
dans la mémoire courte
de tous ceux qui ont cru
qu'avec le temps
ton petit cadavre
n'obstruerait plus l'horizon de leurs forfaits
de tous ceux
proches ou lointains
qui oseraient t'oublier

Non, non
je ne peux pas abandonner mes morts

not remain anonymous
not be the subject
of a family funeral oration
to be buried
in the same tomb of oblivion
after the tears
        the wreaths
                the despairing hugs?

No, no
look here
I take this blowtorch
adjust its short blue flame
and am going coldly to carve
a searing cross
in the short memories
of all those who thought
that with time
your little body
would cease to bulk up the list of their crimes
of all those
near or far
who would dare to forget you

No, no
I cannot abandon my dead

aux simples pétitions
du sacrifice et de l'exemple
Je ne veux pas abandonner mes morts
aux images d'Épinal
de la consolation
Mes morts
sont trop vivants en moi
Je les déterre
vifs et sanguinolents
les déploie
sur le fronton des palais du génocide
pour qu'ils se perpétuent
                                        intenables
châtiment ininterrompu
drapeau jamais en berne
                                        d'insurrections

« Tu parles ou on te tue »
Ils t'ont tuée Évelyne
Tu n'avais pas parlé

Évelyne
un corps minuscule
hâve et ridé
d'enfant empêché de grandir

to mere memorials
of sacrifice and exemplarity
I do not want to abandon my dead
to stereotyped images
meant to console
My dead
are too alive within me
I unbury them
living and bloody
lay them out
on the façade of the palaces of genocide
there to endure
                         unbearable
continual payback
flag of insurrection
                         never at half-staff

"Talk or be killed"
They killed you Évelyne
You did not talk

Évelyne
the tiny body
emaciated and wrinkled
of a child prevented from growing up

Déchaussée
la jupe retirée
les pieds sont attachés
les poignets ficelés
                    rabattus derrière le dos
on fait passer une tringle sous les coudes
des membres entravés
on soulève ainsi le corps
on le suspend en déposant chaque extrémité
de la tringle
sur le bord d'une table en bois
Cinq, dix minutes
La douleur se ramasse
part du centre de la colonne vertébrale
rampe de vertèbre en vertèbre
embrase le dos
traverse la nuque
se verse entièrement dans le cerveau
La tête se met à s'alourdir
grossit grossit
                    roule dans le vide
Un fauve est juché sur le dos
gratte gratte les vertèbres
atteint la moelle épinière

Shoeless
skirt pulled off
feet bound
wrists tied
            behind the back
a rod passed under the elbows
of the hobbled arms
used to lift the body
and hang it up by placing each end
of the rod
on the edge of a wooden table
Five, ten minutes
The pain gathers
radiates from the center of the spine
climbs from vertebra to vertebra
sets the back afire
runs through the nape of the neck
empties completely into the brain
The head begins to feel heavy
swelling swelling
                rolling through a void
A wild beast is clamped to the back
tearing tearing at the spine
reaching the cord

À l'autre bout du corps
le fouet s'abat sur la plante des pieds
siffle
      claque
            cingle
jusqu'à devenir
écho de la flagellation
                        d'un corps inerte
                                  ailleurs

Évanouissement

Évelyne
un corps minuscule
hâve et ridé
d'enfant empêché de grandir
nue
sur un bureau
La prise est branchée
Les pinces sont avancées
griffent les mamelons et s'y fixent
Quelques secondes
et la décharge part
coutelas de feu
qui larde
            taillade

At the far end of the body
a whip strikes the soles of the feet
whistles
              cracks
                        slashes
until it becomes
just an echo of the flogging
                              of an inert body

                                        far away

Unconsciousness

Évelyne
the tiny body
emaciated and wrinkled
of a child prevented from growing up
naked
on a desk
The plug is put in
The clamps approach
clawing at the nipples as they are affixed
A few seconds
and the current flows
a cutlass of fire
that stabs
              slices

pénètre jusqu'à la garde
                              écharpe
Fourmis carnivores
                        dans le sang
Stridences aux tympans
les yeux gonflent
                        chauffent chauffent
Les orbites ne les contiennent plus
les expulsent
Évanouissement

Évelyne
un corps minuscule
hâve et ridé
d'enfant empêché de grandir
nue sur un bureau
Les pinces sont avancées
introduites dans le vagin
s'accrochent
Quelques secondes
et la décharge part
langue à mille fourches
de brasier atomique
marteau-piqueur dans tous les organes
vilebrequin perfore les tempes

sinks in to the hilt
                        hacks
Flesh-eating ants
                        in the blood
Ringing in the ears
the eyes bulge
                        hotter and hotter
The sockets can no longer contain them
and push them out
Unconsciousness

Évelyne
the tiny body
emaciated and wrinkled
of a child prevented from growing up
naked on a desk
The clamps approach
are inserted into the vagina
take hold
A few seconds
and the current flows
tongue with a thousand forks
of a nuclear firestorm
jackhammers in every organ
drill bits perforating the temples

Le cerveau éclate

        se reconstitue

                éclate

Les os tuyaux de caoutchouc

              brûlent

Le corps

       une grande déchirure redoublée sans arrêt

Évanouissement

Fouet

    perchoir

          étouffement à l'eau

                  électrodes

Des heures

       des jours

– On parle toujours

– On finit par parler

– Impossible qu'on ne parle pas

Tu n'avais pas parlé Evelyne

et tes tortionnaires terrorisés

                 sont devenus fous

Non, non Évelyne

je ne peux pas t'abandonner

à un socle froid

The brain explodes
> reconstructs itself
>> explodes

Bones burn
> like rubber pipes

The body
> a great rending endlessly repeated

Unconsciousness

Whip
> perch
>> water torture
>>> electrodes

Hours
> days

"You always talk"
"In the end you talk"
"Impossible not to talk"
You did not talk Évelyne
and it terrorized your torturers
>>> and drove them mad

No, no Évelyne
I cannot abandon you
to a chill pedestal

où je ne pourrais caresser
que la statue pétrifiée de ton héroïsme
car je te sens marcher à côté de moi
sœur inoubliable
et dans ma main
la chaleur de ta toute petite main
hâve et ridée
d'enfant empêché de grandir
tu es
      vivante

Maison centrale de Kénitra, 1974

74

where I could caress
only the petrified statue of your heroism
because I feel you walking beside me
unforgettable sister
with the warmth of your very tiny hand
in mine
emaciated and wrinkled
the hand of a child prevented from growing up
you are
      alive

Kenitra Prison, 1974

BONJOUR SOLEIL DE MON PAYS

Bonjour soleil de mon pays
qu'il fait bon vivre aujourd'hui
que de lumière
que de lumière autour de moi
Bonjour terrain vague de ma promenade
tu m'es devenu familier
je t'arpente vivement
et tu me vas comme un soulier élégant
Bonjour pique-bœuf balourd et philosophe
perché là-haut
sur cette muraille qui me cache le monde
te chatouillant les côtes
à petits coups distraits
Bonjour herbe chétive de l'allée
frissonnant en petites rides opalescentes
sous la caresse taquine du vent
Bonjour grand palmier solitaire
planté sur ton échasse grenue
et t'ouvrant comme une splendide tulipe
à la cime
Bonjour soleil de mon pays
marée de présence annihilant l'exil
Que de lumière
que de lumière autour de moi

GOOD MORNING SUN OF MY LAND

Good morning sun of my land
how good it feels to be alive today
so much light
so much light around me
Good morning empty exercise yard
you have become familiar to me
I cross you with a lively step
and you suit me like an elegant shoe
Good morning ponderous and philosophical oxpecker
perched up there
on the wall that hides the world from me
poking at your ribcage
with distracted little movements
Good morning sparse grass in the alley
quivering in opalescent flurries
at the wind's teasing touch
Good morning great lone palm
erect on your cross-grained trunk
blooming at your peak
like a glorious tulip
Good morning sun of my land
tide of presence abolishing exile
So much light
so much light around me

* * *

J'ai mille raisons de vivre
vaincre la mort quotidienne
le bonheur de t'aimer
marcher au pas de l'espoir

* * *

Tant d'années
à n'avoir jamais connu
la solitude ou l'ennui
tant d'étoiles filantes dans ma tête
La vasque de tendresse murmure
en plein chant
l'étrange bonheur du prisonnier

* * *

La nuit a lâché sa horde de colombes
sur les forêts sensuelles du souvenir
Tu m'apparais
terrifiante de grâces et de promesses
puis c'est le rite
entrecoupé de détonations
de voyeurs hilares puant la cagoule
Je ne suis qu'à moitié homme

I have a thousand reasons to live
to vanquish day-to-day death
the joy of loving you
and walking in step with hope

* * *

So many years
without ever knowing
solitude or boredom
so many shooting stars in my head
The reservoir of tenderness hums
in plainsong chant
the prisoner's peculiar happiness

* * *

Night has released its host of doves
into the sensual forests of memory
You appear to me
terrifying with grace and promise
then comes the ritual
punctuated by explosions
from elated voyeurs stinking of the cagoule
I am half a man only

* * *

L'eau coule dans ma main
Des gouttelettes irisées
absorbent goulûment le soleil
Rêver n'est que le reflet
de ce presque miracle

* * *

Le sourire éclot de lui-même
Je ne l'arrache pas à ma face
oubliée avec tous les miroirs
Sourire inextinguible
c'est comme ça que je résiste

* * *

Les camarades dorment
La prison a cessé de tournoyer dans leur tête
Ils naviguent à cœur ouvert
en haute mer de nos passions inédites
Ils sont beaux dans leur sommeil

* * *

* * *

Water runs onto my hand
Iridescent drops
greedily gobble up the sunshine
Dreaming is merely a reflection
of this near-miracle

* * *

The smile breaks out by itself
I do not wipe it from a face
forgotten along with all mirrors
An inextinguishable smile
my way of resisting

* * *

The comrades are asleep
The prison no longer twists and turns their minds
They are sailing with open hearts
on the high seas of our extraordinary passions
They are beautiful as they sleep

* * *

C'est encore loin le *temps des cerises*
et des mains chargées d'offrandes immédiates
le ciel ouvert au matin frais des libertés
la joie de dire
et la tristesse heureuse

C'est encore loin le temps des cerises
et des cités émerveillées de silence
à l'aurore fragile de nos amours
la fringale des rencontres
les rêves fous devenus tâches quotidiennes

C'est encore loin le temps des cerises
mais je le sens déjà
qui palpite et lève
tout chaud en germe
dans ma passion du futur

Maison centrale de Kénitra, 1978

The *temps des cerises* is still far off
along with hands bearing gifts freely offered
a sky open to the new morning of freedoms
the joy of speech
and happy sadness

The cherry season is still far off
with its cities enchanted by silence
the fragile dawn of our loves
the hunger for encounter
the mad dreams become workaday tasks

The cherry season is still far off
but I feel it already
palpitating and quickening
a warm growing embryo
in my passion for the future

Kenitra Prison, 1978

from

DISCOURS SUR LA COLLINE ARABE

ADDRESS FROM THE ARAB HILL

(1985)

de DISCOURS SUR LA COLLINE ARABE

Si les chaînes t'empêchent de marcher
garde les yeux ouverts
Si ta nuque percluse
t'empêche de lever la tête
garde les yeux ouverts
Si on te ferme les yeux de force
rouvre-les
dedans le continent sismique
de ton corps

* * *

Rien au monde
ne pourra t'obliger
à plier genou
renoncer
à ton identité humaine
Ne mesure pas ta force
à la balance de tes bourreaux

* * *

L'aurore
te restitue ta transparence
Te voilà debout

from ADDRESS FROM THE ARAB HILL

If your chains prevent you from walking
keep your eyes open
If your stiff neck
stops you lifting your head
keep your eyes open
If they shut your eyes by force
reopen them
inside the seismic continent
of your body

* * *

Nothing in the world
can force you
to bend the knee
renounce
your human identity
Do not weigh your strength
on the scales of your tormentors

* * *

Daybreak
restores your clarity
Here you stand

riche de ta nudité
désemparé
comme pour la première fois
devant le cœur et le corps de la bien-aimée
après des années de séparation
Tous tes ennemis ont disparu
il ne reste plus
que les ennemis de l'aurore

* * *

Tandis que la poésie agonise
dans les convulsions du dernier
fou d'amour
et que le règne de barbarie enveloppe
les derniers monuments de notre fragilité
Tandis que les dinosauriens
percent la coquille de l'atavique somnolence
et se répandent parmi les ruines de nos mains
Tandis que le refroidissement de la planète
atteint grièvement le cœur de l'homme
et que les rares survivants émigrent
paniquement
vers un hypothétique équateur
Tandis que des larmes de pierre

rich in your nakedness
as helpless
after years of separation
as the very first time
before the heart and body of your beloved
All your enemies have disappeared
none remain save
the enemies of daybreak

* * *

As poetry agonizes
in the last convulsions
of mad love
and the reign of barbarism envelops
the last monuments of our fragility
As the dinosaur-people
pierce the shell of their atavistic slumber
and spread through the ruins of our hands
As the cooling of the planet
gravely injures the heart of man
and the rare survivors migrate
in panic
towards a hypothetical equator
As tears of stone

brouillent ma vue...
Non
je ne veux pas y croire

* * *

La cellule familière
que je transporte dans ma tête
La petite cour de promenade
que je transporte dans mes pieds
Les grosses clés des grosses serrures
qui tournent et claquent
quotidiennement encore
dans ma poitrine
L'uniforme gris rayé
qui a repoussé
sous mes habits de peau
Les yeux de mes camarades
incrustés dans les yeux
avec lesquels je scrute
le théâtre d'ombres
de la liberté à la petite semaine

* * *

Le tortionnaire s'est réveillé
Près de lui

blur my vision
No
I do not want to believe any of that

* * *

The familiar cell
that I carry in my head
The little exercise yard
that I carry in my feet
The large keys to the large locks
that still turn and clink
every day
in my breast
The striped gray uniform
that has regrown
beneath my suit of skin
The eyes of my comrades
glommed onto the eyes
with which I scrutinize
the shadow play
of freedom on short-term lease

* * *

The torturer has woken up
Beside him

sa femme dort encore
Il se glisse furtivement hors du lit
revêt sa tenue de jungle
et sort
Sur le chemin du réduit
où l'attendent ses instruments
et ses victimes du jour
il pense aux choses ordinaires de la vie
les prix qui grimpent
la maison qui sera trop exiguë
quand viendra le cinquième enfant
les pluies qui tardent de nouveau cette année
le dénouement du dernier feuilleton qui passe à la télé
Il pointe au bureau des entrées
se dirige vers le réduit
ouvre la porte
Les corps sont recroquevillés dans la pénombre
toussotements
puanteur
Lève-toi fils de pute !
crie-t-il
en lançant une ruade
au plexus du premier prévenu
que son pied rencontre

* * *

his wife still sleeps
He slips furtive from the bed
puts his jungle suit back on
and leaves the house
On the way to the lockup
where his instruments await
and his victims of the day
he thinks about the ordinary things of life
rising prices
his house being too cramped
when the fifth baby arrives
the rain that is so late this year
the ending of the latest TV series
He clocks in at reception
Heads for the lockup
opens the door
Bodies curled up in the shadows
muted coughing
stink
Get up you bastard
he shouts
directing a kick
into the belly of the first prisoner
his foot encounters

* * *

Je vous invite à la transparence
je vous invite à l'instant de vérité
Que vaut une vie comme la nôtre
je vous le demande
Observez l'infini des constellations
observez le long cheminement
de notre espèce intelligente
plongez dans le dédale sans issue
de l'homme
mais méditez enfin
arrêtez la machine infernale
de l'accumulation
brisez le temps
du progrès sans mémoire
souvenez-vous de votre infaillible blessure
acceptez ce petit lot de désarroi
Tels
volons au secours du futur

* * *

Entre deux cauchemars
j'ai rêvé
d'une étrange et familière
planète
Tout y était musique

I invite you to be clear
I invite you to a moment of truth
What is a life such as ours worth
I ask you
Consider the infinity of constellations
consider the long journey
of our intelligent species
delve into the endless maze
of mankind
just think it over
then halt the infernal machine
of accumulation
smash the time
of progress without memory
recall your irreparable wound
accept this small share of dismay
And thus prepared
let us fly to the rescue of the future

* * *

Between two nightmares
I dreamt
of a strange and familiar
planet
All was music there

éléments, hommes, faune, flore
Elle roulait
la gredine
de galaxie en galaxie
laissant longuement dans l'espace
son impressionnante traîne d'harmonies
Et j'avais la certitude
que de multiples formes de vie
éclosaient
par-ci par-là
partout
où ma planète était passée
Alors je décidai
dans mon sommeil
de ne plus me réveiller

* * *

Je vais vous dire ma palette
cri Noir d'alerte saccadant l'inaudible
Blanc solennel dardant l'éphémère
Jaune miel reclus dans ma luette
Bleu blême transperçant la transparence
Vert irradiant les marches nocturnes
Rouge taraudant la pacotille des idées
Gris déposant sur l'horizon

elements, humans, fauna, flora
She was rolling along
this waif
from galaxy to galaxy
leaving behind in space
a long and impressive train of harmonies
And I was sure
that myriad life forms
were springing up
here and there
everywhere
my planet passed by
So I decided
in my dream
never again to wake up

* * *

Let me tell you about my palette
Black alarm call punctuating the inaudible
solemn White spearing the ephemeral
Honey Yellow cloistered in my uvula
Pale Blue piercing transparency
Green lighting nighttime walks
Red chastising bogus ideas
Gray laying the trembling embryo

l'œuf vibrant de l'aurore
Rose des vents alliés
soufflant les rides du monde
Des mots
de pauvres mots
pour dompter le taureau invisible des nuées

of the dawn on the horizon
Pink of the winds in alliance
raising the wrinkles of the world
Words
poor words
to tame the invisible bull of the storm clouds

from

L'ÉCORCHÉ VIF

SKINNED ALIVE

(1986)

de L'ÉCORCHÉ VIF

Comme les énigmes de l'inquisiteur sont aisées !
Comparons, dit-il, avec celles
que je n'ose parfois me poser à moi-même :

Par quelle tribu occulte es-tu gangrené ?

Es-tu indemne de tout pouvoir ?

As-tu cassé tous les miroirs ?

De quelles infirmités tires-tu ta force ?

Quels sont les tabous de ta droiture ?

Pourquoi ne reconnais-tu que du bout des lèvres l'ampleur de tes
ignorances ?

Ne t'arrive-t-il pas de te contenter de l'à-peu-près de ce que tu aurais
vraiment voulu dire ? D'être irrité par tes plus justes passions ? De
maudire tes superbes raisons de vivre ?

Ne joues-tu pas un peu au martyr ?

from SKINNED ALIVE

How easy the inquisitor's questions are!
Compare them, he says, with the questions
I sometimes dare not ask myself:

What hidden tribe gave you gangrene?

Are you utterly untainted by power?

Have you broken all the mirrors?

From what weaknesses do you draw your strength?

What taboos govern your rectitude?

Why do you pay only lip service to the scope of your ignorance?

Do you not sometimes settle for a mere approximation of what you
really wanted to say? Are you not sometimes annoyed by your own
most righteous passions? Do you not sometimes tend to curse your
fine reasons for living?

Are you not a little prone to play the martyr?

Ne caches-tu pas ta paresse derrière le tourbillon de tes réalisations ?

Que trahis-tu chaque fois que tu te remets en cause ?

Es-tu comblé par le seul amour qu'on te connaisse ?

Jusqu'où peux-tu aller dans la vérité sur toi-même ?

Do you not hide your idleness behind a whirlwind of activity?

What do you betray whenever you put yourself in question?

Are you fulfilled by the only love you are known to feel?

How far can you go in confronting the truth about yourself?

ÉPILOGUE

Le poète arabe
se met devant sa table rase
s'apprête à rédiger son testament
mais il découvre qu'il a perdu
l'usage de l'écriture
Il a oublié ses propres poèmes
et les poèmes de ses ancêtres
Il veut crier de rage
mais se rend compte
qu'il a perdu l'usage de la parole
De guerre lasse
il s'apprête à se lever
mais il sent qu'il a perdu
l'usage de ses membres
La mort l'a précédé
là où il devait abdiquer
devant la vie

EPILOGUE

The Arab poet
sits down before his bare table
prepares to draw up his will
but discovers that he has lost
the use of writing
He has forgotten his own poems
and the poems of his ancestors
He wants to cry out in fury
but realizes
that he has lost the use of speech
War weary
he prepares to stand up
but he perceives that he has lost
the use of his limbs
Death has preceded him
to the place where
he meant to give up
on life

from

TOUS LES DÉCHIREMENTS

RIFTS EVERYWHERE

(1990)

SOLEILS AUX ARRÊTS

*à Nelson Mandela
et Abraham Serfaty*

Un homme est en prison
Il est noir
les yeux habités de braise et de futur
Il est grand
adossé au volcan rusé de l'histoire
L'arc-en-ciel pleut sur sa langue
y dépose le limon des paroles
qu'un peuple chante en dansant
sur le seuil des mouroirs
Il est trop grand pour sa cellule
quand il s'allonge
ses pieds sortent du judas
et vont folâtrer sur les murailles
Ses mains d'oiseau sans ailes
se tendent vers les étoiles
pour en recueillir le miel natif

Un homme est en prison
Il est blanc
mais vraiment blanc

SUNS UNDER ARREST

for Nelson Mandela
and Abraham Serfaty

A man is in prison
He is black
his eyes inhabited by cinders and by the future
He is tall
his back to history's cunning volcano
The rainbow rains on his tongue
leaving the silt of the words
that a people sings as they dance
on the threshold of the killing chambers
He is too tall for his cell
when he lies down
his feet stick out through the observation window
and scramble up the walls
His hands of a wingless bird
reach for the stars
to gather their native honey

A man is in prison
He is white
but really white

avec sa barbe blanche de dieu en exil
son nez d'aigle nomade
son cœur blanc
ses paumes blanches
où la douleur a gravé
des canaux gigantesques de désirs
des routes en pleine jungle
des lettres affolantes
en calligraphie coufie
une croix énigmatique
un œil sans cils
une charrue et des épis de blé
un petit damier noir et blanc
et une foule de hachures pour autant de naissances

Un homme est en prison
Il est de la couleur dont rêve le peintre
et qu'il n'a jamais pu atteindre
Il est d'un pays
que même les poètes n'ont pas su rêver
Les frontières mythique du sang
ricochent sur le duvet de sa poitrine
et tombent
Il vient du Graal et du Tiers oublié de la planète
des cales de voiliers négriers

with the white beard of an exiled god
the nose of a wandering eagle
a white heart
white palms
where pain has etched
gigantic channels of desires
roads of the deep jungle
bewildering letters
in kufic script
an enigmatic cross
a lashless eye
a plough and ears of wheat
a little black-and-white checkerboard
and a host of hash marks for as many births

A man is in prison
He is the color the painter dreams of
but has never managed to achieve
He is from a country
that even the poets could never dream up
Mythical frontiers of blood
bounce off his chest hair
and vanish
He comes from the Grail and the planet's Forgotten Third
from the holds of slave-running sailing ships

et des réserves de peuples originels à l'encan
Il est arabe et juif
palestinien et chilien
Il est tous les hommes
toutes les femmes
le mutant des langues et des sexes
le doux guerrier de la paix
Il est la boussole du sourire dans les ténèbres

Un homme est en prison
Il est amoureux
d'un amour à faire pâlir Qaïs et Laïla
Abélard et Héloïse
Dante et Béatrice
Tout en lui est amour
Il ne regarde pas les êtres
il les caresse de sa pupille
il ne soulève pas
ne déplace pas
ne dépose pas les choses
il jette à leurs pieds des pétales de rosée
et des fruits de passion
La couche dure est son amante
l'arbre son frère jumeau

and from stocks of indigenous people up for grabs
He is Arab and Jew
Palestinian and Chilean
He is all men
all women
mutant of languages and sexes
gentle warrior of peace
He is the compass of the smile in the shadows

A man is in prison
He is in love
with a love to put Qais and Layla to shame
along with Abélard et Héloïse
and Dante and Beatrice
Everything in him is love
He does not look at beings
but caresses them with his gaze
he does not lift things
or move them
or set them down
he throws petals of dew
and passion fruit
at their feet
A hard bed is his lover
a tree his twin brother

l'eau le liant de son sang
Il est le promis des hirondelles
de la brise
des nuages
l'amoureux transi de la nuit
de la dolente aurore
et de la houle rebelle
Tout en lui est amour

Un homme est en prison
Il n'a rien à ajouter
ayant dit l'essentiel
« Ce que tout cadavre devrait savoir »
ce que les vivants n'écoutent que d'une seule oreille
distraite, oh si distraite
comme ceci :
vivre, la belle affaire
encore faut-il que ça serve à quelque chose
ou ceci : « Si tu veux tracer ton sillon droit
accroche ta charrue aux étoiles »
ou encore ceci :
inutile de chercher loin les tyrans
ils sont sous votre peau
sans oublier ceci :
les hommes naissent esclaves et inégaux

water the binder of his blood
He is the betrothed of swallows
of the breeze
of the clouds
the bashful lover of the night
the doleful dawn
and the rebellious swell
Everything in him is love

A man is in prison
He has nothing more to say
having said the essential
"What every corpse should know"
what the living attend to with one ear only
distractedly, so distractedly
like this:
life is a fine thing
but it ought to be good for something
or this: "If you want a straight furrow
hitch your plough to the stars"
or this:
no need to look far for tyrants
they are right under your skin
not forgetting this:
men are born slaves and unequal

toute la question est qu'ils ne le demeurent pas
Vous le voyez
cet homme n'a rien à ajouter

La prison où se trouve notre homme
est ronde et carrée
proche et lointaine
Elle est d'hier et de demain
souterraine et perdue dans les nuées
carnivore et végétarienne
C'est une baraque près d'une mosquée dans un bidonville
un palais de mauvais goût
dressé sur des béquilles
un immeuble en verre avec vue imprenable
sur un camp d'extermination
C'est une île flottante
un hypermarché
une pyramide renversée
un train sans conducteur
un tamis cachant le soleil
des barreaux plantés dans le désert
une porte fermée
au nez de la mer
un avion désaffecté
un cerveau usé qui pue

the whole point is that they don't stay that way
You see
this man has nothing more to say

The prison that our man inhabits
is round and square
near and far away
It is of yesterday and tomorrow
subterranean and lost in the clouds
carnivorous and vegetarian
It is a hutch near a mosque in a shantytown
a palace in bad taste
supported on props
a glass building with an unspoilt view
of an extermination camp
It is a floating island
a hypermarket
an upside-down pyramid
a train without a driver
a filter keeping out the sun
bars set up in the desert
a door slammed
in the face of the sea
a scrapped airplane
a worn-out brain that stinks

un labyrinthe dans la boule d'une voyante
un fleuve qui tourne en rond
une mouche arrachant ses pattes
pour se dégager de la glu
et surtout elle est en nous
en nous

Un homme est en prison
Il n'est ni le meilleur de ses semblables
ni le pire
On peut dire qu'il connaît bien le bourreau
qu'il a rencontré Dieu
puis l'a perdu de vue
Il a joué à cache-cache avec la mort
escaladé le plus haut sommet du monde
découvert le paradis en enfer
et vice versa
Il a trouvé la meilleure réponse
à la question philosophique du suicide
Il lit comme un talmudiste dans les rêves
et se nourrit à la table du délire
Il est le plus sensuel des saints
Il rit, mais il rit
comme ça n'est pas permis

a labyrinth in a clairvoyant's crystal ball
a river going round in circles
a fly tearing off its legs
as it tries to free itself from glue
and most of all it is within us
within us

A man is in prison
He is not the best among his peers
nor the worst
It can be said that he knows his tormentor well
that he has met God
and then lost sight of him
He has played hide and seek with death
scaled the world's highest peak
found paradise in hell
and vice versa
He has found the best answer
to the philosophical issue of suicide
Like a Talmudist he interprets dreams
and eats at the table of madness
He is the most sensual of saints
He laughs, but laughs so hard
there should be a law against it

Un homme est en prison
Subitement il découvre
le vrai visage de la liberté
cette chatte qui bouffe ses enfants
ce scorpion qui se pique avec son dard
lorsqu'il se sent encerclé
La superbe ogresse
l'amante qui tue pour faire revivre
à prendre ou à laisser
Et il fut preneur sans conteste
de libertés astringentes
humus d'une terre perdue dans l'à venir
émeraude sans rivale à la cheville d'une gazelle
maîtresse d'espéranto et de périples
feuille vierge où seuls les enfants
nés de la vague androgyne
sont appelés à s'inscrire
Liberté de risques bénis et périls
de main coupée célébrant le sang dévastateur
d'orage sur le désert parsemé de famine
de séismes humains
rien qu'humains
vengeant toutes les morts iniques

A man is in prison
Suddenly he discovers
the true face of freedom
mother cat devouring her kittens
scorpion biting itself with its own stinger
when it feels surrounded
Superb giantess
of a lover who kills to bring back life
to be taken or left alone
And he was a taker without question
of cleansing freedoms
humus of an earth lost in the yet-to-be
peerless emerald on the ankle of a gazelle
mistress of esperanto and roundabout journeys
virgin sheet of paper on which only children
born of the wave of androgyny
are invited to sign
Freedom of blessed risks and dangers
of hands cut off to mark blood's devastating power
of storm in the famine-ravaged desert
of human earthquakes
strictly human
avenging all the monstrous deaths

Un homme est en prison
Il parle au mur
au miroir des miroirs
et lui raconte son histoire :
Je suis né entre printemps et automne lors de l'année du Tigre
dans une ville qu'on a depuis lors débaptisée sept fois
Mon pays fait mal lorsqu'on prononce son nom
mais bon sang quel soleil
quel fruit à la bouche des hommes lorsqu'il sourit
quelle folie du matin
répandant l'extrême-onction du jasmin et de la cannelle
Ce pays m'a tant donné
et j'ai voulu lui rendre la pareille
Il paraît que c'était la chose à ne pas faire
« La passion est interdite. Circulez, circulez, clamaient les haut-
parleurs. Faites le grand déménagement dans votre cœur. Fermez
vos yeux, votre nez, vos gueules. Circulez. Il n'y a pas de cochons ici,
gardez vos perles. Et gare, gare aux amants récalcitrants ! »
Pouvais-je résister, ô miroir des miroirs ?
Et me voilà dément authentifié
enchaîné aux parois sourdes de tes reflets
presque heureux de l'être
car je n'ai pas failli à ma passion

A man is in prison
he talks to the wall
to the mirror of mirrors
and tells his story to it:
I was born between spring and fall in the Year of the Tiger
in a village since debaptized seven times
My country pains me whenever its name is uttered
but my god what a sun
what fruit in the mouth of men when it smiles
what morning madness
dispensing its extreme unction of jasmine and cinnamon
This country has given me so much
and I wanted to pay it back in kind
Which was seemingly not the thing to do
"Passion is forbidden. Keep moving, keep moving," boomed the
loudspeakers. "Time for a major house-clearing of your heart. Close
your eyes, your noses. your traps. Keep moving. There are no swine
here, keep your pearls. And beware, beware of recalcitrant lovers!"
How could I resist, oh mirror of mirrors?
And here I am, certifiably insane
chained to the deaf walls
of your reflections
and almost happy about it
because I have not betrayed my passion

Un homme est en prison
Il n'attend pas
il n'a pas de temps à perdre
Il se fait peintre et poète et musicien
Il invite le papillon des mots
à la transe qui fait pousser des racines
Il réfute le sobriquet des couleurs
pour que le blanc de la toile
libère ses démons tapis
Il ravive le cri du silence
pour orchestrer la symphonie du don
Délivré du corps
il marche
il emprunte le chemin secret
qui va de la blessure à l'âme
de l'âme à la graine
de la graine à la tige
de la tige au bourgeon
du bourgeon à la fragile orchidée
de l'espoir
de l'espoir à la lucidité
de la lucidité aux larmes
des larmes à la fureur
de la fureur à l'amour

A man is in prison
He is not waiting
he has no time to waste
He is becoming a painter and a poet and a musician
He invites the butterfly of words
to the trance state that puts down roots
He rejects the sobriquets of colors
to let the white of the canvas
free his crouching demons
He revives the cry of silence
to orchestrate the symphony of the gift
Delivered from his body
he walks
he takes the secret path
that leads from the wound to the soul
from the soul to the seed
from the seed to the shoot
from the shoot to the bud
from the bud to the frail orchid
of hope
from hope to clarity
from clarity to tears
from tears to fury
from fury to love

de l'amour à cette étrange folie
de croire malgré tout aux hommes

A tout hasard
souvenez-vous
un homme est en prison

from love to the strange folly
of believing despite everything in human beings

Just on the off-chance
bear in mind that
a man is in prison

LA GUERRE D'AMOUR

Entre nous
cette brûlure
quand nos mains sont enchaînées

Entre nous
cette soif
quand l'eau multiplie la soif

Entre nous
le désir qui sépare

Voici mon cou
frappe et tranche
il n'y aura pas de sang
mes yeux resteront ouverts
et doux
l'étrange sourire du pendu
étincellera sur mes lèvres
ma tête
ne prendra pas beaucoup de place
dans ton lit
tu ne douteras plus de moi

THE WAR OF LOVE

Between us
this burning
when our hands are clasped

Between us
this thirst
when water makes you thirstier

Between us
the desire that separates

Here is my neck
strike and cut
there will be no blood
my eyes will stay open
and tender
the strange smile of the hanged man
will sparkle on my lips
my head
will not take up much room
in your bed
you will no longer doubt me

Ne m'en veux pas
d'être l'ombre
dont se repaît la lumière

Ce mur que tu ne traverses
est un miroir vermoulu
il suffit d'une pression
de tes mamelons dressés
pour qu'il s'écroule

La folie
raison de plus

Le fleuve te ressemble
il a l'ondoiement de tes courbes
la malice de tes poissons
les berges grasses de ta vulve
les saules pleureurs de tes cils humides
les mouettes convulsives de tes reins
il a ton cri étouffé
et tes larmes
quand je te somme de te retenir
afin de ne pas déranger les voisins

Do not hold it against me
if I am the shadow
that light feeds on

This wall that you cannot get through
is a worm-eaten mirror
all that is needed is the pressure
of your erect nipples
for it to collapse

Madness
a further reason

The river is like you
it has the sinuousness of your curves
the malice of your fish
the lush banks of your vulva
the weeping willows of your moist eyelashes
the convulsive seagulls of your flanks
it has your muffled cry
and your tears
when I tell you to restrain yourself
so as not to disturb the neighbors

Me sont blessure
le parfum scandaleux de ces lis
cette chevelure qui n'en finit pas
d'ameuter les morsures
ce volcan inconscient de sa rage
cette vie plus courte
qu'une corde de potence
ce nuage lyrique
qui déclame ses poèmes
aux seuls oiseaux
ce sein libre
sous la soie de l'interdit
ce train dogmatique
qui n'ose pas utiliser ses ailes
M'est blessure
ta blessure
puisée à la mienne

Aime-moi
au-delà du bien
et du mal

La peur
ne nous ressemble pas
ce n'est qu'un grain d'orge

Wounds to me are
the scandalous scent of these lilies
this hair that never ceases
to incite biting
this volcano oblivious to its fury
this life shorter
than a hangman's rope
this great lyrical cloud
reciting its poems
to the birds alone
this breast free
beneath a barrier of silk
this disciplined pace
that dare not spread its wings
A wound to me
is your wound
drawn from mine

Love me
beyond good
and evil

Fear
does not suit us
it is just a barleycorn

glissé sous notre couche
et qui ne doit pas nous empêcher
de dormir

Manger
est une fête païenne
quand on se regarde dans les yeux
les deux yeux

La pluie
nous surprendra
nous nous déshabillerons
nous étalerons nos branches
nous sortirons nos feuilles
nos bourgeons
nous déploierons nos racines
nous préparerons nos fruits
les arbres
nous reconnaîtront pour leurs

Le désert nous surprendra
tu seras ma chamelle
ou mon guide
je sortirai ma flûte

slipped beneath our bedding
that should not stop us
from sleeping

Eating
is a pagan feast
when we look into each other's eyes
both eyes

The rain
will startle us
we will undress
spread our branches
put out our leaves
our buds
we will extend our roots
we will grow our fruit
the trees
will take us for theirs

The desert will startle us
you shall be my she-camel
or my guide
I will take out my flute

nous laisserons pousser nos cheveux
une oasis naîtra
de cette bonté

L'amour nous surprendra
à deux pas de l'enfer

Le plus bel enfer
des êtres marqués
à la gorge éblouie éblouissante
aux narines de faucon pris au piège
aux pupilles égarées
dans la montée intrépide du désir
ce voyou

Ma tête a blanchi, mon amie
tout d'un coup
Cela s'est passé
comme toutes les choses de chez nous
Là-bas
il n'y a ni printemps
ni automne
il n'y a que l'impitoyable été
et le rude hiver

we will let our hair grow long
an oasis will be born
from these good things

Love will startle us
two steps from hell

That finest hell
of marked beings
breast dazzled dazzling
nostrils of a trapped falcon
eyes wandering astray
with the fearless rise of desire
that bad boy

My hair turned white, my love
all of a sudden
It happened
like everything in our country
Over there
there is neither spring
nor fall
just the pitiless summer
and the brutal winter

Je me suis toujours soumis
à tes larmes

Qui aime
en moi
Qui
me tue ?

S'il n'y avait
que ton désir dans le miroir
j'aurais les traits
de ton visage d'adolescente
tu serais de nouveau violée
sous les yeux crevés d'Œdipe
ton ventre
redeviendrait de marbre

Sans toi
je ne pourrai pas remplir ma tombe
lorsqu'il faudra bien
se résigner au silence

Ne m'aime pas mort
mais ne jette pas mes poèmes

I have always surrendered
to your tears

Who loves
in me
Who
kills me?

Were there nothing
but your desire in the mirror
I would see
the features of your adolescent face
you would be violated once again
under the sightless gaze of Oedipus
your belly
marble once more

Without you
I will not be able to fill my tomb
where resigning oneself to silence
is unavoidable

Do not love me dead
but do not throw away my poems

La bougie se consume
et me consume
quelqu'un viendra la moucher
dans mes yeux

Derrière la brume
une femme languide
allongée au soleil
sa toison s'écarte
je bois à la source brûlante
Un oiseau éclate
dans ma bouche
je ne comprends pas

Nous recueillerons
le nom du printemps
nous soignerons ses blessures
nous éloignerons de lui
les convoitises de l'hiver
mais au premier souhait qu'il formulera
nous lui rendrons sa liberté

Nous y voilà
nulle part

The candle burns out
and burns me out
someone will come to snuff it
in my eyes

Beyond the mist
a languid woman
lies in the sun
her fleece parts
I drink at the burning spring
A bird explodes
in my mouth
I don't understand

We shall pluck
the name of spring
dress its wounds
and keep at bay
winter's covetous glances
but at its first expressed wish
we shall restore its freedom

Here we are
nowhere

Cette terre est belle
disait mon grand frère turc
mais qui la suit du regard
dévore l'ascension de ses jambes
la chute vertigineuse de ses reins
la fraise énigmatique
de son sourire
ses ongles rongés jusqu'au sang
Qui en croit encore ses yeux ?

La terre
me fait tourner la tête
Ah si elle pouvait être
immobile et plate

Je ne suis pas
de n'importe quelle terre
la mienne est terriblement possessive
elle ne chasse
que ses amants orgueilleux
et stériles

Ma terre
est suceuse et dévoreuse
elle n'hésite pas à faire couler le sang

This land is beautiful
my Turkish big brother used to say
but anyone who runs their eyes over her
devours the rise of her legs
the vertiginous fall of her flanks
the mysterious strawberry
of her smile
her nails bitten to the quick
Who could still believe their eyes?

The land
makes my head spin
If only she could be
motionless and flat

I am not
from any old land
my land is terribly possessive
she chases away
only arrogant
and impotent lovers

My land
sucks you dry and devours you
never shrinks from spilling blood

et saigner à son tour
Ma terre est volage
sans être oublieuse
elle adore les outrances de langage
et les délices de sodomie
C'est une barbare
qui se rit des civilités
Elle ne baise pas avec la tête
et ne prend pas la pilule
ma terre
ma putain sacrée
la dernière femme fidèle
Elle me ressemble et ne me suit pas
C'est une terre
comme on n'en fait plus

Je ne me prosterne pas
non plus
devant le cul de ma terre

Ce pacte qui nous lie
est celui des enfants
que nous volons
à la porte des abattoirs

and bleeding in her turn
My land is flighty
though not forgetful
she adores outrageous language
and the delights of sodomy
She is a barbarian
who scorns civility
She does not fuck with her head
and does not take the pill
my land
my sacred whore
the last faithful woman
She is like me and does not follow me
A land
of the kind
they don't make anymore

Nor do I prostrate myself
before the ass of my land

The pledge that binds us
is that of the children
we snatch
at the door to the slaughterhouses

Quand je me noie
ma terre
ne me croit pas

Je t'attends
en ordre dispersé
je veux ne rien te dire
je veux que tu comprennes tout
Dos à dos
la foudre nous coulera
dans un moule définitif

Tout à toi
ma déraison
quand ta braise craque
entre les lèvres
le creux de l'oreille
et m'exile
Tu passes
caravane après caravane
comme si tu montais au ciel
pendant que je tremble
de t'avoir déjà perdue

When I drown myself
my land
does not believe me

I wait for you
in disarray
I want to tell you nothing
I want you to understand everything
Back to back
a lightning strike will pour us
into a permanent mold

I am all yours
my unreason
when your heat
slips between my lips
or into the corner of my ear
and exiles me
You pass
caravan after caravan
as though ascending to heaven
while I tremble with fear
of having already lost you

Dans le noir
tu es plus excitante
car j'ai envie
d'éclairer

J'ai appris
à offrir des fleurs
à en nommer chaque espèce
à les disposer artistiquement
dans un vase
mais je refuse d'apprendre
le langage des fleurs

Sans te regarder
je sais que tu me veux
nous parlons déjà pour ne rien dire
nous avons perdu l'appétit
nous éteignons la dernière cigarette
la pièce se met à tournoyer
le vaisseau décolle
soulevant un nuage de perdrix enceintes
C'est encore moi
qui tendrai ma main vers ton embouchure
tu dresseras la table
pour nos bruyantes ripailles

In the dark
you are more exciting
because I want
to put the light on

I have learnt
how to give flowers
to name every variety
to arrange them artistically
in a vase
but I refuse to learn
how to say it with flowers

Without looking at you
I know that you want me
we are already talking without saying a thing
we have lost our appetites
we put out our last cigarettes
the room begins to swirl
The craft takes off
raising a cloud of pregnant partridges
It is I once again
who will reach for your cleft
as you set the table
for our noisy revels

Nous ne parlons pas
le même langage
heureusement
sinon
comment pourrions-nous dialoguer ?

Je veux aimer
à ma manière
loin des yeux ou près du cœur
mes promises dans mon épouse
plusieurs en un
l'enfant, l'ami
le camarade perdu en cours de route
ce qu'aucune femme ne peut donner
le coup de foudre et l'habitude
les transes du désir
et la présence rassurante
ce qui ressemble à la résurrection
quand il ne reste plus rien à brûler
Je veux aimer
au-delà de l'amour

Ne me caresse pas
quand j'écris
dans ma tête

We do not speak
the same language
fortunately
otherwise
how could we converse?

I want to love
in my own way
far from eyes or close to the heart
all my fiancées in my wife
several in one
child, friend
comrade lost along the way
what no woman can give
wild love and routine both
the raptures of desire
along with a reassuring presence
something like a resurrection
once there is nothing left to burn
I want to love
beyond love

Do not caress me
when I am writing
in my head

Toutes les guerres finissent
sauf celle
d'amour

All wars end
save the war
of love

de POÈMES TOMBÉS DU TRAIN

Les larmes montent
aux yeux du sphinx
tant l'énigme a tué

L'oiseau
disons la tourterelle
se moque du désordre
son chant
n'est pas une réponse
aux inquiétudes de l'éphémère

Cette lumière
n'est pas à décrire
elle se boit
ou se mange

La feuille tremble
ou ne vit pas

Le poème s'inquiète
des menaces d'extermination
il ramasse des pierres
au cas où…

from POEMS FALLEN FROM THE TRAIN

Tears flood
the eyes of the sphinx
for the riddle has killed so many

The bird
let us say the turtle-dove
cares not a jot about disorder
his song
is not a response
to worries about the ephemeral

This light
is not for describing
it is drunk
or eaten

A leaf trembles
or does not live

The poem is concerned
by the threat of extermination
it gathers stones
just in case. . .

Le jaune attend le bleu
qui s'attarde avec le vert
le blanc sourit
à cette scène ordinaire
du dépit amoureux

Le vin est licite
bois, ô compagnon
tu n'as rien à oublier
c'est en buvant que tu te souviens

Habiter son corps
n'est pas aisé
c'est une maison hantée
un champ de mines
Il faudrait pouvoir le louer
juste pour des vacances

Ce qui est beau
l'est immédiatement
universellement

Est-ce une injustice
si les femmes sont plus belles
que les hommes ?

Yellow is waiting for blue
who is dallying with green
white smiles
at this ordinary scene
of amorous resentment

Wine is permitted
drink, comrade
you have nothing to forget
by drinking you remember

Inhabiting your body
is not easy
it is a haunted house
a minefield
One ought to be able to rent it
just for the holidays

What is beautiful
is beautiful immediately
universally

Is it an injustice
if women are more beautiful
than men?

La laideur
en tout cas
est injuste

L'amandier en fleur
ne souffre pas la critique

Si j'écris
c'est pour ne pas me mépriser

Toute femme qui dort
fait l'amour

Majesté de l'arbre
il trône sans gouverner
sans sévir
sans prélever d'impôt
sans appeler les jeunes
sous les drapeaux
sans consommer de vierge
chaque nuit
sans devoir mentir
Il est le monarque
parfaitement juste

Ugliness
in any case
is unjust

The almond-tree in flower
is not subject to criticism

If I write
it is so as not to despise myself

Every woman sleeping
is making love

Majesty of the tree
he reigns but does not rule
does not take harsh measures
does not raise taxes
does not draft the young
does not possess a virgin
every night
does not need to lie
He is the perfectly just
monarch

Je veux bien
me charger de vos tristesses
mais pourquoi la mienne
devrait-elle vous rester étrangère ?

Si je me jetais
sous les roues d'un train
j'aurais vraiment pitié de vous

Vouloir la lune
devrait être
le plus petit dénominateur commun

Lire parfois
c'est être humilié de ne pas écrire

La rosée
ce n'est que de l'eau
mais c'est une eau amoureuse

Aujourd'hui
les mots s'étirent d'aise
et bâillent
ils ont un teint de pêche

I am quite willing
to shoulder your woes
but why should mine
not concern you?

If I threw myself
under the wheels of a train
I would truly pity you

Asking for the moon
should be
the lowest common denominator

Reading sometimes means
being humiliated for not writing

The dew
is just water
but it is water in love

Today
words stretch luxuriously
and yawn
they are peach-hued

Ce sont les défaites
qui nous apprennent
la générosité

Je ne le nie pas
l'écriture est un luxe
mais c'est le seul luxe
où l'homme
n'exploite que lui-même

Le prophète détruit les idoles
le tyran
édifie des statues

Je connais
quelques maladies
compatis à toutes les autres
mais je n'ai jamais compris
la maladie de l'argent
et du pouvoir
Dois-je compatir aussi
à celle-ci ?

Les privilèges rabaissent

Defeats
are what teach us
generosity

I don't deny it
writing is a luxury
but it is the only luxury
whereby man
exploits only himself

The prophet destroys idols
the tyrant
erects statues

I have suffered from
a few diseases
and feel for sufferers
from all others
but I have never understood
the disease of money and power
Should I empathize
there too?

Privileges demean

Je ne mérite rien
rien ne me mérite
Je suis quitte
avec la gratitude
et l'ingratitude

L'Histoire jugera, dit-on
Encore un procès !

Attendre
c'est ma bête noire

J'ouvre la fenêtre
de mon jardin secret
Les prédateurs ont tout saccagé
ils ont emporté
jusqu'au secret de mon jardin

Souvent
je me sens diminué
fautif quelque part
quand on vient me féliciter

I deserve nothing
Nothing deserves me
I am done
with gratitude
and ingratitude

Let History judge, they say
Another trial!

Waiting
is my bête noire

I open the window
to my secret garden
The predators have pillaged everything
they have even taken
the secret of my garden

Many a time
I feel diminished
even guilty in a way
when people congratulate me

Je lis beaucoup
dans le sourire des autres
mais je ne sais pas de quoi est fait
le mien

J'ai condamné mes enfants
au fardeau que je porte
Dois-je le déposer
pour qu'ils s'en libèrent ?

Je suis inquiet
quand je ne rêve plus

Il devrait y avoir
une banque du rêve
à l'instar des banques du sang

Le sourire
ne s'apprend pas
c'est un don

Je n'attends rien de la vie
je vais
à sa rencontre

I read much
in the smiles of others
but I don't know what my own
is made of

I have condemned my children
to the burden I carry
Should I put it down
to free them of it?

I get anxious
when I no longer dream

There should be
a dream bank
after the fashion of blood banks

The smile
cannot be learnt
it is a gift

I expect nothing of life
I go
to meet it

La morsure des jours. L'amour en jachère. Le cheval écartelé. L'encre
sauvage. La rose contagieuse. L'île de marbre. Les vomissures de
l'aveugle. Le nom de la boue. Le dieu distrait. Les balles savantes.
Les draps mutilés. La cage du ciel. Le café blanc. Le sanglot des
choses. La lèpre du Nord. Les petits lacs de la bouche. La fosse
commune des couronnes. La flamme nomade. La cendre des mots.

On peut avoir le coup de foudre
pour un mot
Un mot vient à votre rencontre
et vous tend
la clé de l'œuvre

The bite of the days. Fallow love. The quartered horse. Wild ink. The contagious rose. Isle of marble. Blind man's vomit. The name of mud. The absent-minded god. Wise bullets. Crippled sheets. The cage of the heavens. White coffee. The sobbing of things. Northern leprosy. The mouth's little lakes. Potter's field of crowned heads. The nomad flame. Ashes of words.

You can fall head over heels in love
with a word
A word comes to meet you
and gives you
the key to the whole work

from

LE SOLEIL SE MEURT

THE SUN IS DYING

(1992)

de LE SOLEIL SE MEURT

Le soleil se meurt
une rumeur d'homme à la bouche
C'est une étrange soif
quand grisonnent les idées
et que l'amour
à peine commence

* * *

Les voilà débarrassés du rêve
hommes et femmes aux hanches étroites
Ah ils respirent enfin
se mettent à leurs calculatrices
ouvrent les vannes du bruit
pour remplir leur assiette
avant de se coucher
dans leurs lits séparés

* * *

Qui parle
de refaire le monde ?
On voudrait simplement
le supporter

from THE SUN IS DYING

The sun is dying
with human murmurs on its lips
A strange thirst comes
when ideas go gray
and love is only just
beginning

* * *

Here they are, unburdened of the dream
men and narrow-hipped women
Phew! they can breathe at last
as they turn to their calculators
open the floodgates of noise
and fill their plates
before getting into
their separate beds

* * *

Who's talking
about remaking the world?
We merely wish
to support it

avec une brindille
de dignité
au coin des lèvres

* * *

O dieu
si tu es homme
frère de l'homme
renonce à tes mystères
sors de ta grotte
Dis à tes partisans
la vanité de leurs temples
Plonge-les dans la cécité
Lève l'étendard de la révolte
Joins-toi à ceux
qui n'ont que leurs chaînes
pour labourer le malheur
Viens donc
leur embrasser les pieds

* * *

Demain l'incertain
encore plus incertain que l'hier
Il faudra pour se rendre

by putting a sprig
of dignity
in the corner of its mouth

* * *

O god
if you are a man
brother of man
give up your mysteries
come out of your cave
Tell your supporters
how pointless their temples are
Strike them blind
Raise the banner of revolt
Join with those
who have only their chains
to tackle their misery
And come on down
and kiss their feet

* * *

Tomorrow is the uncertain
even more so than yesterday
To visit the sun's bedside

au chevet du soleil
trouver les fleurs vivantes
les oranges non traitées
le sourire à peu près sincère
se présenter et dire
dans le charabia qui reste :
De quel mal souffres-tu ?
Est-il humain
rien qu'humain ?

* * *

Il ne sait plus dire
je t'aime
avec les vieux mots de l'amour
Se dévêtir comme le tonnerre
en jetant ses habits aux nuées
Caresser
avec les mains imaginatives du laboureur
Prier devant l'autel de l'anarchie
Regarder ce qu'il boit et mange
comme une collision mortelle
Embrasser sa proie
le long de ses blessures
Se coucher aux pieds de sa souveraine

we'll need to find fresh flowers
unsprayed oranges
a more or less genuine smile
introduce ourselves and say
in the patter that remains:
What seems to be the trouble?
Is it human
strictly human?

* * *

He can no longer say
I love you
with the old words of love
No longer undress like a thunderclap
hurling his clothes into the clouds
Or caress
with a laborer's knowing hands
Pray at the altar of anarchy
Treat everything he drinks and eats
like a fatal collision
Kiss his prey
the length of its wounds
Or lie down at the feet of his sovereign

comme une panthère apprivoisée
Il ne voit plus que son fantôme
dans les prunelles absentes
de l'ogresse repentie

* * *

Les barbares
nos semblables
Ils ont toujours craché sur les merveilles
pissé sur les livres
coupé les têtes savantes
répandu du sel
sur les ruines de Sodome
pour finir dans une alcôve
au milieu d'almées au pubis rasé
de devineresses naines
et d'eunuques hilares

* * *

L'époque est banale
moins étonnante que le tarif d'une prostituée
Les satrapes s'amusent beaucoup
au jeu de la vérité

like a tame panther
All he can see is his ghost
in the distracted gaze
of the reformed ogress

* * *

Barbarians
our like
always spat on the marvelous
pissed on books
beheaded the wise
sprinkled salt
on the ruins of Sodom
and ended up in fleshpots
amid dancing-girls with shaven vulvas
midget fortune-tellers
and laughing eunuchs

* * *

The times are pedestrian
less surprising than the price of a whore
The satraps have great fun
playing the game of truth

Les déshérités se convertissent en masse
à la religion du Loto
Les amants se séparent
pour un kilo de bananes
Le café n'est ni plus ni moins amer
L'eau reste sur l'estomac
La sécheresse frappe les plus affamés
Les séismes se plaisent à compliquer
la tâche des sauveteurs
La musique se refroidit
Le sexe guide le monde
Seuls les chiens continuent à rêver
tout au long des après-midi et des nuits

* * *

Il y aura une grande attente
avant la dite résurrection
Et le fils de l'homme
rendu à l'illusion
s'écriera : Qu'ai-je ?
Et les anges
peseurs du bien et du mal
s'écrieront : Qu'a-t-il ?
Et le ciel restera muet
comme au temps de la grande attente

The disinherited are converting en masse
to the religion of Lotto
Lovers break up
over a kilo of bananas
The coffee is neither more nor less bitter
Water sticks in the craw
Drought strikes the starving first
Earthquakes love complicating
the work of the rescuers
Music grows cold
Sex rules the world
Only dogs still dream
all afternoon and all night long

* * *

There will be a long wait
before the so-called resurrection
And the son of man
an illusion once more
will cry: What's the matter with me?
And the angels
who weigh good and evil
will cry: What's the matter with him?
And heaven will remain silent
as it has done throughout the long wait

*   *   *

Il y aura ce grand feu de veille
qui éloigne les fauves
et rassemble ceux
qui vont découvrir l'outil
Et le griot aux paroles qui blessent
se lèvera et frappera sept coups
au gong en bois de la mémoire
Et l'homme qui va faire fondre le métal
bondira et crachera au visage du griot
Et la femme aux sept maris reconnus
jettera au feu l'enfant disputé

*   *   *

Il y aura
au fond d'une grotte ou d'un désert
le survivant attitré des holocaustes
catastrophes nucléaires
épidémies informatiques
D'aucuns imaginent déjà son bonheur
l'affublent de l'ingéniosité de Crusoé
l'incitent à quitter son trou
pour rééditer la genèse
faire sortir de sa cuisse la femelle

There will be a great watch fire
to keep wild animals away
and muster those
who are to discover the tool
And the griot with the words that wound
will rise and strike
the wooden gong of memory
seven times
And the man who is going to melt the metal
will spring up and spit in the griot's face
And the woman with seven official husbands
will cast into the fire the contested child

* * *

Deep in a cavern or a desert
there will be
the certified survivor of holocausts
nuclear catastrophes
network viruses
Some already picture his satisfaction
credit him with a Crusoe-like ingenuity
urge him to come out of his den
and repeat Genesis

et concevoir
Mais lui finit par se coucher
se recouvrir de sable
Il décide d'entamer
la grève de la vie

* * *

Personne ne parlera
dans la langue archaïque de l'âme
avec cette musique de cœur qu'on écorche
et ce murmure de larmes fendant la pierre
Avec ces mots taillés dans les racines
et le bec recourbé de l'aigle
Avec le tonnerre qui ricane
le feu qu'on avale et recrache
Avec la panique
et la promesse des sept fléaux
Avec l'étoile qui apparaît
et le délire qui fait sens
Avec la horde en prière
et les tyrans qui meurent
d'un étrange mal de tête
Mais où sont les prophètes d'antan ?

producing a female from his thigh
and multiplying
But he eventually goes to bed
covers himself with sand
and decides to call
a strike on life

* * *

No one will speak
in the ancient language of the soul
with the music of the ravaged heart
and the murmur of tears splitting stone
With words hewn from the roots
and the curved beak of the eagle
With mocking thunder
and fire swallowed and spat out
With the panic
and the promise of the seven plagues
With the star that appears
and madness that makes sense
With praying crowds
and tyrants dying
from a strange headache
Oh where are the prophets of yesteryear?

*　*　*

Ce siècle qui n'en finit pas
et le suivant qui devra compter
cent unités
pas une de moins
sans que l'on sache
s'il y a vraie vie
paradis quelque part
sans qu'un signe indique
s'il y a commencement ou fin
Mais où sont les apocalypses d'antan ?

*　*　*

Mais il faudra
une immense écoute
des yeux, de la langue
de la matrice
des sexes incandescents
Que les enfants se réveillent
de leur naïve hibernation
Que les femmes reviennent
de leur double exil
Que les mâles se mettent enfin
en quête de leur identité

This interminable century
and the next which is bound
to reach a hundred
not a single year less
without our ever learning
if real life exists
a paradise somewhere
without a sign to indicate
if there is a beginning or an end
Oh where are the apocalypses of yesteryear?

* * *

But an immense attentiveness
will be required
from eyes, tongue
womb
and incandescent genitals
Let children awake
from their naïve hibernation
Let women return
from their double exile
Let men begin at last
to seek their identity

Il faudra qu'une soif inconnue
nous tenaille
Il nous faudra une nudité
que même la peau ne pourrait travestir

* * *

Il était une fois
le lys et le basilic
les bons et les méchants
la cité
ses portails et murailles
ses chats aux sept âmes
ses saints déguisés en mendiants
ses rois d'un jour
ses vierges brûlant sur un chandelier
sa boue montant jusqu'aux genoux
ses fêtes où le pardon frappe aux portes
en babouches et djellaba blanche
Il était une fois
une fois seulement
la quiétude

* * *

An unprecedented thirst
must tear at us
We need a nudity
that even skin cannot disguise

* * *

Once there were
lilies and basil
good people and bad people
the city
its gates and walls
its cats with nine lives
its saints disguised as beggars
its kings for a day
its virgins lighting candles
its mud knee-deep
its feast days with clemency knocking at doors
in babouches and a white djellaba
Once
but only once
there was quiet

* * *

L'enfant s'éloigne
tirant avec une ficelle
son petit coffre en bois
Cercueil ou berceau ?
Il ne sait
Il marche
parce qu'on lui a parlé de la mer
comme d'un âge adulte de l'eau
et des îles
comme de villes de cristal
érigées dans un jardin
L'enfant s'éloigne
et sa tête blanchit
à la vitesse de la rumeur

* * *

Maître de la lumière
voici le désert
sa page impitoyable
et loyale
Etends tes doigts sur la flamme
et supporte
Puis écris la vague qui te tourmente
vocalise-la

The child goes off
pulling his little wooden box
on a string
Coffin or cradle?
He doesn't know
He is walking
because he has been told that the sea
is a kind of grown-up water
and islands are
like crystal cities
built in a garden
The child goes off
and his hair turns white
at the speed of rumor

* * *

Master of light
look at the desert
light's merciless
and faithful page
Hold you fingers over the flame
and bear the pain
Then write of the force that torments you
voice it

Fais que ta main soit l'artisane
de cette migration amoureuse
dans le silence des braves
Ne te retourne pas
pour contempler ton œuvre
Déjà le vent apocryphe
s'acharne sur la trace
et le désert lave sa planche
l'enduit de glaise
pour l'égaré
ton imprudent sosie
qu'une autre vague tourmente

* * *

La fenêtre est là
A quoi sert de l'ouvrir
tant qu'elle donnera sur une porte close
avec cet incroyable numéro
18611 ?
Il faut apprendre à vivre en enfer
avec les hétaïres sacrées
les imprécateurs bègues
les saints affectés de coïtus interruptus
les fourmis carnivores

Make your hand the artisan
of this amorous migration
in the silence of the brave
Do not look back
to behold your work
Already the apocryphal wind
is hot on the trail
the desert is clearing its slate
and covering it with loam
for the one who is lost
your reckless double
whom another force torments

* * *

The window is there
Why bother opening it
so long as it gives onto a closed door
bearing the incredible number
18611?
You must learn to live in hell
with sacred hetairai
stammering blasphemers
saints afflicted by coitus interruptus
flesh-eating ants

que même Satan n'a pu suborner
Apprendre à jouer des coudes
pour étaler son tapis de prière
là où il y a urgence
de compassion

* * *

La fenêtre cédera un jour
lorsque les hommes n'y pourront rien
et qu'ils n'auront en guise de mains
que des moignons pourris
peu habiles à compter l'argent
Lorsqu'ils perdront la vue
à force d'éviter le regard de leurs semblables
Lorsque la bête les aura rongés
jusqu'à la corde de leur graisse d'orgueil
Lorsque la puanteur de leurs idées
fera fuir même les dieux
qu'ils ont calomniés d'existence

* * *

that even Satan could not corrupt
And learn to jostle your way through
to lay your prayer carpet
where there is an urgent call
for compassion

* * *

The window will yield one day
when men can do nothing to help it
when for hands all they have is
rotten stumps
hardly useful for counting money
When they lose their sight
from avoiding the gaze of their peers
When the beast has chewed
the flab of their pride
down to the bone
When the stench of their ideas
repels even the gods
that they falsely accuse of existing

* * *

Sûr
que cette planète a la nausée
Elle n'en peut plus
de devoir dispenser
le message de rosée
les éblouissements
la rage des beautés
qu'on ne peut enfermer dans un nom
le bruissement de tout fragile
les fragrances d'oasis boréales
Mille riens invisibles
qui font lianes
autour du sexe écartelé
où éclot le nouveau-né
Sûr qu'elle n'a plus envie
d'être lyrique

                                                 * * *

Paix
ne serait-ce qu'une minute
pour rendre au matin
ce qui appartient au matin
l'offrande et l'allégeance
le sein dardant ses rayons

Be sure
that this planet is nauseated
It can no longer stomach
having to spread
messages about the dew
dazzling wonders
the cult of beauty
beyond naming
the frail rustle of everything
the scents of boreal oases
The horde of invisible trivialities
encircling like lianas
the outspread sex
whence the newborn springs
Be sure the earth no longer wishes
to wax lyrical

* * *

Peace
if only for a moment
to render unto the morning
those things that are the morning's
offerings and allegiance
the breast shooting forth its rays

la salive attendrissant la chair
sous la dent
le fabuleux sourire des amants
délicieusement inconscients
Et bénie soit la tourmente !

* * *

Ah il ne s'agit pas d'oublier
Quoi qu'en pensent les poètes
nous avons été heureux quelques fois
Le simple mot de liberté
nous a fait pleurer comme des Madeleines
Des hommes comme nous
nous ont semblé être
des dieux de bonté et de miséricorde
Nous avons baptisé places et rues
en autant de soleils fraternels
Nous avons laissé pousser barbe et cheveux
pour que la douceur soit autant virile
que féminine
Nous avons dansé, chanté, bu
et fait l'amour toute la nuit
sur la paillasse crasseuse
du vieux monde

saliva softening flesh
under the tooth
the marvelous smile of lovers
so delightfully unconscious
And blessed be the tempest!

* * *

Oh it's not about forgetting
Whatever the poets may think
we were happy now and again
The simple word freedom
made us weep rivers
Men just like us
we took for
gods of goodness and mercy
We named squares and streets
after such fraternal suns
We let our beards and hair grow long
to make gentleness as manly
as feminine
We danced, sang, drank
and made love all night
on the filthy mattress
of the old world

* * *

Nous en avons aboli des murailles
des prisons
autour de nous
en nous
Nous en avons investi des citadelles
déplacé des montagnes
Et nous n'avons pas hésité
à balayer devant notre porte
au point d'être impitoyables
envers nous-mêmes
Nous avons refermé les livres
petits et grands
pour n'apprendre que de l'intuition
de nos blessures
Nous avons ouvert les yeux
sur notre planète si fragile
monté la garde autour de ses poumons
Ah nous en avons appris des choses
de nos défaites

* * *

We have torn down walls
of prisons
around us
and within us
We have occupied citadels
moved mountains
And not shrunk
from sweeping up in front of our doors
to the point of being unforgiving
toward ourselves
We have closed books
short and long
so as to learn solely by intuition
from our injuries
We have opened our eyes
to our so fragile planet
and stood guard over its lungs
Oh yes, we have learnt much
from our defeats

* * *

Avec cependant ce doute
qui donne à l'espoir
l'amertume tonique de son ivresse
Avec cependant cet espoir
qui donne au doute
le lyrisme de sa méthode
Avec des hauts et des bas
des couples qui foutaient le camp
des enfants qui crachaient dans la soupe
Avec des amis qui disparaissaient
et reparaissaient en nœud papillon
Avec des exclusions et contre-exclusions
Avec la bouillie des dogmes
dont il restait toujours quelque chose
Avec la fureur rentrée réveillant les ulcères
Nous avons tenu autant que possible
dans ce radeau de fortune

* * *

Le soleil se meurt
une rumeur d'homme à la bouche
Le chaos viendra balayer la scène
de cette vieille tragédie
racontée mille et une fois

Even with the doubt
that lends hope
the tonic bitterness of its excess
Even with the hope
that lends doubt
the lyricism of its constancy
Even with the ups and downs
the couples who packed it in
the kids who spat in the soup
The friends who disappeared
only to pop up again in bow-ties
The expulsions and counter-expulsions
The hodgepodge of dogmas
that always left something behind
Even with the bottled-up ulcer-arousing anger
We held on as best we could
to our makeshift raft

* * *

The sun is dying
with human murmurs on its lips
Chaos will come and clear the stage
of this old tragedy
told a thousand times

par un idiot
devant une salle vide
Ce sera une autre éternité
d'absence trouble
de duel entre masques
et de manque à écrire

Créteil, 1990

by an idiot
in an empty theater
There will be another eternity
of roiled absence
dueling masks
and the failure to write

Créteil, 1990

ÉLOGE DE LA DÉFAITE

Ce matin plus calme
Les bourgeons s'enhardissent
pas les mots
encore blessés
souillés
Une mouche seule
fait le printemps

La mort s'est lassée

Même la paix est laide

Loin du corps qui fut
le sang rampe
entre les rives dévastées
du cœur

Babylone
a détruit
Babylone

Que s'édifie
le Mur de l'Hilarité !

IN PRAISE OF DEFEAT

A calmer morning
The buds are getting bolder
Not words
still wounded
soiled
A single fly makes
a spring

Death is weary

Even peace is ugly

Far from the body that was
blood crawls
between the devastated banks
of the heart

Babylon
has destroyed
Babylon

Let the Wall of Mirth
be built!

On viendra
s'y cogner le front
les dents
le sexe
On crèvera de rire
jusqu'au dernier
si cela peut soulager la terre

Ah je l'ai arpentée
cette terre
Partout imploré
le ciel humain
Et maintenant
parfois je trouve
que ma cellule
m'a été plus clémente

L'arbre
peut-il mentir
lui aussi ?

D'une cohue l'autre
je cherche les yeux
qui cherchent les miens

We'll come
and bang our heads
teeth
sexual organs
against it
We'll die laughing
to the last man
if it can relieve the earth

Oh I have walked
this earth
And everywhere beseeched
the human heavens
And now
I sometimes think
that my cell
was more forgiving

Can
the tree
lie too?

From one throng
to the next
I seek eyes
that seek mine

Les passants
ont-ils encore des yeux ?

La peur de vivre
a remplacé
la peur de mourir

Assis sur la chaise de Van Gogh
devant un bûcher froid
je me tords l'oreille
et défie les tournesols

L'amour s'insinue
et dit :
Si je déserte
que restera-t-il ?

Les pluies
ne tarderont pas
Elles rouleront leur acide
sur l'ardoise des toits
noirciront les bagues
aux doigts des forsythias
La menace des nuages
se confirme

Do passersby
still have eyes?

The fear of living
has replaced
the fear of dying

Sitting in Van Gogh's chair
by a cold fireside
I twist my ear
and challenge sunflowers

Love sneaks in
and says:
If I quit
what will be left?

The rains
will not be long coming
They will roll their acid
over the roof slates
darken the rings
on the fingers of the forsythia
The menace of the clouds
is borne out

Derrière les nuages affairés
le miroir brûle
comme un torchon

Ah mon frère
mon semblable
Tu es donc ainsi ?

Les mots me fuient
Je partage leur méfiance

Mais que faire
quand ce sont les morts qui lancinent
Rien d'audible
Juste un signe
de sous les décombres
« Enterrez-nous dignement ! »

La guerre
dites-vous
Quelle guerre ?

Voilà
je démissionne du genre humain
Je vais me faire chien

Behind the busy clouds
the mirror burns
like a rag

Ah my brother
my like
So this is how you are?

I scare words away
I share their mistrust

But what to do
when it is the dead who plead
Nothing audible
Just a signal
from under the rubble
"Bury us with dignity!"

War
you say
What war?

Alright then
I resign from the human race
I'll turn myself into a dog

ou plutôt chienne
Je vais apprendre à flairer
le mal
de loin
de très loin

Si les chiens me rejettent
je demanderai aux magnolias
de m'accepter pour fleur
le temps que dure
une fleur de magnolia

Sinon
j'irai me terrer dans une fourmilière
Réapprendre ce qu'est le travail
invisible
que les géants écrasent
plus ou moins par mégarde

J'irai de l'autre côté
Celui où le temps n'est pas une machine
à broyer la vie
Celui où l'espace
n'est pas un obstacle à la vue
Là où je me confondrai

or rather a bitch
I'll learn to sniff out
evil
from far away
very far away

If dogs turn me down
I'll ask the magnolias
to take me as a flower
for as long as
a magnolia flower lasts

Failing that
I'll go and hole up in an anthill
to rediscover what the invisible work
is like
that giants crush
more or less by mistake

I'll go over to the other side
Where time is not a machine
for grinding up life
Where space
is not an obstacle to sight
Where I'll be indistinguishable

avec un corps aimant-aimé
qui n'a point enfanté
et qui n'a point été enfanté

Je serai l'ermite invisible
l'instrument du désert

Je serai bref
et entier
pour ne pas rompre l'harmonie
de l'univers

Ah j'aimerai
d'amour
le seul être
que je n'ai pas entendu blasphémer
le nom de l'homme

Elle m'aura rejoint
dans ma petitesse
mon aimée aux ongles rongés
et nous vivrons jusqu'à la fin
d'une goutte d'eau
et d'une amande

from a body loving and loved
that has never given birth
and has never been born

I shall be the invisible hermit
tool of the desert

I shall be brief
and whole
so as not to break the harmony
of the universe

Ah I shall love
with a true love
the only being
whom I have not heard taking
the name of man
in vain

She will have joined me
in my insignificance
my beloved with her chewed fingernails
and we shall live till the end
on a drop of water
and an almond

Partagerez-vous
un rêve
si menu ?

Non
le temps n'est pas au rêve
C'est impudique un rêve
et inutile
comme les larmes du poète

Il n'y a de monde
que ce monde-ci
A lui nous appartenons
et à lui nous retournons
Que sa raison soit sanctifiée
Que son règne demeure

Il y a tout dans ce monde
tant décrié
Le soleil, la lune
les vaches, les cochons
la mer, la glèbe
l'amour, la haine
la joie, la tristesse

Would you share
in a dream
so small?

No
these times are not for dreams
Dreams are improper
and as useless
as a poet's tears

There is no world
but this one
To it we belong
and to it we return
May its purpose be sanctified
May its reign endure

In this world so disparaged
you have everything
The sun, the moon
cows, pigs
the sea, the soil
love, hate
joy, sadness

la paix, la guerre
les hauts et les bas
Que voulez-vous donc de plus ?

Ce monde n'est pas parfait
mais c'est le seul qui existe
Trouvez-nous-en un autre !

Si j'avais des réponses
je ne me brûlerais pas aux questions

Je voudrais croire
à la réalité de mon corps
de ses besoins
Mais je ne sais d'où vient
cette voix
qui se refuse aux apparences

Je voudrais me soumettre
corps et âme
comme une femme
ou comme un homme
converti à l'amour

peace, war
highs and lows
What more could you ask?

This world is not perfect
but it is the only one that exists
See if you can find us another!

If I had answers
I would not be consumed by questions

I would like to believe
in the reality of my body
and its needs
But I don't know
where this voice comes from
that balks at appearances

I would like to submit
body and soul
like a woman
or like a man
converted to love

Je voudrais dormir
un siècle ou deux
et me réveiller
avec d'autres idées
d'autres passions
Mon troisième œil bien ouvert
au front
ou mieux dans la nuque

Je voudrais
chaque fois que j'ouvre la main
dans mon sommeil
qu'une main anonyme
s'insinue dans la mienne
et m'invite
par petites pressions universelles
au partage d'un repas
qui ne serait pas celui de la trahison

Je voudrais
sortir maintenant de ma chambre close
et trouver au tournant de la rue
Saïda Menebhi
plus vivante que quand elle était vivante

I would like to sleep
for a century or two
and wake up
with different ideas
different passions
My third eye wide open
on my forehead
or better at the nape of my neck

I would like it if
every time
I opened my hand in my sleep
an anonymous hand
crept into mine
and invited me
with little universal squeezes
to share a meal
that was not the supper of betrayal

I would like
to leave my closed room now
and at the street corner
run into Saïda Menebhi*
more alive even than when she was alive

* Militant and prison mate. Died in 1977 during a hunger strike.

tenant par la main une petite fille
qui lui ressemblerait comme deux gouttes d'eau
Et la petite fille
me tendrait une orchidée noire
en disant : Ça, c'est pour la peine du poète

Je voudrais
qu'un oiseau-rokh
vienne m'empoigner sans ménagement
me fasse voler dans les airs
et me dépose dans ce pays
où la vallée des roses
aurait absorbé la vallée des larmes
Maroc mien
que je dénommerais Levant de l'âme

Je voudrais abattre le conditionnel
et dire au présent :
Lève-toi Lazare
la vraie vie t'attend

Je voudrais
m'arrêter d'écrire
sans avoir mauvaise conscience

holding the hand of a little girl
who was her spitting image
And the little girl would give me a black orchid
saying: This is for the suffering of the poet

I would like a roc
to come and seize me without mercy
and have me fly through the air
and land in a country
where a vale of roses
has absorbed the vale of tears
in a Morocco of mine
that I would call the Levant of the Soul

I would like to abolish the conditional
and say in the present tense:
Arise Lazarus
real life awaits

I would like
to stop writing
without having a guilty conscience

O nuages immaculés
Ne partez pas
Soyez cléments
En vain je vous livre ma planche
pour que vous effaciez le cauchemar
et me fassiez jouir
de l'oubli
En vain

Je suis
la proie
de moi-même

J'arrache
et je bouffe
Jette les os
derrière mon épaule gauche
Et ça n'en finit pas

A croire
qu'un géant masochiste et paresseux
a choisi de m'habiter
pour que je fasse à sa place
cette triste besogne

Oh immaculate clouds
Do not leave
Be merciful
In vain I hand you my slate
for you to erase the nightmare
and have me delight
in forgetfulness
In vain

I am
my own prey

I tear
and gobble
Toss the bones
over my left shoulder
And there is no end to it

As though
a lazy masochistic giant
had chosen to dwell within me
to have me perform this bleak task
in his stead

Mais nul corps
n'est incessant
L'infini
c'est ce qui le relie
à la banale souffrance

La guerre
dites-vous
Quelle guerre ?

Celle-là
qui se déroule sous nos pieds
aphasiques
bien avant Caïn
Ah quand l'ennemi se découvrit
dans la matière cannibale
Le sec contre l'humide
Le dur contre le friable
Pousse-toi que je m'y mette
Arbres titans contre tritons de laves
Gaz contre gaz
Le vaste dessin animé
de la Création
Dieux jaloux
déesses perverses

But no body
is immortal
The infinite
is what connects it
to ordinary suffering

War
you say
What war?

The one
waged beneath our aphasic feet
well before Cain
Ah! when the enemy revealed itself
within cannibal matter
Dry versus wet
Hard versus friable
Move over let me get at it
Titanic trees versus Tritons of lava
Gas against gas
The immense animated cartoon
of Creation
Jealous gods
perverse goddesses

lois d'adultère et d'inceste
Chaos enfantant le chaos
Prix de l'ordre

La guerre
dites-vous
Quelle guerre ?

Celle-là
qui va de la graine au pain
du nuage au verre de thé
du regard oblique
au poignard dans le dos
de la caresse
à la strangulation
du berceau à la tombe
L'homme empêtré
dans ce nœud de pulsions
Victime
bourreau
bourreau du bourreau
et qui ne sait où donner du cœur
de la tête
vaincu chaque fois
se donnant des airs de vainqueur

adultery and incest taboos
Chaos generating chaos
The price of order

War
you say
What war?

The one
that leads from the seed to the loaf
from the cloud to the cup of tea
from the sideways look
to the stab in the back
from a caress
to a strangling
from cradle to grave
The man tied up in
this knot of impulses
is victim
executioner
executioner of executioners
and knows not where to direct
heart or head
defeated at every turn
he parades as a victor

Et que dire de l'enfant
qui ne sait que regarder ?

Viens mon enfant
Baptise ton aïeul
convertis-le à ton regard muet
Verse dans sa paume
quelques gouttes du baume

La guerre
dites-vous
Quelle guerre ?

Appelons-la
« Guerre des Arabes »
On pourra ainsi
plus tard
y faire allusion

Est-ce le soleil qui se lève
ou l'ultime lueur
d'un astre qui s'éteint ?

Ils ont refermé le livre
du désert

And what of the child
who knows only how to watch?

Come my child
Baptize your grandfather
convert him to your mute gaze
Pour onto his palm
a few drops of your balm

War
you say
What war?

Let us call it
"The War of the Arabs"
In that way
later on
we can refer to it

Is it the sun rising
or the last rays
of a dying star?

They have closed the book
of the desert

revêtu les longs manteaux
de la ressemblance
décrété la chasse à l'homme
sur toute la planète

Ils se sont improvisés juges
avocats
jurés
Ils ont rempli la salle
de leurs sbires
et fait vider le box des accusés

Ils ont divisé
le père et la mère
la sœur et le frère
l'amant et l'amante

Ils ont détourné
le fleuve
de la vérité

Et toi
perdu

donned the long cloaks
of resemblance
declared a manhunt
all over the planet

They have appointed themselves judges
lawyers
jurors
They have packed the court
with their
lackeys
and emptied
the defendants' dock

They have torn apart
father from mother
sister from brother
lover from lover

they have diverted
the river
of truth

And you
lost

au milieu de cette clameur toxique
titubant dans la fournaise
Homme lointain
n'ayant plus de l'homme
ni la qualité
ni la quantité
Hirsute
dans la bourrasque délétère
Maintenant que le ciel a disparu
que reste-t-il à tes yeux
ton index
pour invoquer la miséricorde ?
Qui te croira
même si tu blasphèmes
et dis : J'ai vu l'enfer
Dieu en est innocent ?
On te clouera à tes atavismes
ta fatalité
et tu n'en seras pas
à ta dernière leçon
Il te faudra de nouveau
te couvrir de l'antique manteau
sous la neige et la lave
les huées et les insultes
répéter à voix basse

amid this toxic hullabaloo
tottering into the furnace
Man is far away
bereft now
of either qualitative
or quantitative
humanity
Shaggy
in the ravaging blasts
Now that heaven has vanished
what remains of your eyes
or forefinger
with which to call for mercy?
Who will believe you
even if you blaspheme
and say: I have seen hell
Can God be innocent of this?
You will be nailed to your atavism
your fate
and that won't be the end of it
You will be obliged once more
to cover yourself in the ancient mantle
against snow and lava
against hoots and insults

jusqu'à l'évanouissement
ton credo suspect
Pleure mon ami
tu n'en seras pas plus méprisé
Et cela fait du bien

O vaincus de tous les temps
voici venir l'ère
de votre humble message
Prenez garde
Ne vous mettez pas en tête
d'écrire l'Histoire
Laissez-la aux vainqueurs
Racontez plutôt
ce que nous avons perdu
dans le dédale de l'aveuglement
Faites-le en énigmes
contes, devinettes, charades
petits poèmes rimés ou en prose
N'écrivez rien
racontez
Que la parole s'emboîte dans le souffle
et remplisse la bouche
Qu'elle se déverse de vos lèvres

reciting your suspect credo
under your breath
until you pass out
Weep my friend
you will not be the more scorned for it
And it helps

Oh losers of all time
the moment for your
humble message
is at hand
Do not take a notion
to write History
Leave that to the victors
Tell instead
what we have lost
in the labyrinth of blindness
Do so by means of enigmas
tales, riddles, charades
in little rhymes or prose
Write nothing
recount
Let speech walk in step with breath
and fill your mouth
Let it pour from your lips

tantôt miel
tantôt coloquinte
Rendez sa vigueur
à la mémoire en miettes
sauvegardez-la
Et puis procréez
faites passer le message
Parlez au-dessus de la haine
de la rancœur
Couvrez-les de vos voix prophétiques
et des cendres de cette planète
qui se refroidit
et s'éteint
faute d'amour

Montlouis-sur-Loire, 1991

like honey
or colocynth
Restore speech's vigor
to shattered memory
preserve it
And then propagate
pass along the message
Speak beyond hate
beyond rancor
Cover these with your prophetic voices
with the embers of this planet
which is cooling
and dying
for want of love

Montlouis-sur-Loire, 1991

from

L'ÉTREINTE DU MONDE

THE WORLD'S EMBRACE

(1993)

LES ÉCROULEMENTS

Regarde mon amour
ce monde qui s'écroule
autour de nous
en nous
Serre bien ma tête contre ta poitrine
et dis-moi ce que tu vois
Pourquoi ce silence ?
Dis-moi simplement ce que tu vois
Les étoiles contaminées tombent-elles
de l'arbre de la connaissance
Le nuage toxique des idées
nous submergera-t-il bientôt ?

Dis-moi ce que tu vois
Brûle-t-on déjà les livres sur les places publiques
Rase-t-on la tête des femmes avant de les lapider
Y a-t-il des processions d'hommes à cagoule
brandissant croix et cimeterres
Pourquoi ce silence, mon aimée
Sommes-nous sur une île flottante
ou voguons-nous sur une torpille
Sommes-nous seuls

COLLAPSES

Look my love
at this world collapsing
around us
within us
Hold my head tight against your breast
and tell me what you see
Why this silence?
Tell me simply what you see
Are contaminated stars falling
from the tree of knowledge
Will the toxic cloud of ideas
soon engulf us?

Tell me what you see
Are they burning books yet on public squares
Are they shaving women's heads before stoning them
Are there processions of hooded men
brandishing crosses and scimitars?
Why this silence, my love
Are we on a floating island
or riding on a torpedo
Are we alone

ou enchaînés à d'autres frères d'infortune
Quel jour sommes-nous
Quelle heure est-il ?

Serre bien ma tête contre ta poitrine
et si tu peux
ouvre ton ventre et accueille-moi
au creuset de ta force
Fais-moi remonter le fleuve
jusqu'à la source des sources
Replonge-moi dans la vasque de vie
et verse sur ma fontanelle
sept poignées d'orge
en fredonnant la chanson de Fayrouz
celle que tu chantes mieux qu'elle

Pourquoi pleures-tu
As-tu peur pour le monde
ou pour notre amour
Ne peux-tu rien pour moi ?
Alors dis-moi simplement ce que tu vois
De quel mal meurt-on aujourd'hui
Quelle est cette arme invisible qui extirpe l'âme
et le goût à nul autre pareil de la vie
Quelle est cette caravane qui dévore ses chameaux

or shackled to other companions in misfortune
What day are we
What time is it?

Hold my head tightly against your breast
and if you can
open your belly and welcome me
into the crucible of your strength
Carry me upstream
to the spring of springs
Plunge me into the cauldron of life
and sprinkle seven handfuls of barley
upon my fontanel
as you hum Fayrouz's song
the one you sing better than her

Why are you crying
Are you afraid for the world
or for our love
Can you do nothing for me?
Then tell me simply what you see
What ailment is killing us today
What is this invisible weapon that destroys the soul
and the unrivaled taste for life
What is this caravan that devours its camels

et vide ses outres d'eau dans le sable
Quel est ce magicien
qui fait de la guerre un acte d'amour ?

Pourquoi ce silence
Crois-tu toi aussi que les mots sont si souillés
qu'ils ne servent même plus à demander son chemin
Crois-tu qu'il n'y a plus rien à dire
et que mes pauvres versets
ne sont que dérision sur dérision
Veux-tu que je me taise
pour te laisser regarder ces écroulements
dans la dignité du silence ?

Serre bien ma tête contre ta poitrine
et berce-moi
Dans le cocon soyeux de tes mains
ma tête se fera toute petite
Le gros abcès des idées crèvera
et je redeviendrai l'enfant d'un autre siècle
effrayé par le tonnerre
et qui se donne du courage
en ânonnant un vieil alphabet
à la lueur d'une bougie
dans la maison interdite de Fès

and empties its waterskins into the sand
Who is this magician
who turns war into an act of love?

Why this silence
Do you too believe that words are so corrupted
that they no longer serve even to ask the way
Do you think there is nothing left to say
and that every one of my poor verses
is more ridiculous than the next
Do you want me to go quiet
and let you contemplate these collapses
in dignified silence?

Hold my head tightly against your breast
and rock me
In the silky cocoon of your hands
my head will get very small
The great abscess of ideas will burst
and I will once more become the child of another century
scared by thunder
and building up my courage
by muttering an old alphabet
by candlelight
in the forbidden house of Fez

près d'un brasero où brûlent encens et fenugrec
et éclate dans l'alun le mauvais œil
Berce cet enfant qui n'a point été bercé
afin qu'il revive et fasse revivre entre tes bras
un monde englouti, saccagé, volé
dont il ne reste
qu'un âcre parfum d'innocence

Pourquoi ce silence mon aimée
Ai-je réveillé en toi ta douleur tue
ou le même besoin d'être bercée
Celui d'une petite fille née dans une autre guerre
partie au-delà des mers
pour rencontrer le soleil de ses livres d'images
en caresser les fruits d'or dans un verger
gardé par des légionnaires ?
Toi ignorant ce vain tourment des racines
plus près de l'homme que de sa rumeur
apprenant vite les langues méprisées
sachant semer là où saigne la glèbe
planter là où l'arrachement s'acharne
Tout cela, en faisant mine de passer
avec la loyauté des oiseaux migrateurs
et ce vague à l'âme qui les déchire en douceur
entre nid et périple

by a brasero where incense and fenugreek are burning
and the evil eye gleams from the alum
Rock this child who has never been rocked
that he may return to life in your arms
and revive a world swallowed up, pillaged, stolen
of which nothing remains
save a bitter scent of innocence

Why this silence my love
Have I awakened in you your silenced pain
or the same need to be rocked
That of a little girl born during another war
gone away overseas
to find the sun of her picture books
and caress golden fruit in an orchard
guarded by legionnaires?
You who know nothing of the useless torment of roots
who are closer to man than to man's clamor
quick learner of scorned languages
knowing how to sow where the soil bleeds
to plant where plants are continually uprooted
All of it with an air of passing by
as faithfully as migratory birds
and the sadness that gently torments them
between nest and journey

Pourquoi pleures-tu
Est-ce pour ce monde englouti
ou pour ce monde qui s'écroule
Pour l'enfant ou pour l'adulte
Pouvons-nous choisir entre deux adieux
nous résoudre à l'adieu
alors que le miracle est là
nos pouls qui battent paisiblement
jouent leur symphonie
poignet contre poignet
même si les armes parlent
à la place des poètes ?

Serre bien ma tête contre ta poitrine
et dis-moi ce que tu vois
avec l'œil que nous avons patiemment cultivé
au plus noir des ténèbres
quand les jours de l'année se comptaient à l'envers
quand le printemps nous dévorait le sexe
quand l'automne était une hirondelle de cire
sur notre oreiller
quand l'été nous marquait au fer rouge dans ses fourgons
et l'hiver nous accordait une miette de miséricorde
Quand quelques mots d'amour lancés à travers les grilles
nous nourrissaient pendant une interminable semaine
Quand je souriais à la conquête de ton sourire

Why are you crying
Is it for a world swallowed up
a world that is collapsing
For the child or for the adult
Can we choose between two farewells
or opt for farewell at all
when the miracle is here
when our pulses beat peacefully
play their symphony
wrist to wrist
even if weaponry speaks
instead of poets?

Hold my head tightly against your breast
and tell me what you see
with the eye that we so patiently trained
in the darkest of shadows
when the days of the year were counted backwards
when spring gnawed at our sexual parts
when fall was a wax swallow
on our pillow
when summer branded us with its red-hot pokers
and winter granted us a crumb of mercy
When a few words of love slipped between bars
nourished us through an endless week
When I smiled at winning a smile from you

et que tu versais la larme que je me refusais
Quand je faisais sortir de ma tête un pigeon
pour que tu l'arbores fièrement sur ton épaule
dans les files d'attente

Dis-moi ce que tu vois
avec cet œil de chair et d'acier
familier des ténèbres
vieux comme la conscience
contempteur de l'oubli
témoin irrécusable
Pourquoi ce silence mon aimée
Cet œil ne peut s'éteindre, n'est-ce pas ?
Alors dis-moi ce que tu vois
A-t-on commencé à détruire Grenade
Les barbares sont-ils à nos portes
Comment sont les barbares
Parlent-ils une langue inconnue
Viennent-ils vraiment d'une autre galaxie
d'une autre dimension du temps
En quoi nous ressemblent-ils
Quoi en eux est si terrifiant ?

Dis-moi ce que tu vois
Le fleuve des images monte-t-il toujours
Pour quand prévoit-on le déluge

and you shed the tear that I forbade myself
When I produced a dove from my head
for you to show off with pride on your shoulder
in the waiting lines

Tell me what you see
with that eye of flesh and steel
so accustomed to the shadows
as old as consciousness
scorner of forgetfulness
irreproachable witness
Why this silence my love
Surely that eye can never close?
So tell me what you see
Have they begun to destroy Granada
Are the barbarians at our gates
What are the barbarians like
Do they speak an unknown language
Do they really come from another galaxy
from another dimension in time
In what ways are they like us
What is so terrifying about them?

Tell me what you see
Is the river of images still rising
When is the flood expected

Se bat-on déjà aux abords de l'arche
Que fait-on des chevaux blessés
des enfants qui ne peuvent pas marcher
Les femmes ont-elles pris les armes à leur tour
Y a-t-il au milieu de la horde un prophète perdu ?

Pourquoi ce silence mon aimée
Me condamnerais-tu à devoir imaginer
ce que je n'aurais jamais accepté d'imaginer
dussé-je me crever les yeux
Comment aurais-je pu croire que j'exercerais un jour
le métier réprouvé du corbeau
ou même le sombre office du cygne
Moi l'artisan fils de l'artisan
laboureur de l'antique beauté
tisserand de l'espérance
veilleur de l'âtre jusqu'aux cendres
berger sans gourdin du troupeau
que je dressais contre le chien-loup
Moi l'artisan fils de l'artisan
guettant l'arc-en-ciel
pour ne pas me tromper sur les couleurs
en me fiant à leurs noms
les recueillant une à une
dans la marmite en cuivre de ma génitrice
comme autant d'épices rares

Is fighting already going on around the ark
What is being done with the wounded horses
and the children who cannot walk
Have the women taken up arms in their turn
Is there a lost prophet somewhere in the horde?

Why this silence my beloved
Would you condemn me to imagining
what I would rather gouge my eyes out
than ever agree to imagine
How could I have believed that I would one day
carry out the crow's reprehensible task
or even the grim duty of the swan
I, craftsman and craftsman's son
carver of ancient beauty
weaver of hope
keeper of the hearth down to the embers
shepherd crook-less of the flock
I used to muster against the wolf-dogs
I, craftsman and craftsman's son
studying the rainbow
so as not to get its colors wrong
relying on their names
collecting them one by one
in the copper cooking pot of my progenitress
like so many rare spices

destinées aux joies humaines
au partage d'un repas qui ne devient licite
que si les pauvres le bénissent et l'honorent ?

Comment aurais-je pu croire
que ce rêve qui m'a converti à l'homme
deviendrait un cauchemar
que les héros de ma jeunesse
scieraient l'arbre de mon chant
que les livres où j'avais rencontré mes sosies
jauniraient au fond de ma bibliothèque
que mon errance vouée à la rencontre
manquerait à ce point du gobelet d'eau
et de la galette déposés au bord de la route
par Celui ou Celle qui veille sur l'errance ?

Comment aurais-je pu croire
au mirage d'un si beau chemin
aux chaînes d'un si fol horizon
au ver dans un si beau fruit
Où donc était la faille ?

Pourquoi ce silence mon aimée
veux-tu attiser encore plus en moi la parole
me faire vaticiner, blasphémer
refaire avec les mots ce que les hommes

to enhance human enjoyment
at a common meal illicit
unless blessed and honored by the poor?

How could I have believed
that the dream that converted me to mankind
would turn into a nightmare
that the heroes of my youth
would fell the tree of my song
that the books where I had found my doubles
would yellow in the depths of my library
that my wanderings in quest of encounter
would so lack so much as the glass of water
and the loaf left by the wayside
by He or She who takes care of the wanderer?

How could I have believed
that so beautiful a road was a mirage
that so wild a horizon hid chains
that so fine a fruit had a worm
For where was the flaw?

Why this silence my beloved
are you out to stoke the fire of speech in me even more
have me prophetize, blaspheme
redo with words what men

ont défait avec les mots
retrouver sens à ce qui s'est ligué contre le sens
arrêter d'un cri l'engrenage qui a pris tout mon corps
et ne m'a laissé que ce semblant de voix
Mais qui parle en moi
Est-ce toi, ô mon œil
ou ma parole en deuil ?
Alors va, parole
délie-moi
délire-moi
rends à ma langue ses langues perdues
ses antiques croyances
les frelons ingouvernables de ses mots
ses jungles et leurs réducteurs de têtes froides
Délivre-moi de l'étau de toute raison
Prends mes peaux de loup et d'agneau
mon encrier fossile, mes crayons
le pain des funérailles sur lequel j'ai prêté serment
Prends ce bâton de pèlerin
qui a cru guider un aveugle
Prends la dernière cigarette et jette le paquet

Va ma parole
délie-moi
délire-moi

have undone with words
find meaning in what has allied against meaning
halt with a single cry the chain reaction
that has taken over my whole body
and left me nothing but this travesty of a voice
But who speaks in me
Is it you, oh my eyes
or is it my grieving voice?
Come on then, voice
unleash me
let me rave
give my tongue back the tongues it has lost
its long-gone beliefs
its ungovernable hornets of words
its jungles with their shrinkers of cool heads
Deliver me from the vise of all rationality
Take my wolf and lamb skins
my fossil inkwell, my pencils
the funeral bread on which I swore my oath
Take this pilgrim's staff
that thought it was guiding a blind man
Take the last cigarette and throw away the pack

Come on my voice
unleash me
let me rave

sois drue, âpre, rêche, ardue, hérissée
Monte et bouillonne
Déverse-toi
Lave les mots traînés dans la boue
et les bouches putrides
Fais qu'en toi la vague se soulève
et d'un bond inexplicable quitte la mer
avec tous les poissons qui refusent la fatalité aquatique
Fais qu'en toi un autre magma se forme
d'un limon aguerri
et qu'il nous promette une genèse têtue
sans enfer ni paradis
lente comme la caresse qui enflamme le désir

Va ma parole
ma loyale
Maintenant, corps entier
je parle
avec tous mes avortements
Vaincu, je ne me rends pas
Je vais ouvrir un grand chantier dans ma mémoire
allumer des torches avec les prunelles de mes martyrs
battre le tambour avec leurs mains
Nous allons danser la danse
des soleils qu'on nous a volés

be firm, fierce, rough, difficult, quarrelsome
Come to the boil
Overflow
Cleanse words dragged through the mud
and mouths that are putrid
Cause a wave to rise within you
and leave the sea in a baffling leap
along with all the fish that reject their watery fate
Cause a new magma to form within you
from hardened silt
may it assure us of an obstinate genesis
without heaven or hell
slow as the caress that sparks desire

Come on my voice
my loyal voice
Now, my body whole
I speak
despite all my miscarriages
Defeated, I do not surrender
I am going to open up a great building site in my memory
light torches with the eyes of my martyrs
beat the drum with their hands
We shall dance the dance
of the suns stolen from us

des taureaux égorgés
et jetés avec nous dans nos cellules
des danseuses sacrées brûlées pour délit de danse

Ah ma parole
Ne laisse en jachère nul organe
arrose-les d'un suc de grossesse et de jouvence
Danse-moi
Danse-nous
Ruines ou pas ruines
chaos ou abysse
Dieu mort ou vif
danse toute
Je viens de toi à toi
pauvre et nu comme il se doit
avec une poignée de sel dans la bouche
les ongles noircis et longs
foulant les braises ardentes
dans un nuage de santal et de viscères fumants
levant l'étendard jaune et noir des femmes folles
prêtresses des trous dans la terre
Je viens à vous
ô mère et père
rejoindre le cortège et la robe
nouer ma foi à la corde de votre foi

of the bulls slaughtered
and tossed with us into our cells
of the sacred dancing women burnt for the sin of dancing

Ah my voice
let no organ lie fallow
bathe them all in the sap of fertility and youthfulness
Dance me
Dance us
Ruins or not
chaos or abyss
God dead or living
dance voice the whole of you
I come from you to you
poor and naked as befits
with a pinch of salt in my mouth
nails blackened and long
walking on hot coals
in a cloud of smoking sandalwood and guts
raising the yellow and black banner of crazy women
priestesses from holes in the ground
I come to you
oh mother and father
to join the procession and don the robes
and tie my faith to the cord of yours

J'apporte un bouc, des cierges décorés de Salé
trois pains de sucre
et un bouquet de menthe de Meknès
O faites-moi place
pour que je danse depuis le commencement
et que mon sang noir gicle sur le pavé
indique le chemin du sanctuaire
où nul Imam ne se cache
Ce sanctuaire oublié même de vous
Là où le rebelle échappe aux lois humaines
et peut vivre en homme libre

Ah parole
danse-moi
danse-nous
Je te confie ces corps en transe salutaire
ces tumeurs bénignes et non bénignes
ces talismans incrustés dans la peau
pour instiller la patience du roc
et rendre le sort moins vorace
Je te confie
ce cortège hésitant entre frénésie et soumission
Je te confie
tambours, crotales
et violons suborneurs

I bring a goat, decorated candles from Salé
three sugarloaves
and a bunch of mint from Meknes
Oh make room for me to dance
from the beginning
so my dark blood may splash the pavement
and show the way to the sanctuary
where no imam is hiding
That sanctuary forgotten even by you
That place where the rebel escapes human laws
and can live as a free man

Ah voice
dance me
dance us
I entrust you with these bodies in healthy trance
these tumors benign and malignant
these talismans embedded in the skin
to instill a rock-like patience
and render fate less voracious
I entrust you
with this procession havering between frenzy and submission
I entrust you
with drums, castanets
and seductive violins

Je te confie
la bouilloire et les aiguières
le chaudron, le feu et ses serveurs
Je te confie
la vierge et les esprits qui l'habitent
son cri multiplié de fausse parturiente
ses seins aveuglants
ses hanches de bateau ailé fendant la nuit
Je te confie
ô maîtresse imprévisible
les vannes de cette nuit
afin que tu les lâches
à l'heure dite
sans faiblir
sur les ravisseurs de l'aube

Ah parole
d'où viendrais-je, sinon de toi
et où irais-je ?
Je n'ai plus que ce cheveu
pour porter mes pas d'un précipice l'autre
rejoindre quelques étoiles amies
qui s'obstinent à briller dans la désolation du ciel
remonter les cercles d'un enfer incohérent
où d'aucuns ont cru que je me complaisais

I entrust you
with the kettle and the pitchers
the cauldron, and the fire and its minders
I entrust you
with the virgin and the spirits that possess her
her repeated scream of a woman in feigned labor
her dazzling breasts
the winged boat of her hips cleaving the night
I entrust you
oh unpredictable mistress
with the sluicegates of the night
so that you may open them
without hesitation
at the appointed time
upon the ravishers of the dawn

Ah voice
where could I have come from, if not from you
and where would I go?
I have nothing left but a hair
to guide my steps from one precipice to the next
rejoin a few friendly stars
stubbornly shining in the desolation of the sky
and go up through the circles of a chaotic hell
where some once thought I was content

Je n'ai plus que cet empan
d'un royaume
où je n'ai même pas droit à une tente
et dont je ne peux entendre le nom
sans avoir mal
là où aucun fil ne peut recoudre les blessures
Dois-je t'appeler patrie
pour me consoler ou me venger des patries
ou dois-je te laisser libre toi aussi
souveraine de racines, hérésies, amour
en permanence insurgée ?

Ah parole
ma redoutable
toi seule peux me bannir
quand nul tyran ne peut m'exiler
Toi seule peux seller ma monture
lui choisir mors, étriers
et l'engager dans d'effroyables pistes
où tu te complais à me faire lire comme un débutant
dans le sable, les cailloux et les traces refroidies
Toi seule, ô femme jalouse
ne peux accepter ni défaillance ni infidélité
Et voilà que tu me jettes tel un mouchoir en papier

I now have only this strip
of a kingdom
where I am allowed not so much as a tent
and cannot hear its name
without feeling pain
where no thread can stitch up the wounds
Should I call you fatherland
for consolation or take revenge on fatherlands
or should I leave you free also
sovereign of roots, heresies, love
in permanent rebellion?

Ah voice
my formidable voice
only you can banish me
no tyrant can send me into exile
Only you can saddle my mount
select its bit and stirrups
and send it down terrifying paths
where you love to make me
like a novice
trace the signs in the sand, the pebbles, the cold trails
You alone, oh jealous woman
can abide neither failure nor faithlessness
And look, you toss me like a paper handkerchief

dans ce chaos
Voilà que tu me donnes en exercice
cette fin de monde
avec pour tâche de déceler dans les décombres
la pierre noire ou blanche
la graine manquante
l'anneau de bois
ou l'organe tombé en déshérence
l'un ou l'autre de ces chaînons
qu'il faudra ajuster à l'âme
quand viendra l'ère
d'une autre vie aventureuse
Et j'obtempère
je cherche
j'ajoute mon désordre au désordre du monde
J'écris pour ne pas me perdre, ne pas tomber
J'écris en regardant fiévreusement ma montre
la course du soleil
l'ombre portée sur le mur
Je cherche dans le sable pollué
le bout de bois rond
le moindre éclat de pierre blanche
Je guette les oiseaux qui se posent
pour aller leur disputer la fameuse graine

into this chaos
And present me
with this end of the world
as an exercise
my task being to discover in the rubble
a black or white stone
a missing seed
a wooden ring
or an organ in escheat
one or another of these links
needing to be adapted to the soul
with the coming of the era
of a new adventurous life
And I comply
I search
I add my confusion to the world's
I write so as not to get lost, not to fall
I write while frantically checking my watch
the progression of the sun
the shadow thrown on the wall
I search in the filthy sand
for a round piece of wood
the slightest gleam of a white stone
I watch the birds landing
ready to fight with them for the famous seed

Je fouille dans mes artères
pour trouver quelque organe
dont on ne m'a pas appris l'existence à l'école
Et puis, dis-moi
comment déceler une pierre noire dans les ténèbres ?

J'écris avec le tout et le rien
l'énergie du désespoir
et Dieu sait si elle est grande
Je travaille aussi dur qu'un pauvre maçon
que le sort a désigné pour construire des villas de riches
qu'un mineur qui s'acharne sur le ventre de la terre
pour se venger de sa stérilité
qu'il reproche bien sûr à sa femme

J'écris comme d'autres prient
font pénitence
et acceptent le Mystère
J'ai parfois des joies comme eux
des éblouissements
mais j'ai souvent des doutes qu'ils ignorent
des tourments qui donnent à ma prière
ses accents de vérité défiant la foi

I rummage in my arteries
to find some organ
they didn't teach me about at school
And anyway, tell me
how do you find a black stone in the pitch dark?

I write with everything and nothing
with the energy of despair
and God knows it is great
I work as hard as the poor mason
whom fate has chosen to build villas for the rich
or as the miner hacking at the belly of the earth
to avenge a sterility
that he naturally blames on his wife

I write as others pray
do penance
and accept the Mystery
Like them I feel joy at times
bedazzlement
but often I have doubts unknown to them
agonies that lend my prayer
notes of truth that defy faith

J'écris
quand tu m'écris
ô parole
et j'ajoute des choses qui t'échappent
quand je soumets tes mots à l'ordalie
réveille en eux la mémoire qui te précède
Quand je cesse de les traiter comme des esclaves
et les caresse dans le sens de la dignité
Quand je leur donne des rendez-vous amoureux
et arrive avant l'heure pour déguster mon attente
Quand je les invite après le verre de courtoisie
à un repas où nous mangeons avec les doigts
dans le même plat
Quand je n'exige rien d'eux
hormis ce que nous devons
à notre souveraine liberté

J'écris par compassion
en tendant ma sébile
et peu importe si je n'y récolte que des crachats

Ah parole
vois comme tu m'as endurci
Je suis devenu ton enclume
Les marteaux du monde peuvent frapper
je ne me courberai pas

I write
when you write me
oh voice of mine
and I add things that escape you
when I put your words to the test
awaken memories in them that predate you
When I stop treating them as slaves
and rub their dignity the right way
When I make romantic dates with them
and arrive early to savor the wait
When I invite them after the formal cocktail
to a meal eaten with our fingers
from a common bowl
When I ask nothing from them
beyond what we owe
to our sovereign freedom

I write out of compassion
holding out my begging bowl
and if I am spat on for my pains no matter

Ah voice
see how you have hardened me
I have become your anvil
But all the hammers in the world can strike
I shall not buckle

J'attendrai qu'ils s'épuisent
pour me préparer au monde suivant
Et qu'il prépare lui aussi ses marteaux !

Ai-je dormi, mon amour
Qu'ai-je dit de ce que j'ai cru voir
D'où vient ce cheveu
que j'ai, noué autour de la langue
Pourquoi suis-je tout courbatu ?
Mes pieds sont enflés
Ma tête s'est comme vidée d'une eau lourde
Mais je me sens apaisé
prêt à voir et à entendre
me dégager de ton étreinte
et me présenter devant la Balance
pour peser mon âme
ce que mes deux paumes ont pu posséder
y déposer les quelques plumes qui restent de mes ailes
le mouchoir brodé que j'ai oublié dans ma poche
Je ne garderai sur moi que notre bague commune
Ni l'ange du bien ni l'ange du mal ne me la prendra
Je la défendrai avec mes dents et mes ongles
ma rage de grand handicapé
Je la garderai
et comme dans les vieux contes

I'll let them tire
before I prepare myself for the next world
Let it too get its hammers ready!

Did I sleep, my love
What did I say about what I thought I saw
Where did this hair come from
that I find tied around my tongue
Why am I all stiff?
My feet are swollen
My head feels drained of some heavy fluid
But I feel calm now
ready to see and hear
to free myself from your embrace
and to come before the Scales
to weigh my soul
whatever I have been able to hold between my two palms
leaving the few feathers that remain of my wings
the embroidered handkerchief forgotten in my pocket
I shall keep on me only the ring we share
Neither the angel of good nor the angel of evil shall take it
I will defend it tooth and nail
with all the fury of the seriously handicapped
I'll hang on to it
and as in the old tales

je la ferai tourner
quand le geôlier aura cru fermer toutes les issues
Il y aura un grondement et une tour de fumée
un tremblement et un vol impromptu de perdrix
Et le miracle sera là
nos pouls qui battent paisiblement
jouent leur symphonie
poignet contre poignet
pendant que nous voguons
sur l'empan de notre île
avec une nouvelle provision de mots
un peu d'eau douce
quelques fruits
en sachant que notre esquif est de ce monde
qui s'écroule autour de nous
en nous
Notre esquif est de ce monde
encore plus perdu que nous
Notre esquif est de ce monde
éberlué
trop jeune ou trop vieux
pour comprendre
qu'une petite bague
peut faire un miracle

Créteil, March 1992

I'll turn it
when the jailor thinks he has locked all the exits
There will be a rumbling and a puff of smoke
a trembling and an impromptu passing partridge
And the miracle will be at hand
our pulses beating peacefully
play their symphony
wrist against wrist
as we sail the length
of our island
with a new supply of words
a little fresh water
some fruit
in the knowledge that our skiff is of this world
which is collapsing about us
within us
Our skiff is of this world
even more astray than us
Our skiff is of this world
deluded
too young or too old
to grasp
that a little ring
can work a miracle

Créteil, March 1992

LES RÊVES VIENNENT MOURIR SUR LA PAGE

Un à un
les rêves viennent mourir sur la page
Ils se sont donné le mot
ils viennent de partout
pour mourir sur la page
comme les éléphants dans leur cimetière
J'assiste à leurs convulsions
ne peux tendre un verre d'eau
Je les regarde pour la première fois
pour la dernière fois
avant de les envelopper dans le suaire de mes mots
et les déposer sur la barque menue
qui fut jadis leur berceau
Le courant les emporte
et bien vite me les ramène
comme si le large n'était pas là-bas
mais ici sur la page

DREAMS COME TO DIE ON THE PAGE

One by one
dreams come to die on the page
The word was passed around
They come from everywhere
to die on the page
like elephants in their graveyard
I witness their convulsions
cannot offer them a glass of water
I look at them for the first time
for the last time
before wrapping them in the shroud of my words
and placing them in the tiny boat
that was once their cradle
The current carries them off
but very soon brings them back to me
as though the open sea were not over there
but here on the page

JE SUIS L'ENFANT DE CE SIÈCLE

Je suis l'enfant de ce siècle pitoyable
l'enfant qui n'a pas grandi
Les questions qui me brûlaient la langue
ont brûlé mes ailes
J'avais appris à marcher
puis j'ai désappris
Je me suis lassé des oasis
et des chamelles avides de ruines
Etendu au milieu du chemin
la tête tournée vers l'Orient
j'attends la caravane des fous

I AM THE CHILD OF THIS CENTURY

I am the child of this pitiful century
a child who has never grown up
the questions that used to burn my tongue
have burnt my wings
I had learned to walk
then I unlearned
I grew tired of oases
and camels searching avidly for ruins
Stretched out in the middle of the road
with my head turned toward the East
I await the caravan of the mad

J'OSE PARLER DE MES TÉNÈBRES

J'ose parler de mes ténèbres
Je suis dans les ténèbres
et n'implore ni planche ni salut
Je vais habiter ce chaos
le meubler comme on meuble une cellule
me faire une couche avec la paille de mes livres
me ligoter les mains
pour ne pas succomber à la tentation
tailler avec ma flamme noire
une fenêtre dans le mur de la nuit
Je vivrai, veillerai ainsi
épouvantail dressé
dans le champ des ténèbres

I DARE TO SPEAK OF MY DARKNESS

I dare to speak of my darkness
I am in the darkness
and beg for no lifeline
I am going to live in this chaos
furnish it as you would a cell
make myself a bed from the straw of my books
tie my hands
to defeat temptation
carve out a window in the wall of the night
with my black flame
Thus I shall live, keep watch
like a scarecrow standing
in a field of shadows

LE DÉSESPOIR, C'EST MON ENFANT

Ne vous réjouissez pas trop vite de mon désespoir
Le désespoir
c'est mon enfant handicapé
Il me raconte avec ses yeux
l'histoire de la hache d'amour
Ses doigts crochus sont ma boussole
je les embrasse et ne les compte pas
Sa douleur est ma source
Sa soif me fait inventer l'eau
La nourriture que je porte à sa bouche
il faut que je l'arrache de ma chair
Le désespoir
c'est mon enfant handicapé
Il me tient éveillé
et somme toute m'aide à marcher
aussi bien que la canne de l'espoir

DESPAIR IS MY CHILD

Do not rejoice too readily at my despair
Despair
is my disabled child
Its eyes tell me
the story of love's ax
Its crooked fingers are my compass
I kiss and do not count them
Its pain is my spring
Its thirst makes me invent water
The food I bring to its mouth
I have to wrench from my flesh
Despair is my disabled child
It keeps me awake
and in a word helps me walk
as much as the cane of hope

IL Y A UN CANNIBALE QUI ME LIT

Il y a un cannibale qui me lit
C'est un lecteur férocement intelligent
un lecteur de rêve
Il ne laisse passer aucun mot
sans en soupeser le poids de sang
Il soulève même les virgules
pour découvrir les morceaux de choix
Il sait lui que la page vibre
d'une splendide respiration
Ah cet émoi qui rend la proie
alléchante et déjà soumise
Il attend la fatigue
qui descend sur le visage
comme un masque de sacrifice
Il cherche la faille pour bondir
l'adjectif de trop
la répétition qui ne pardonne pas
Il y a un cannibale qui me lit
pour se nourrir

THERE IS A CANNIBAL WHO READS ME

There is a cannibal who reads me
A ferociously intelligent reader
an ideal reader
He lets no word get past him
without measuring its weight in blood
He even removes the commas
in search of choice passages
He knows full well that the page resonates
with a superb respiration
Such emotion! Strong enough to make his prey
mouth-watering and already submissive
He waits for fatigue
to cloak the face
like a sacrificial mask
He looks for the weak spot before pouncing
the otiose adjective
the unpardonable repetition
There is a cannibal who reads me
for nourishment

LA LANGUE DE MA MÈRE

Je n'ai pas vu ma mère depuis vingt ans
Elle s'est laissée mourir de faim
On raconte qu'elle enlevait chaque matin
son foulard de tête
et frappait sept fois le sol
en maudissant le ciel et le Tyran
J'étais dans la caverne
là où le forçat lit dans les ombres
et peint sur les parois le bestiaire de l'avenir
Je n'ai pas vu ma mère depuis vingt ans
Elle m'a laissé un service à café chinois
dont les tasses se cassent une à une
sans que je les regrette tant elles sont laides
Mais je n'en aime que plus le café
Aujourd'hui, quand je suis seul
j'emprunte la voix de ma mère
ou plutôt c'est elle qui parle dans ma bouche
avec ses jurons, ses grossièretés et ses imprécations
le chapelet introuvable de ses diminutifs
toute l'espèce menacée de ses mots
Je n'ai pas vu ma mère depuis vingt ans
mais je suis le dernier homme
à parler encore sa langue

MY MOTHER'S LANGUAGE

I haven't seen my mother for twenty years
She let herself starve to death
They say she used to take her headscarf off
every morning
and knock seven times on the floor
cursing heaven and the Tyrant
I was in the cave
the one where the convict reads in the darkness
and paints the bestiary of the future on the walls
I haven't seen my mother for twenty years
She left me a Chinese coffee service
whose cups are breaking one by one
though they are so ugly I don't mind
But I love coffee all the more for it
Today, when I am alone
I assume my mother's voice
or rather she speaks through my mouth
with her oaths, obscenities and imprecations
her inimitable rosary of pet names
the whole threatened species of her words
I haven't seen my mother for twenty years
but I am the last person
who still speaks her language

LES LOUPS

J'entends les loups
Ils sont bien au chaud dans leurs maisons de campagne
Ils regardent goulûment la télévision
Pendant des heures, ils comptent à voix haute
les cadavres
et chantent à tue-tête des airs de réclame
Je vois les loups
Ils mangent à treize le gibier du jour
élisent à main levée le Judas de service
Pendant des heures, ils boivent un sang de village
encore jeune, peu fruité
à la robe défaite
le sang d'une terre où sommeillent des charniers
J'entends les loups
Ils éteignent à minuit
et violent légalement leurs femmes

THE WOLVES

I hear the wolves
They are nice and warm in their country houses
They watch television hungrily
For hours they count the corpses aloud
and sing advertising jingles at the top of their lungs
I see the wolves
Thirteen at table eating the day's kill
electing their Judas of the moment on a show of hands
For hours they drink a local blood
still young, not too fruity
pallid as to color
the blood of a land where mass graves slumber
I hear the wolves
They turn their lights out at midnight
and rape their wives legally

EN VAIN J'ÉMIGRE

J'émigre en vain
Dans chaque ville je bois le même café
et me résigne au visage fermé du serveur
Les rires de mes voisins de table
taraudent la musique du soir
Une femme passe pour la dernière fois
En vain j'émigre
et m'assure de mon éloignement
Dans chaque ciel je retrouve un croissant de lune
et le silence têtu des étoiles
Je parle en dormant
un mélange de langues
et de cris d'animaux
La chambre où je me réveille
est celle où je suis né
J'émigre en vain
Le secret des oiseaux m'échappe
comme celui de cet aimant
qui affole à chaque étape
ma valise

IN VAIN I EMIGRATE

I emigrate in vain
In every city I drink the same coffee
and put up with the po-faced waiter
The laughter of my fellow customers
interrupts the melody of the evening
A woman passes by for the last time
In vain I emigrate
and try to convince myself of my distance
In every sky I rediscover a crescent moon
and the obstinate silence of the stars
I talk in my sleep
a jumble of languages
and animal cries
The room where I awake
is the one where I was born
I emigrate in vain
The secret of the birds eludes me
as does that of the magnet
Which at every way-station
puts my suitcase in an uproar

DEUX HEURES DE TRAIN

En deux heures de train
je repasse le film de ma vie
Deux minutes par année en moyenne
Une demi-heure pour l'enfance
une autre pour la prison
L'amour, les livres, l'errance
se partagent le reste
La main de ma compagne
fond peu à peu dans la mienne
et sa tête sur mon épaule
est aussi légère qu'une colombe
A notre arrivée
j'aurai la cinquantaine
et il me restera à vivre
une heure environ

TWO HOURS ON THE TRAIN

During two hours on the train
I rerun the film of my life
Two minutes per year on average
Half an hour for childhood
Another half-hour for prison
Love, books, wandering
take up the rest
the hand of my companion
gradually melts into mine
and her head on my shoulder
is as light as a dove
When we arrive
I'll be fifty or so
and still have
about an hour
to live

LES MIETTES SOUS LA TABLE

Je rends leur noblesse
à ces miettes sous la table
Je me baisse humblement
les ramasse, les embrasse une à une
et les dépose dans la haute fissure
O mur qui menaces ruine
Hirondelles averties
qui déménagez déjà vos nids
O monde échoué comme un superbe voilier
voici ces miettes rendues à leur noblesse
Je les dépose dans la haute fissure
et dis : Ceci est mon esprit
ramassé sous la table

CRUMBS UNDER THE TABLE

I restore their nobility
to these crumbs under the table
I lean down humbly
gather them up, kiss them one by one
and place them in this high crevice
Oh wall verging on collapse
Oh swallows forewarned
already packing to leave your nests
Oh world like a fine sailing ship aground
here are these crumbs with their nobility restored
I am placing them in this high crevice
and I say: This is my spirit
picked up under the table

UNE MAISON LÀ-BAS

Une maison là-bas
avec sa porte ouverte
et ses deux tourterelles
récitant inlassablement le nom de l'absent
Une maison là-bas
avec son puits profond
et sa terrasse aussi blanche
que le sel des constellations
Une maison là-bas
pour que l'errant se dise
j'ai lieu d'errer
tant qu'il y aura une maison là-bas

A HOUSE BACK THERE

A house back there
with its open door
and its two turtle-doves
tirelessly repeating the name of the absentee
A house back there
with its deep well
and its terrace as white
as the salt of the constellations
A house back there
so that the wanderer can tell himself
I have good reason to stray
so long as there is a house back there

ABRÉGÉ D'ÉTERNITÉ

Sur le radeau, j'allumerai un cierge
et j'inventerai ma prière
Je laisserai à la vague inspirée
le soin d'ériger son temple
Je revêtirai de ma cape
le premier poisson
qui viendra se frotter à mes rames
J'irai ainsi par nuit et par mer
sans vivres ni mouettes
avec un bout de cierge
et un brin de prière
J'irai ainsi
avec mon visage d'illuminé
et je me dirai
ô moitié d'homme, réjouis-toi
tu vivras si tu ne l'as déjà vécu
un abrégé d'éternité

A SHORT VERSION OF ETERNITY

On the raft I shall light a candle
and invent my prayer
I'll leave it to the inspiration of the waves
to build their temple
I'll drape my cape
over the first fish
to come and rub against my oars
Thus shall I go by night and by sea
without victuals or seagulls
with my candle end
and my fragment of prayer
Thus shall I go
with my visionary's face
and I'll say to myself
oh half-man, rejoice
you are about to live
if you have not already lived
a short version of eternity

LA VIE

La vie
Il me suffit de m'être réveillé
le soleil dans ma droite
la lune dans ma gauche
et d'avoir marché
depuis le ventre de ma mère
jusqu'au crépuscule de ce siècle
La vie
Il me suffit d'avoir goûté à ce fruit
J'ai vu ce que j'ai dit
je n'ai rien tu de l'horreur
j'ai fait ce que j'ai pu
j'ai tout pris et donné à l'amour
La vie
Ni plus ni moins que ce miracle
sans témoins
Ah corps meurtri
âme meurtrie
Avouez un peu votre bonheur
Avouez-le
rien qu'entre nous

LIFE

Life
Enough for me to have awoken
with the sun in my right hand
the moon in my left
and to have walked from my mother's belly
to the dusk of this century
Life
Enough to have tasted this fruit
I saw what I said I saw
I hid nothing of the horror
I did what I could do
I took everything from love
gave everything to love
Life
Neither more nor less than a miracle
unwitnessed
Ah battered body
battered soul
Admit your happiness a little
Admit it
just between you and me

LE MANUSCRIT

Je ne savais pas que Satan – Iblis pour les intimes – était de petite taille et qu'il était si indiscret, voleur de surcroît.

J'étais à mon bureau en train d'écrire quand il est venu s'asseoir en silence à mes côtés. Moi qui ne suis pas un géant, je le dépassais d'une tête. Je le détaillai donc avec assurance, relevai un à un ses signes distinctifs. De profil, son nez paraissait long. Son œil unique n'avait pas de cils. Une étoile à sept branches était tatouée à la commissure de ses lèvres.

L'ayant ainsi dévisagé et reconnu, je me suis remis sereinement à l'ouvrage. Tiens, un poème sur Iblis, me dis-je. Il a suffi que j'émette cette pensée pour que mon compagnon s'agite. J'ai vu une main très fine sortir de sa poche et se poser sur ma feuille. A chaque mot que j'écrivais il ajoutait un autre, avec un sens réel de l'à-propos je dois dire. Mais si l'une de ses trouvailles ne me plaisait pas et que je la raturais, il me rendait immédiatement la pareille.

Nous écrivîmes et corrigeâmes ainsi longtemps jusqu'au moment où la sonnerie du téléphone retentit. Je décrochai, attendis que mon interlocuteur se présente. Mais il n'y avait personne à l'autre bout du fil. Je finis par raccrocher avec rage.

Iblis avait mis à profit cet intermède pour disparaître, emportant avec lui notre manuscrit.

THE MANUSCRIPT

I did not know that Satan – Iblis to his intimates – was so short and so indiscreet, not to mention a thief.

I was at my desk busy writing when he came and sat in silence beside me. Though no giant, I was a head taller. I inspected him therefore with confidence, noting his distinguishing features one by one. In profile, his nose seemed long. His sole eye had no lashes. A seven-pointed star was tattooed at the join of his lips.

After thus scrutinizing and recognizing him, I calmly returned to my work. Very well, I told myself, let's have a poem on Iblis. No sooner had I had this idea than my neighbor went into motion. I saw a very fine hand leave his pocket and settle on my paper. Every time I wrote a word he would add another, and this, I must say, with a great sense of pertinence. But if one of his finds failed to satisfy me and I crossed it out, he would immediately return the compliment.

We went on writing and correcting in this way for a good while until the telephone rang. I answered and waited for the caller to introduce himself. But there was nobody on the line. Eventually I hung up in annoyance.

Iblis had taken advantage of this interruption to disappear, taking our manuscript with him.

LE SOUFI ÉLÉGANT

Quand le soufi découvrit le drap anglais, le cachemire et le foulard de soie, il déchira sa tunique de laine grossière : « Je me sentirai mieux dans ces étoffes, se dit-il. Elles donneront de la grâce à mes génuflexions. Je vais me couper cheveux et barbe, me brosser les dents trois fois par jour, utiliser comme déodorant une bonne eau de Cologne, jeter aux orties ma natte pourrie et la remplacer par un vrai tapis zemmour. Je me présenterai net et propre devant Dieu et m'est avis que mes prières gagneront en pureté. Dorénavant je ne vivrai plus d'aumônes. Je vais me trouver un travail honnête et d'un rapport honorable. Je me mêlerai à mes semblables, connaîtrai leurs soucis, apprendrai leurs blasphèmes, m'initierai à leurs amours terrestres, goûterai à leurs vins terrestres et peu à peu les ramènerai sur la voie du Mystère. Au fond, ma vie ne changera que de forme mais j'aurai inauguré une nouvelle voie mystique, celle des soufis élégants. »

THE ELEGANT SUFI

When the sufi discovered English bed linen, cashmere, and silk scarves, he ripped up his rough wool garments. "I will feel more comfortable in these materials," he told himself. "They will lend grace to my genuflections. I am going to cut my beard and hair, brush my teeth three times a day, use a good eau de Cologne as a deodorant, throw out my rotten old mat and replace it with a genuine Zemmour rug. I shall stand before God fresh and clean and I know that my prayers will be the purer for it. From now on I shall no longer live on charity. I am going to find honest and honorably remunerated employment. I shall mingle with my fellows, experience their troubles, learn their oaths, initiate myself into their secular loves, savor their worldly wines, and gradually bring them back to the way of the Mystery. At bottom my life will change in form only, but I shall have opened up a new mystical path, the path of the elegant Sufis."

LA VIE REPREND LE DESSUS

La scène est banale. Après l'enterrement, le repas des funérailles est assez joyeux. La viande est tendre. La salade de fruits exotiques parfumée à la fleur d'oranger est délicieuse. La place attitrée du défunt est occupée par un boute-en-train que sa jeune voisine dévore des yeux. L'ami intime découvre subitement l'étrange beauté de la veuve. Dans la pièce d'à côté, ceux que l'on appelle toujours les enfants commentent bruyamment la retransmission d'un match de tennis.

– Baissez un peu le son, leur crie-t-on.

– Où en étais-je ? reprend le boute-en-train. Ah oui, il paraît qu'on a découvert dans les effets de tous les soldats irakiens tués un coran miniature et un linceul cousu, prêt à servir. En dehors de cela, rien, pas la moindre boîte de conserve ou un bout de biscuit. Allez comprendre avec ça quelque chose à la mentalité orientale !

– Ouf ! on l'a échappé belle, commente son admiratrice.

– On a beau dire, l'Amérique est un grand pays, conclut l'ami intime.

– Reprenez un peu de salade, propose la veuve. Je vais mettre l'eau à chauffer. Café, thé ou tisane ?

– Je viens t'aider, souffle l'ami intime.

La vie reprend le dessus, comme on dit.

Le voyeur, car il y a un voyeur, quitte sans regret le trou de la serrure.

LIFE RETURNS TO NORMAL

The scene is banal. After the burial, the funeral meal is quite jolly. The meat is tender. The tropical fruit salad perfused with orange blossom is delicious. The traditional place of the deceased is occupied by a life-and-soul-of-the-party type whom a young table companion cannot take her eyes off. The closest friend is suddenly finding the widow strangely beautiful. In the next room, those always referred to as the children are noisily commenting on the replay of a tennis match.

"Turn the volume down in there!" goes the cry.

"Where was I?" the life-and-soul guy goes on. "Oh yes, apparently they discovered that the packs of all the dead Iraqi soldiers contained a miniature Koran and a sown-up winding-sheet ready for use. Apart from that, nothing. Not so much as a can of food or a scrap of hard bread. Go figure what that says about the Oriental mentality!"

"Lucky we escaped that!" observes his admirer.

"Say what you like, America is a great country," adds the closest friend.

"Have a little more salad," suggests the widow. "I'll boil some water. Coffee, tea, herb tea?"

"I'll come and help you," says the closest friend quietly.

Life is returning to normal, as they say.

The voyeur, for there is one, leaves his keyhole without regret.

LES CONVIVES

Ma table est mise et mes convives sont en retard.

Ont-ils oublié mon invitation, perdu mon adresse en cours de route ? Quel mal a-t-il pu leur arriver ?

Depuis des heures, j'attends, « mon oreille suspendue à la porte ». Je ne sais pas combien seront mes convives, s'ils porteront des habits d'hiver ou d'été, en quelle langue ils lanceront leur salut en entrant.

Ma table est mise. J'attendrai le temps qu'il faut et qu'il ne faut pas. Et si j'étais victime d'une illusion, je m'entêterais. J'inventerais des amitiés rares, des visages ouverts, faciles à lire comme des livres d'enfants, des voix aux accents délicieux et des bouches petites qui partageraient jusqu'au grain de couscous.

Ma table est mise. J'y ai disposé toutes mes cultures, avec amour. La musique m'aide à supporter l'attente. Elle attendrit mes ragoûts, fait briller mes olives, libère les parfums de mes épices.

Enfin, j'entends des bruits de pas. Je me lève pour aller ouvrir. Mais la porte vole en éclats. Sont-ce là mes convives ? Des hommes sans visage font irruption, l'arme au poing. Ils ne font pas attention à moi.

Ils tirent sur la table jusqu'à la réduire en miettes et se retirent sans dire mot. La musique s'arrête.

Bon, il ne me reste plus qu'à faire le ménage et préparer un nouveau repas.

GUESTS

My table is set and my guests are late.

Have they forgotten my invitation, or lost my address on the way? What could have befallen them?

For hours now I have been waiting with my ears "glued to the door." I don't know how many guests there will be, whether they will be wearing winter or summer clothes, or in what language they will greet me when they come in.

My table is set. I shall wait as long as need be, or as need not be. And if ever I am suffering from a delusion, I'll stubbornly persist. I'll invent rare friendships, open faces as easy to read as children's books, voices with delightful intonations, and little mouths ready to share everything down to a single grain of couscous.

My table is set. I have laid out all my creations with love. Music helps me to put up with the wait. It softens my ragouts, makes my olives gleam, releases the tang of my spices.

At last I hear footsteps. I get up to open the door. But the door explodes in smithereens. Can this be my guests? Faceless men burst into the room, weapons in hand. They pay no attention to me.

They open fire on the table, reducing it to splinters, then leave wordlessly. The music stops.

Very well. All I have to do now is clear up and make another meal.

L'ARBRE À POÈMES

Je suis l'arbre à poèmes. Les savants disent que j'appartiens à une espèce en voie de disparition. Mais personne ne s'en émeut alors que des campagnes ont été lancées récemment pour sauver le panda du Népal et l'éléphant d'Afrique.

Question d'intérêt, diront certains. Question de mémoire, dirai-je. De temps en temps, la mémoire des hommes sature. Ils se délestent alors du plus encombrant, font de la place en prévision du nouveau dont ils sont si friands.

Aujourd'hui, la mode n'est plus aux vieilles essences. On invente des arbres qui poussent vite, se contentent de l'eau et du soleil qu'on leur mesure et font leur métier d'arbre en silence, sans état d'âme.

Je suis l'arbre à poèmes. On a bien essayé sur moi des manipulations, qui n'ont rien donné. Je suis réfractaire, maître de mes mutations. Je ne m'émeus pas à de simples changements de saison, d'époque. Les fruits que je donne ne sont jamais les mêmes. J'y mets tantôt du nectar, tantôt du fiel. Et quand je vois de loin un prédateur, je les truffe d'épines.

Parfois je me dis : Suis-je réellement un arbre ? Et j'ai peur de me mettre à marcher, parler le triste langage de l'espèce menteuse, m'emparer d'une hache et m'abattre sur le tronc du plus faible de mes voisins. Alors je m'accroche de toutes mes forces à mes racines. Dans leurs veines infinies je remonte le cours de la parole jusqu'au cri primordial. Je défais l'écheveau des langues. J'attrape le bout du

THE POEM TREE

I am the poem tree. The experts say that I belong to a species on the way to extinction. But nobody is concerned about it, even though campaigns have recently been launched to save the Nepalese panda and the African elephant.

Some will say that it's a question of profit. For myself I say the issue is memory. From time to time to time the memory of men gets saturated. At which point they jettison the most cumbersome items and make room for the novelties that so infatuate them.

Today old varieties are no longer fashionable. Trees are invented that grow quickly and are satisfied by water and sunshine dosed out for them, and perform their job as trees with no display of emotion.

I am the poem tree. Of course they have tried manipulating me, but to no avail. I am recalcitrant, master of my mutations. I am unaffected by mere changes of season or era. The fruits I bear are never the same. Sometimes I fill them with nectar, sometimes with venom. And when I spot a predator a long way off, I spike them with thorns.

Sometimes I wonder: Am I really a tree? And I am afraid of setting off, speaking the sad language of the lying race, grabbing an ax and hacking at the trunk of the weakest of my neighbors. So I cling with all my might to my roots. Through their endless veins I retrace the course of language all the way back to the primordial cry. I unravel the skein of all language. I grasp the end of the thread and

fil et je tire pour libérer la musique et la lumière. L'image se rend à moi. J'en fais les bourgeons qui me plaisent et donne rendez-vous aux fleurs. Tout cela nuitamment, avec la complicité des étoiles et des rares oiseaux qui ont choisi la liberté.

Je suis l'arbre à poèmes. Je me ris de l'éphémère et de l'éternel.

Je suis vivant.

pull, liberating music and light. Images surrender to me. From them I create the buds I like and arrange meetings with flowers. All of this in the night, with the complicity of the stars and of the rare birds that have chosen freedom.

I am the poem tree. I scoff at the ephemeral and the eternal alike.

I am alive.

from

LE SPLEEN DE CASABLANCA

CASABLANCA SPLEEN

(1996)

de LE SPLEEN DE CASABLANCA

Dans le bruit d'une ville sans âme
j'apprends le dur métier du retour
Dans ma poche crevée
je n'ai que ta main
pour réchauffer la mienne
tant l'été se confond avec l'hiver
Où s'en est allé, dis-moi
le pays de notre jeunesse ?

                                    * * *

O comme les pays se ressemblent
et se ressemblent les exils
Tes pas ne sont pas de ces pas
qui laissent des traces sur le sable
Tu passes sans passer

                                    * * *

Visage après visage
meurent les ans
Je cherche dans les yeux une lueur
un bourgeon dans les paroles
Et j'ai peur, très peur
de perdre encore un vieil ami

from CASABLANCA SPLEEN

In the noise of a soulless city
I am learning the tough job of returning
In my ripped pocket
I have only your hand
to warm mine
so much does summer now resemble winter
Where has it gone, tell me
the land of our youth?

* * *

Oh how alike countries are
and how alike exiles
Your steps are not the kind
that leave prints in the sand
You pass by without passing

* * *

Face after face
the years die
I look for a gleam in people's eyes
a burgeoning in their words
And I am afraid, very afraid
of losing yet another old friend

Ce gris matin est loyal
Je lui sais gré du spleen qu'il répand
de la douleur qu'il recueille
de la gerbe des doutes qu'il m'offre
en bon connaisseur

* * *

Si je sors
où irai-je ?
Les trottoirs sont défoncés
Les arbres font pitié
Les immeubles cachent le ciel
Les voitures règnent
comme n'importe quel tyran
Les cafés sont réservés aux hommes
Les femmes, à raison
ont peur qu'on les regarde
Et puis
je n'ai de rendez-vous
avec personne

* * *

* * *

This gray morning is true
I am grateful for the spleen it propagates
for the pain it distils
for the bouquet of doubts
it offers me
as a fine connoisseur

* * *

If I go out
where shall I go?
The sidewalks are potholed
The trees pitiful
The buildings block the sky
The cars rule
like any old tyrant
The cafés are reserved for men
The women, with good reason
are afraid of being looked at
And what is more
I have an appointment
with no one

* * *

Je ne suis pas ce nomade
qui cherche le puits
que le sédentaire a creusé
Je bois peu d'eau
et marche
à l'écart de la caravane

* * *

Le siècle prend fin
dit-on
et cela me laisse indifférent
Quoique le suivant
ne me dise rien qui vaille

* * *

Dans la cité de ciment et de sel
ma grotte est en papier
J'ai une bonne provision de plumes
et de quoi faire du café
Mes idées n'ont pas d'ombre
pas plus d'odeur
Mon corps a disparu
Il n'y a plus que ma tête
dans cette grotte en papier

I am not the sort of nomad
who seeks the well
that a resident has dug
I drink little water
and I walk
well away from the caravan

* * *

This century is coming to an end
so they say
and that leaves me cold
But the next one to my mind
has nothing going for it

* * *

In the city of cement and salt
my cave is of paper
I have a good reserve of pens
and the means of making coffee
My ideas cast no shadow
nor do they have an odor
My body has vanished
All that remains in this paper cave
is my head

***

J'essaie de vivre
La tâche est ardue

***

Quel sens donner à ce voyage
Quelle autre langue
me faudra-t-il apprendre
Lequel de mes doigts
devrai-je sacrifier
Et si mes lèvres repoussent
saurai-je encore embrasser ?

***

Aujourd'hui
une étoile a dû naître
dans une galaxie
qu'on finira bien par découvrir
J'imagine la joie mauvaise
de cette garce
qui va survivre
à mes petits-enfants

***

I am trying to live
An arduous task

What meaning to give to this journey
What other language
will I have to learn
Which of my fingers
will I have to sacrifice
And if my lips grow back
will I still know how to kiss?

Today
a star must have been born
in a galaxy
that will surely be discovered some day
I can imagine the mean joy
of that bitch
who will outlive
my grandchildren

Mère
je t'appelle
alors que tu n'es plus que poussière
Il faut que je te dise :
Je suis ton éternel enfant
Grandir
est au-dessus de mes forces

* * *

Poète
réjouis-toi de ces questions
qui te réveillent
au milieu de la nuit
et ne pâlissent pas à l'aube
avec les étoiles

* * *

Les grandes feuilles m'intimident
Je les coupe en deux
pour écrire
des demi-poèmes

* * *

Mother
I am calling you
though now you are merely dust
I have to tell you:
I am your child forever
Growing up
is more than I can do

* * *

Poet
delight in the questions
that wake you up
in the middle of the night
and do not fade away at dawn
like the stars

* * *

Large sheets of paper scare me
I cut them in half
to write
half-poems

* * *

Verre après verre
nous réveillons la vie
Elle ouvre un œil
nous sourit vaguement
et se rendort

* * *

Le soleil est là
Je n'ai plus à l'acheter
Et bien vite je l'oublie
comme si j'étais fasciné
par les ténèbres

* * *

Les pays
maintenant
se valent
en férocité

* * *

Les livres qui portent mon nom
et que je n'ose ouvrir
de peur

Glass after glass
we awaken life
It opens one eye
smiles at us vaguely
and goes back to sleep

* * *

The sun is here
I no longer have to buy it
And very soon I forget it
as though fascinated
by the darkness

* * *

Countries
are now
equal
in ferocity

* * *

The books that bear my name
and that I dare not open
for fear

qu'ils ne tombent en poussière
entre mes doigts

* * *

A force de côtoyer le monstre
l'odeur du monstre
te colle à la peau

* * *

Réveille-toi
rebelle
Le monde croule
sous les apparences
Il va crever
de résignation

* * *

Quand j'avais froid
et faim
(j'ai connu cela
ne vous en déplaise)
la vie m'était presque douce
et fécondes mes insomnies
Je pensais chaque nuit aux autres

of their turning to dust
in my hands

* * *

Keep knocking about with the monster
and the smell of the monster
will stick to your skin

* * *

Wake up
rebel
The world is crumbling
beneath the weight of appearances
It is about to die
of resignation

* * *

When I was cold
and hungry
(which I have been
believe it or not)
life was almost sweet for me
and my sleeplessness fruitful
I thought every night of others

(aux laissés-pour-compte
ne vous en déplaise)
et chaque matin
un soleil fraternel
venait me rendre visite
et déposait à mon chevet
deux ou trois
morceaux de sucre

* * *

J'ai besoin d'un répit
le temps que vous voudrez bien m'accorder
pour ouvrir une fenêtre
sur un temps que je n'ai pas encore visité
une île de chair princière
qui s'offrira à moi pour de bon
Je pousserai cette fenêtre bleue
et je ferai vite avant qu'elle ne se referme
Je ne dirai pas ce que j'aurai vu
Ce que j'aurai éprouvé
ira rejoindre le mystère
Si seulement vous m'accordiez ce répit
M'est avis que je vous rendrais
friands d'énigmes

(of the dispossessed believe it or not)
and every morning
a fraternal sun
paid me a visit and left
by my bed
two or three lumps of sugar

* * *

I need respite
the time you would be willing to grant me
to open a window
onto a time I have not yet visited
an island of princely flesh
offering itself to me in earnest
I'll push that blue window open
and hurry before it closes again
I will not tell you what I see
What I experience
will return to the realm of mystery
If only you granted me this respite
I feel sure
I would make you
eager for enigmas

* * *

Le poète invente une rose
mais ne sait quelle couleur lui donner
Comment est-ce la couleur du secret ?
Tiédeur reconnaissable au creux de l'oreille
Visage rayonnant du père
emporté par la mort douce
Ride naissante au flanc de l'aimée ?
Rien de cela ne définit une couleur
L'invention de notre poète
restera donc incomplète

* * *

Il paraît que la porte de l'enfer
avoisine celle du paradis
Le grand menuisier les a conçues
dans le même bois vulgaire
Le peintre manitou les a barbouillées
de la même couleur
Comment les distinguer dans cette pénombre ?
Voyons
As-tu les clés
Quelle est la bonne
Et puis pourquoi te risquerais-tu

* * *

The poet invents a rose
but does not know what color to make it
What color does a secret have?
A warmth whispered in the ear
The radiant face of a father
taken by a painless death
Beginning of a wrinkle
on the side of the beloved?
None of these suggest a color
Our poet's invention
must therefore remain unfinished

* * *

They say the gate of hell
is just next to the gate of heaven
The great carpenter made them
from the same plain wood
The painter-god daubed them
the same color
How can you tell them apart in the half-darkness?
Let's see
Do you have the keys
Which is the right one

à ouvrir
ce qui ne pourrait donner
que sur le néant ?

* * *

La nuit
un semblant de pays
s'absente de lui-même
Il sort ses mandibules
pour happer les images sulfureuses
des galaxies promises
Il boit mange et se masturbe
aux frais de la princesse
Et quand à l'aube
le muezzin appelle à la prière
il se met à ronfler
comme n'importe quel mécréant

* * *

Je tire les rideaux
pour pouvoir fumer à ma guise
Je tire les rideaux
pour boire un verre
à la santé d'Abou Nouwas

And why should you risk
opening a door
that leads only
to nothingness?

* * *

At night
a semblance of a country
leaves itself behind
Opens its jaws
to snap up sulfurous images
of promised galaxies
Drinks eats and masturbates
on the public purse
And when at daybreak
the muezzin calls to prayer
starts snoring
like any old infidel

* * *

I draw the curtains
to smoke at my leisure
I draw the curtains
to raise a glass

Je tire les rideaux
pour lire le dernier livre de Rushdie
Bientôt, qui sait
il faudra que je descende à la cave
et que je m'enferme à double tour
pour pouvoir
penser
à ma guise

* * *

Les gardiens sont partout
Ils règnent sur les poubelles
les garages
les boîtes aux lettres
Les gardiens sont partout
dans les bouteilles vides
sous la langue
derrière les miroirs
Les gardiens sont partout
entre la chair et l'ongle
les narines et la rose
l'œil et le regard
Les gardiens sont partout
dans la poussière qu'on avale

to the health of Abu Nuwas
I draw the curtains
to read Rushdie's latest book
Before long, who knows
I shall have to go down to the cellar
and double-lock myself in
to be able to think
as I please

* * *

Guards are everywhere
They rule over the trashcans
the garages
the mailboxes
Guards are everywhere
in empty bottles
under the tongue
behind mirrors
Guards are everywhere
between flesh and fingernail
nostrils and rose
eye and gaze
Guards are everywhere
in the dust we swallow

et le morceau qu'on recrache
Les gardiens croissent et se multiplient
A ce rythme
arrivera le jour
où nous deviendrons tous
un peuple de gardiens

* * *

On m'a volé mon pays
Vous qui connaissez les lois
et savez vous battre
dites-moi
Où puis-je déposer une plainte
Qui pourra me rendre justice ?

Ce ne pourra pas être un pays
avec des drapeaux hissés
au-dessus des maisons
Une langue unique pour prier
Un nom que les tribuns prononcent
la bouche pleine de majuscules
en fermant les yeux de béatitude

Ce ne pourra pas être un pays
qu'il faille quitter ou retrouver

in the bit of food we spit out
Guards increase and multiply
At this rate
the day will come
when we are all turned into
a race of guards

* * *

They have robbed me of my country
You who know the law
and know how to fight
tell me
Where can I file a complaint
Who can bring me justice?

It cannot be a country
with flags flying
over the houses
A sole language for prayer
A name that tribunes utter
with mouths full of capital letters
and their eyes closed in bliss

It cannot be a country
that you must leave or return to

avec les mêmes déchirements
l'obscure litanie du deuil
et ce sanglot des racines
hélant d'improbables rivages

Ce ne pourra pas être un pays
qu'on doive apprendre à l'école
à la caserne
en prison
avec la hantise
de se tromper de pays

Ce ne pourra pas être un pays
juste pour le ventre
ou la tombe
et rien d'autre
hormis le fardeau des peines
qu'on n'ose plus confier
même à l'ami

Ce ne pourra pas être un pays
qui ne sait plus rire
vivre à en être meurtri

with the same old rifts
the same dark litany of grief
and that sob from the roots
hailing improbable shores

It cannot be a country
you must learn about at school
in the barracks
in prison
with the haunting sense
of having picked
the wrong country

It cannot be a country
for the belly
or the tomb
and nothing else
except the weight of suffering
that you no longer dare speak of
even to your friend

It cannot be a country
that can no longer laugh
or live to the bruising point

peupler la nuit de ses excès
jusqu'à déchirer d'amour
les draps de l'aube

Ce ne pourra pas être un pays
parmi la cohorte des pays
cynique
avare
dur d'oreille
engraissant les voyous
leur offrant le glaive et la balance
alignant les suaires
et payant jusqu'aux pleureuses
pour les doux

Ce ne pourra pas être un pays
qui dans le cœur
chasse un autre pays
pour ériger des murailles
entre le désir et le désir
et vouer au blasphème
l'humble joie de l'errant

Ce ne pourra pas être un pays
qui ferme sa porte à l'hôte

or fill the night with its excesses
until love has torn to shreds
the dawn's bedsheets

It cannot be a country
amid the cohort of countries
cynical
miserly
hard of hearing
fattening gangsters
offering them sword and scales
lining up shrouds
and even paying weepers
for the meek

It cannot be a country
that in its heart
drives out another country
to build walls
between desire and desire
and condemn
the wanderer's humble joy
as blasphemy

It cannot be a country
that closes its door to guests

l'étranger
époux de l'étoile
émissaire de nos antiques amours
survivant de la marche
celle des origines
quand la vie nous visitait encore
et que nos pas s'aventuraient
de sillon en sillon
dans ce continent englouti
disparu
avant de nous livrer la clé du rêve
qu'il a fait glisser dans nos songes

Ah c'est un pays encore à naître
dans la soif et le dénuement
La brûlure qui rend l'âme à l'âme
et de la mer morte
des larmes
soulève la houle des mots

C'est un pays encore à naître
sur une terre coulant de source
éprise d'infini

foreigners
spouses of the star
emissaries of our ancient loves
survivors of the journey
from the beginnings
when life still visited us
and our steps ventured forth
from furrow to furrow
on a continent that was swamped
and vanished
before giving us the key to the dream
that he slipped into our reveries

Ah it is a country yet to be born
in thirst and destitution
The fire that renders soul to soul
and from the dead sea
of tears
raises the swell of words

It is a country yet to be born
upon an earth rising from the source
in love with the infinite

drapée du bleu de l'enfance
aussi fraîche que la cascade
du premier soleil

C'est un pays encore à naître
dans la lenteur du lointain
et du proche
Dans la langueur de l'espérance
mille fois trahie
Dans la langue éperdue
et retrouvée

C'est un pays encore à naître
sur le chemin
qui ne fait que reprendre
et ne conduit à nul pays

O pays qui m'écarte
et m'éloigne
Laisse-moi au moins te chercher

draped in the blue of childhood
fresh as the cascading rays
of the first sun

It is a country yet to be born
at the slow pace of far
and near
In the languor of hope
a thousand times betrayed
In language lost
and found

It is a country yet to be born
on a road
forever beginning again
and leading to no country

Oh country that pushes me aside
and away
Allow me at least to go in search of you

from

FRAGMENTS D'UNE GENÈSE OUBLIÉE

FRAGMENTS OF A FORGOTTEN GENESIS

(1998)

de FRAGMENTS D'UNE GENÈSE OUBLIÉE

[. . .]
Au commencement était le cri
et déjà la discorde

Voici l'homme
l'héritier
doutant de tout
aux prises avec lui-même

Il parle
la peur au ventre
la bouche de travers

Il crache ses mots
vide l'abcès de son crâne
de son foie
dans le grand entonnoir de l'indifférence

Il parle
ou se parle
comme s'il se donnait des gifles
et s'esclaffait de sa trouvaille :

from FRAGMENTS OF A FORGOTTEN GENESIS

[...]
In the beginning was the cry
and, already, discord

Behold the man
the heir
doubting everything
at odds with himself

He speaks
with fear in his belly
and a twisted mouth

He spits out his words
draining the abscesses of skull
and liver
into the great funnel of indifference

He speaks
or speaks to himself
as if delivering slaps
and bursting out laughing at a discovery:

Homme dites-vous ?
Admettons

Je mets par commodité ce nom
sur mon visage
prends la place désignée
dans la barque

Que peut dire un galérien
de ses chaînes
de ces genèses apocryphes
au bout desquelles
il se retrouve
dans la même arche trouée
avec les mêmes compagnons d'infortune
drogués
guettant en vain la terre promise ?

Tant de chaînons manquent
à la belle aventure
et je suis le chaînon de trop

Il suffit que je bouge
que j'inspire ou expire
pour que l'harmonie se rompe

Man you say?
Let's suppose so

I inscribe this word for convenience
on my face
and take my assigned place
in the boat

What can the galley slave say
about his shackles
about those false beginnings
at whose end
he finds himself
in the same leaky ark
with the same companions of misfortune
drugged
and vainly looking out for the promised land?

So many links are missing
for a great adventure
and I am a link too many

All it takes is that I budge
that I breathe in or out
for harmony to be broken

et qu'une chape de laideur
s'abatte sur la tendre palette de l'aube

Il suffit d'un lapsus
d'une bulle qui crève
dans la mare délétère de mes manques
pour que le monstre se réveille
et bondisse dans l'arène
affamé
inventif
amoureux à l'insu de sa proie
plus vif que la gazelle de l'utopie

Il suffit d'un faux pas
d'un moment d'inattention
pour que le sablier de ma mémoire
se renverse
et que je m'ébranle à reculons
vers ma mort
en un vagissement de bête blessée
par la vie

Il suffit d'un passage à vide
pour que je me méprise

for a curtain of ugliness
to fall over dawn's delicate palette

All it takes is a slip
a bubble bursting
in the noxious pond of my shortcomings
for the monster to wake
and bound into the arena
famished
resourceful
unknowingly in love with his prey
livelier than the gazelle of utopia

All it takes is one false step
a moment of distraction
for the hourglass of my memory
to turn upside down
for me to stumble backwards
towards my death
whimpering like an animal wounded
by life

All it takes is a bad patch
for me to fall into self-contempt

D'une nuit blanche
pour que je change de couleur
de religion
et d'habits de clown

Il suffit d'un tremblement
aux contours des objets
pour que la connaissance s'envenime
et m'apparaisse le gnome du ridicule

Il suffit d'une seule confidence
pour que je me retrouve
sans défense
nu
malade de ma vérité

Homme dites-vous ?
Admettons

Je me joins au troupeau
qui s'achemine gaiement vers l'abattoir
et je bêle à pleins poumons

Ma petite cervelle de mouton
ne m'avertit pas du danger

Or a sleepless night
for me to change color
religion
and clown suit

All it takes is a tremor
in the contours of things
and knowledge becomes venomous
and the gnome of ridicule appears to me

All it takes is a single confidence
and I find myself
defenseless
naked
sick with my truth

Man you say?
Let's suppose so

I join the flock
gaily making its way to the slaughter
and I bleat with all my might

My little sheep's brain
warns me of no danger

Et la rumeur court
s'amplifie
L'heure a sonné
C'est le jour des comptes et châtiments
Voici la balance
les videurs du paradis
les péripatéticiennes de l'enfer
et le visage hilare du dieu vainqueur

Courage ô mes brebis
nous mourrons à quatre pattes
dignes
comme il sied à l'espèce des ruminants

According to a rumor
growing louder and louder
The hour is nigh
The day of judgment and retribution is at hand
As witness the scales
the bouncers of paradise
the streetwalkers of hell
and the laughing face of a triumphant god

Courage oh my ewes
we shall die on our four hooves
with dignity
as befits the race of ruminants

[. . .]

J'ai appris à lire et à écrire
pour mon malheur

Que disait le texte
gribouillé dans la langue oubliée
maudite ?

Seul l'évadé pourra le déchiffrer

Tends-moi la main ô mon frère proscrit
Je n'ai pas ton courage
car j'ai encore peur pour les miens

J'ai peur de ne trouver auprès de toi
qu'un paysage minéral
sans la caresse de l'amie
ni la fille prodigue du raisin

J'ai du mal à quitter
ce qui me fait mal
et me dresse contre le mal

[. . .]
Unfortunately for me
I learnt to read and write

What was the meaning
of that text scribbled
in a forgotten
and accursed language?

Only the escapee could decipher it

Give me your hand oh my banished brother
I do not have your courage
for I still fear for my kin

At your side I am afraid to find
only a mineral landscape
without the touch of a woman
without the prodigal daughter of the grape

I find it hard to quit
what hurts me
and braces me to fight it

Frère
tends-moi la main
non pour m'attirer à toi
avec ta violence légendaire
mais pour m'offrir la clé
dont tu n'as que faire

Toi
tu es libre maintenant

Dégagé de la connaissance
et du sens

De la lutte
et de la représentation

De la vérité
et de l'erreur

De la justice des hommes et des dieux

Dégagé même de l'amour
et de la ménagerie des désirs

Brother
hold out your hand
not to draw me to you
with your legendary violence
but to offer me the key
that you have no more use for

As for you
you are free now

Detached from knowledge
and meaning

From struggle
and from representation

From truth
and error

From the justice of men and gods

Detached even from love
and the menagerie of desires

Tu manges peu
et bois à peine

Tu ne redoutes plus les yeux inquisiteurs

L'apaisement t'indiffère

Tu n'attends plus du soir
le supplément d'âme de sa musique
et de l'aurore
ses promesses rarement tenues

Ta couche
c'est là où te surprend le rêve
où tu te meus avec des ailes ou sans

Un coin frais
derrière une porte
sur un banc
tout lieu est le lieu
où viennent s'offrir à toi les prémonitions
d'une vie
que l'on n'a pas besoin de vivre
pour en être rempli

You eat little
and barely drink

You no longer dread inquisitorial eyes

Relief means nothing to you

From the evening you no longer expect
soul-strengthening music
nor from the dawn
its promises rarely kept

Your bed
is where dreams take you by surprise
where you move with wings or without

A cool corner
behind a door
on a bench
anywhere
is where
premonitions offer themselves to you
of a life
that one does not need to live
in order to be filled by it

Qui aurait l'idée de t'enseigner
de te convaincre
toi qui as cessé de vouloir convaincre
et ne parles
que pour les reptiles facétieux de ta tête

Qui pourrait t'en vouloir
toi qui as renoncé à tout ?

Who would ever think
of trying to teach you
to convince you
you who no longer wish to convince
and speak only
for the facetious reptiles in your head

Who could have anything against you
you who have given up on everything?

Je te connais bien mon frère

Nous nous sommes rencontrés souvent
au fil des épreuves

La première fois, c'est le tortionnaire qui nous a présentés l'un à
l'autre. Même avec le bandeau sur les yeux, nous nous sommes
reconnus. Puis je t'ai entendu crier, crier, et j'avais hâte de prendre ta
place, d'offrir ma chair à l'insupportable qui vrillait ta chair.
Plus tard, nous nous sommes retrouvés dans l'attente. Le mur
qui nous séparait était si friable. Nous en avons fait un cahier de
musique. Chaque nuit, nous échangions de sobres partitions :
– Qu'as-tu mangé
– Que lis-tu
– As-tu reçu une lettre
– Qu'as-tu vu dans la lune
– Le moineau à la patte cassée t'a-t-il rendu visite
– L'aimée a-t-elle répandu du parfum sur ton oreiller ? Lilas ou
jasmin ? Musc ou ambre ?

Parfois je t'entendais crier dans ton sommeil et je revivais la scène.
Toi ou moi, aux prises avec la forme et son ombre. Ta poitrine ou
la mienne ouverte par un rat-chirurgien fouillant dans nos viscères,
cherchant on aurait dit à extirper notre âme.

I know you well my brother

We have often met
in the course of our ordeals

The first time, it was the torturer who introduced us. Even
blindfolded we recognized one another. Then I heard you screaming,
screaming, and was eager to take your place, to offer my own flesh up
to the unbearable drilling of yours.
Later we met again as we waited. The wall dividing us was so flimsy.
We used it to make music. Each night we exchanged sober vocal
partitions:
"What did you eat"
"What are you reading"
"Did you get a letter"
"What did you see on the moon"
"Did the sparrow with the broken leg visit you"
"Did your beloved sprinkle perfume on your pillow? Lilac or
jasmine? Musk or amber?"

Sometimes I heard you crying out in your sleep and I relived the
scene. You or I grappling with form and shadow. Your chest or mine
opened up by a rat of a surgeon pawing through our innards, striving,
apparently, to destroy our soul.

Bien plus tard, c'est dans un désert glacial que nous nous sommes croisés. Un écran de neige nous séparait, et nous avions du mal à trouver belle la neige. Ta bouche nommait l'exil avant d'être scellée. Et sur tes yeux, je voyais palpiter le papillon de la dernière image. Une terrasse blanche où pousse cette plante aux fleurs jaunes appelées « crottes de chat ». Faute de maison, une terrasse chaulée où flotte le linge de l'enfance telles les voiles du prodigieux navire.

Je te connais bien mon frère
et tu me connais
aussi bien que la poche lourde
aqueuse
de ta tête

Alors
tends-moi la main
donne-moi la clé
dont tu n'as que faire

Much later on it was in a frigid desert that we ran into one another. A sheet of snow separated us, and it was hard for us to find the snow beautiful. Your mouth named the place of exile before being closed forever. And in your eyes I saw the flashing butterfly of the last image. A white terrace where the yellow flowers known as cat droppings grow. For want of a house, a whitewashed terrace where the laundry of childhood flaps like the sails of a magical ship.

I know you well my brother
and you know me
as well as the heavy
watery
pouch
of your head

So
hold out your hand
give me the key
that you have no more use for

[...]
Homme dites-vous ?
Admettons

Ceci
ou autre chose
à quoi bon se torturer ?

Peu importe l'enveloppe
l'étiquette
le masque que l'on ne peut plus ôter
sans décoller la peau

Je fais face
faussement serein
mais je fais face

Dans ce périple
je n'ai choisi ni la monture
ni l'itinéraire

À peine si j'y ai mis
mon grain de sel

[. . .]
Man you say?
Let's suppose so

That
or something else
why rack our brains?

What matter the envelope
the label
the mask you cannot remove
without ripping off skin

I face up to it
my calm is fake
but I face up to it

On this journey
I chose neither mount
nor route

I hardly had
a word to say about it

Je me suis rendu invisible
pour essayer l'autre regard
et ne pas me voir du dehors
pantin parmi les pantins

Je compte derechef les jours

Diable ce qu'ils sont longs
et affreusement courts

De banalité en banalité
je m'étiole
me rétrécis

Je suis là
dans la marge qui m'a choisi
tenant à la main
ma fleur
poussée dans le béton

Qui voudra de ma fleur ?

Personne ne m'appellera ici
par mon nom
ne poussera ma porte

I made myself invisible
to test the other's scrutiny
and to avoid seeing myself from outside
just another puppet

From now on I count the days

My god how long they are
and how horribly short

From one triviality to the next
I fade
I shrink

Here I am
on the fringe that is my lot
holding in my hand
my flower
grown in concrete

Who would like my flower?

No one here will call me
by my name
or push my door open

pour demander de l'aide
ou une pincée de sel

Il pleut
et fait soleil
bonnet blanc et blanc bonnet

Le vent n'a pas de voix

Les oiseaux se cachent
pour chanter

Les volcans sont loin
les séismes frappent ailleurs

Dans la rue
les passants
y compris les chiens
ne sont que des passants

Faute d'un visage rayonnant
je dis bonjour au magnolia du coin
à la branche de menthe plantée hier
à la chaise vide devant moi

to ask for help
or a pinch of salt

It rains
the sun shines
six of one and half a dozen of the other

The wind has no voice

The birds hide
before they sing

Volcanoes are far away
earthquakes strike elsewhere

In the street
the passersby
including the dogs
are just passersby

Seeing no radiant face
I say good morning to the magnolia on the corner
the sprig of mint planted yesterday
and the empty chair in front of me

Est-elle vraiment vide ?

Je sais que non

Nombreux sont ceux qui viennent s'y asseoir
sans rien dire

Chacun d'eux
a pris de moi quelque chose

Curieux cette façon qu'ont les fantômes
de vous piller
et de vous rappeler vos défauts

Je vis et laisse vivre

La chaise est solide
elle nous survivra à tous

J'écris
je ne sais dans quelle langue
l'oubliée ou la maudite
j'imite les caractères du talisman
qui m'a révélé le labyrinthe

Is it really empty?

I know the answer is no

Many are those who come and sit there
without a word

Every one of them
took something from me

Odd the way ghosts have
of robbing you
and reminding you of your shortcomings

I live and let live

The chair is solid
it will outlive all of us

I write
I don't know in which language
forgotten or accursed
I copy the characters of the talisman
that showed me the labyrinth

Je m'applique comme je peux

Me relis sept fois
pour ne pas contrevenir à la règle

De phrase en phrase
je m'étiole
me rétrécis

La page elle
s'élargit
se rallonge
jusqu'à recouvrir entièrement la table
et déborder

Mon calame m'échappe
saute par la fenêtre

Le ciel me claque sa porte au nez

J'assiste
impuissant
à la rébellion de mes outils

I apply myself as best I can

Re-reading myself seven times
so as not to break the rule

From one sentence to the next
I fade
I shrink

As for the page
it grows larger
longer
until it covers the whole table
and goes over the edge

My quill slips from my fingers
flies out of the window

Heaven slams the door in my face

Helplessly
I witness
the rebellion of my tools

Il est temps de se taire
de ranger les accessoires
les costumes
les rêves
les douleurs
les cartes postales

Il est temps de fermer la parenthèse
arrêter le refrain
vendre les meubles
nettoyer la chambre
vider les poubelles

Il est temps d'ouvrir la cage
des canaris qui m'ont prodigué leur chant
contre une vague nourriture
et quelques gobelets d'eau

Il est temps de quitter
la maison des illusions
pour le large d'un océan de feu
où mes métaux humains
pourraient enfin fondre

Time to stop talking
to put away my effects
suits of clothes
dreams
pains
postcards

Time to close the parentheses
halt the refrain
sell the furniture
tidy up the bedroom
empty the trashcans

Time to open the cage
of the canaries who have offered me their song
against some vague food
and a few dishes of water

Time to leave
the house of illusions
for an ocean main of fire
where my human metals
may melt at last

Il est temps de quitter l'enveloppe
et s'apprêter au voyage

Nos chemins se séparent
ô mon frère l'évadé

J'ai de la folie
mon grain propre

Un choix autre
de la séparation

J'ai ma petite lumière
sur les significations dernières
de l'horreur

Une fois
une seule fois
il m'est arrivé d'être homme
comme l'ont célébré les romances

Et ce fut
au mitan de l'amour

Time to leave the envelope
and get ready for the journey

Our paths are diverging
oh my escapee brother

I have my own
touch of madness

Another way of choosing
separation

I have my little light to shine
on the ultimate meaning
of horror

Once
just once
I was able to be a man
of the kind celebrated in the Romances

And it was
in the midst of love

L'amour
quoi de plus léger pour un havresac

Alors je m'envole
sans regret
j'adhère au cri
l'archaïque
rougi au feu des déveines
et je remonte d'une seule traite
la chaîne des avortements

Je surprends le chaos
en ses préparatifs

Je convoque à ma transe noire
le peuple majoritaire des éclopés
esprits vaincus
martyrs des passions réprouvées
vierges sacrifiées au moloch de la fécondité
aèdes chassés de la cité
dinosaures aussi doux que des colombes
foudroyés en plein rêve
ermites de tous temps
ayant survécu dans leurs grottes
aux bulldozers de l'histoire

Love
what could be lighter in a knapsack

So I fly off
with no regrets
I endorse the cry
the ancient cry
reddened in the fires of ill fortune
and in a single stint trace back
the whole chain of miscarriages

I take chaos by surprise
during its preparations

To my dark trance I invite
the majoritarian people of cripples
defeated souls
martyrs to censured passions
virgins sacrificed to the Moloch of fertility
ediles banished from the city
dinosaurs gentle as doves
blasted as they dream
hermits of all time in their caves
who have survived
the bulldozers of history

Je ne me reconnais d'autre peuple
que ce peuple
guéri du rapt et du meurtre
du vampirisme des besoins
des adorations
des soumissions
et des lois stupides

Je ne me reconnais d'autre peuple
que ce peuple
non issu de la horde
nuitamment nomade
laissant aux arbres leurs fruits
aux animaux la vie sauve
se nourrissant du lait des étoiles
confiant ses morts
à la générosité du silence

Je ne me reconnais d'autre peuple
que ce peuple
impossible

Nous nous rejoignons dans la transe

I acknowledge no people
other than this people
survivors of rape and murder
of the vampirism of needs
pieties
submissions
and stupid laws

I acknowledge no people
other than this people
not sprung from the horde
nomadic by night
who leave fruit on trees
and let animals live
feeding on the milk of the stars
and entrusting their dead
to the generosity of silence

I acknowledge no people
other than this impossible
people

We all join together in the trance

La danse nous rajeunit
nous fait traverser l'absence

Une autre veille commence
aux confins de la mémoire

Dancing rejuvenates us
carries us across absence

Another watch begins
at the frontiers of memory

La saison du dire est close

De tout ce que l'homme a proféré
que restera-t-il ?

Çà et là
quelques bribes

La saveur des mots
qui ont donné la vie
et l'ont reprise

L'histoire d'un amour vaincu

Le chant désespéré
d'une espérance folle

Une clé
jetée au fond d'un puits

Le dernier râle d'un taureau
traîné comme une loque
hors de l'arène

The talking season is closed

Of everything man has offered
what will remain?

A few traces
here and there

The flavor of words
that gave life
and renewed it

The history of a defeated love

The desperate song
of a mad hope

A key
tossed down a well

The last roar of a bull
dragged like an old rag
from the ring

Un collier d'énigmes
au cou translucide de la beauté

La saison du dire est close

Derrière la parole
se profile l'oubli

Avec sa lyre enchantée

Ses grandes mains effaceuses

Sa toge d'apparat aux mille replis

Et les rubis fondants de sa coupe

L'oubli
ce suborneur
sans délicatesse aucune

Il regagne la taverne de ses aïeux
s'installe sur son trône
et verse à ses ouailles
le breuvage illicite

A collar of enigmas
about the translucent neck of beauty

The talking season is closed

Behind words
lurks Oblivion

With his enchanted lyre

His great eraser hands

His ceremonial toga with its thousand folds

And the fading rubies of his chalice

Oblivion
that suborner
so devoid of delicacy

He returns to the tavern of his forebears
settles on his throne
and serves forbidden libations
to his flock

À son banquet
personne ne manque à l'appel

Il y a là
tout excités
les convertis de la vingt-cinquième heure
les vieux routiers de l'utopie
amers et sombres
les tortionnaires à la retraite
grands-pères et jardiniers émérites
les généraux
poètes du dimanche
tueurs du lundi et des autres jours
les banquiers des organes
et du sang impur
les marins fabulateurs
les faiseuses d'anges
les terrassiers de la juste voie
les petits artisans de la corruption
les ténors de la prudence
les maquereaux du ciel
les rois nus
coiffés de bonnets d'âne
les clowns du désert
les dompteurs du rêve

Nobody is missing
at his banquet

Here
in high excitement
are converts of the twenty-fifth hour
hardened seekers of utopia
bitter and somber
retired torturers
venerable grandfathers and gardeners
generals
Sunday poets
Monday killers (also other days)
bankers of organs
and impure blood
fable-spinning seamen
backstreet abortionists
roadbuilders of the correct path
petty craftsmen of corruption
tenors of prudence
pimps of heaven
naked kings
in their dunce's caps
clowns of the desert
dream tamers

la meute au complet
des délateurs

Il y a là
vautrés au pied du trône
la masse des repentis
les fatigués du voyage
des libertés pour rien
de la misère sans fond
de la roue arracheuse de vérité

Il y a là
derrière le trône
posant pour la photo
l'aréopage des anciennes victimes
au torse bombé
armées jusqu'aux dents

Il n'y a là
que des vieux
ou des jeunes vieillis avant l'âge
des enfants sadiques
au cou ridé
aux mains velues

and the whole pack
of informers

Here
prostrate at the foot of the throne
are the mass of penitents
those weary of the journey
of worthless freedoms
of depthless poverty
of the wheel that snatches away the truth

Here
behind the throne
posing for a photo
is the areopagus of former victims
bodies bent
armed to the teeth

Here
are only the old
or the young old before their time
sadistic children
with wrinkled throats
and hairy hands

des femmes à la poitrine plate
au cheveu rare

La taverne est bondée
l'odeur irrespirable

On n'attend plus que le dîner
qui enfin arrive

Les serveurs
en tenue rayée de bagnard
remplissent les assiettes
d'énormes quartiers de chair
crue
avariée
et disent
à qui veut les entendre :
Mangez-vous les uns les autres !

Les convives s'en donnent à cœur joie
déchirent
avalent
et se pourlèchent

women with flat chests
and thinning hair

The tavern is chock-full
the stench insufferable

They wait only for dinner now
which arrives at last

The servers
in convicts' stripes
pile the plates high
with enormous hunks of meat
raw
tainted
and say
to any who care to listen:
Go on, devour one another!

The guests have at it delightedly
tearing at the food
swallowing
and licking their lips

La boisson coule à flots

Une musique « moderne » fuse

Les plus vaillants quittent les tables
forment une ronde
se déhanchent comme ils peuvent

La musique devient vulgaire
les hommes aussi

Les femmes quittent leurs habits
le reste de leur féminité

L'orgie
si l'on peut dire
bat son plein

L'oubli trône
au fond de la taverne

Déguste son pouvoir

Drink flows abundantly

"Modern" music erupts

The boldest leave their tables
form a circle
and loosen their hips as best they can

The music becomes vulgar
the men too

The women shed their clothes
and what is left of their femininity

The orgy
so to speak
is in full swing

Oblivion
sits on his throne
at the back of the tavern

Savoring his power

La taverne de l'oubli
est maintenant vide

Les reliefs du banquet
dispersés par le vent

La horde a repris ses chemins obscurs
ses tribulations

La scène est prête
pour accueillir d'autres drames

Pas de répit pour les saltimbanques
pas de pitié
pour les éternels spectateurs

Tiens
une parodie de l'apocalypse !

Ce qu'il faut pour frapper les esprits
jusqu'à l'extinction de l'esprit

Il y aura
cette fin de règne
et les appétits qu'elle réveille

The tavern of oblivion
is empty now

The remains of the feast
blown away by the wind

The hordes are back on their obscure paths
with their tribulations

The stage is set
to welcome other dramas

No respite for the performers
no pity
for the eternal spectators

Hey
a parody of the apocalypse!

Just what is needed to unsettle minds
until the mind is no more

There will be
this end of a reign
and the appetites it awakens

Les signes
de la grande cassure
au centre de la terre
au cœur des idées

La dérive de la raison
et son morcellement

L'opaque dressant son airain
entre la chose et son contraire

Les fléaux et les miracles habituels.
Mal inconnu à la racine. Mutation du sang. Confusion des cinq sens.
Dérèglement de la lumière, des métaux, du coït.
Un siècle de pluies. Un siècle de sécheresse.
L'éclipse annoncée de longue date, souvent reportée. L'arbre qui
saigne. Les statues somnambules. La licorne qui s'anime, saute de sa
tapisserie et s'envole par la cheminée.
Réapparition de l'espèce éteinte des lutins. Disparition de l'île des
rencontres. Morts suspectes au moment de la prière amoureuse.
Évasion collective de tous les asiles et des bagnes secrets. Tarissement
de la source de vérité, de l'océan intérieur. Suicides en série des
athlètes et des tribuns adorés par le peuple. Invasions de sauterelles
mécaniques, de puces hautement intelligentes.

The signs
of the great break
at the center of the earth
at the core of thought

The drift
and crumbling
of reason

Opacity placing its iron bar
between the thing and its opposite

The usual plagues and miracles.
Evil of unknown origin. Mutation of the blood. Confusion of the
five senses. Disordering of the light, of metals, of copulation.
A century of rains. A century of drought.
The long-foretold eclipse, so often postponed. The bleeding tree.
Sleepwalking statues. The unicorn that comes to life, leaps from his
tapestry and flies off up the chimney.
Reappearance of the extinct race of pixies. Disappearance of the
island of encounters. Suspicious deaths at the moment of the loving
prayer. Mass breakout from all asylums and secret prisons. Drying up
of the spring of truth, the inner ocean. Serial suicides of athletes and
leaders beloved of the people. Invasions of mechanical locusts and
highly intelligent fleas.

Avancée allègre
du désert
dans les cœurs

Il y aura
dans les bagages du désert
le messager
le mal-aimé de son vivant

Candidat au martyre

Il sortira de la dune
aux sept vierges enterrées vivantes
du manuscrit aux pages arrachées
de la légende
ou d'une baraque de bidonville

Il aura les yeux de l'albinos
le visage mal rasé des mutins
le nez sans équivoque du loup de mer
les mains brûlantes
de l'esclave-laboureur

Il avancera
sous le soleil livide

Lively progression
of the desert
into hearts

In the desert baggage train
will be
the messenger
ill-loved in his lifetime

Candidate for martyrdom

He will emerge from the dune
of the seven virgins buried alive
from the legendary manuscript
with pages ripped out
or from a hovel in a shantytown

He will have an albino's eyes
a mutineer's unshaven face
a sea dog's unmistakable nose
and the burning hands
of a slave laborer

He will proceed
under a pallid sun

au milieu de la horde incrédule
dans le décor des misères morales

On entendra
les hurlements de la trompe archaïque
une rafale de caquètements
un coup de gong au goût de rouille

Puis dans le silence précurseur
des hauts récits
qui vont accéder à la mémoire
il essuiera de ses lèvres
les relents du mensonge
fixera les rangées de têtes immatures
avant de dire :
Voici venir l'ère
des famines
et de l'égorgement

Ô peuple de cancrelats lubriques
prépare-toi à l'épreuve

La roue des destinées a tourné
et s'est arrêtée

through the incredulous horde
against a backdrop of moral poverty

The wail of the ancient horn
will be heard
a burst of clucking
a rusty-sounding gong struck

And then in the silence preceding
the grand testimony
about to be lodged in memory
he will wipe the remnants of the lie
from his lips
look straight at the ranks of immature heads
and say:
The time
of famine
and slaughter
is at hand

Oh people of lustful cockroaches
prepare for the ordeal

The wheel of destiny has turned
and stopped

Tu as joué
et perdu

Tu n'as su lire aucun signe

Du jardin qui t'a été confié
tu as fait un dépotoir

De la graine sacrée
déposée en toi
tu as tiré le pain amer
qui ne peut se partager

Tu as consacré l'intelligence
aux alibis des crimes parfaits

Tu as ôté aux pauvres
la bouée de l'espérance

Aux femmes
la parure de l'être

You have played
and lost

You were unable to interpret any sign

You have treated
the garden entrusted to you
as a garbage heap

From the sacred seed
planted within you
you have created the bitter bread
that cannot be shared

You have devoted your intelligence
to alibis for perfect crimes

You have deprived the poor
of their buoy of hope

Women
of the adornment of their being

À tes enfants
tu as légué tes œillères
l'appât du gain
et le lexique de la haine

À ceux qui t'ont offert un miroir
pour débusquer le monstre en toi
et compter tes lâchetés
tu as crevé les yeux

Et moi
moi qui te parle et te préviens
je sais quel sort tu me réserves

Voilà
j'offre mon corps à l'absurde
de ton ingéniosité sadique

Je te maudis
et maudis en même temps
cette tradition de l'holocauste
qui me fait m'agenouiller
écarter les bras
tendre le cou
pour que tu t'éprouves

To your children
you have bequeathed your blinkers
the lust for money
and the lexicon of hate

You have gouged out the eyes
of those who handed you a mirror
to discern the monster within you
and to inventory your acts of cowardice

And as for me
speaking to you and warning you
I know what fate you have reserved for me

Here then
I offer my body to the absurdity
of your sadistic ingenuity

I curse you
and at the same time I curse
the tradition of the burnt offering
that makes me kneel
stretch my hands wide
present my neck
so that you will put yourself to the test

avant de trancher la gorge
de l'agneau sans défense que je suis
et dont l'âme
s'il a une âme
ne trouvera jamais le repos

before cutting the throat
of the defenseless lamb that I am
a lamb whose soul
if it has one
will never find rest

Le messager prêchera longtemps
dans le vide

La curée qu'il redoutait
et désirait
n'aura pas lieu

La foule se détournera de lui

Il restera seul
torturé par ses visions

S'enfoncera peu à peu
dans le sable

Le soleil continuera à éclairer
l'ordinaire horreur

La nuit à recouvrir
le sordide inavouable

Le ciel ne se prononcera pas

L'apocalypse ne sera pas
une resucée du déluge
après la destruction des cités pécheresses

The messenger will preach for a long time
in a void

The spoils that he feared
and wished for
are not forthcoming

The crowd will turn their backs on him

He will remain alone
tormented by his visions

Sinking little by little
into the sand

The sun will continue to light up
everyday horror

The night to obscure
unmentionable squalor

Heaven will have no comment

The apocalypse will not be
a replay of the flood
that followed the destruction of the sinful cities

Pour ceux qui auront appris à lire
elle se déroulera
en un coin perdu
dans la boue d'une tente de réfugiés
là où un enfant décharné
couvert de vermine
exhale son dernier souffle

Dans ses yeux
qui prennent la moitié du visage
il n'y a ni question
ni réponse

Il n'y a rien de ce que les humains partagent
ou se disputent

Rien de ce qui les attache
à ce que l'on appelle vie :
la chamade de la pluie
quand elle embaume la terre
la fenêtre de l'aube
ouverte sur le jasmin
et le beignet ruisselant de miel
la litanie pieuse d'une tourterelle
semant le trouble

For those who have learnt to read
it will take place
in a dim corner
in the mud of a refugee tent
where an emaciated child
crawling with vermin
breathes its last

In his eyes
that fill half his face
is no question
no answer

Nothing of what human beings share
or fight over

Nothing of what attaches them
to what we call life
the drumbeat of the rain
perfuming the earth
the window of dawn
opening onto jasmine
and a pastry dripping with honey
a turtledove's devout litany
prompting anxiety

dans le cœur fermé au mystère
le pain chaud
qu'on recouvre avec une serviette à carreaux
les fruits qu'on dépose amoureusement sur la table
la coupe
dont on contemple la robe
avant de la défaire
à petites gorgées savantes
la caresse qui s'attarde
sur chaque grain de la peau
et se dirige vers la source des sources
la vue de la mer
après une longue incarcération
– miracle des vagues libres
délices de l'horizon
poème qui s'énonce clairement –
le seuil frais d'une maison
où les vieux jours s'égrènent
en rêveries aux couleurs de friandises
la nouvelle de la chute d'un despote
celle de la mort d'un ami
les nuits blanches
où l'alezan de l'espoir
s'ouvre les veines
les coquelicots du bord de la route

in hearts immured against mystery
warm bread
covered by a check napkin
fruit placed lovingly on the table
the glass of wine
whose hue we contemplate
before emptying it and savoring each sip
the caress that lingers
on every pore of the skin
as it makes for the spring of springs
the sight of the sea
after a long imprisonment
– the miraculous freedom of the waves
the delight of the horizon
a poem so clearly voiced –
the cool threshold of a house
where the days of old age
pay themselves out
in candy-colored revery
news of a dictator's fall
or of a friend's death
sleepless nights
when the palomino of hope
opens its veins
poppies by the wayside

quand le train ralentit
laisse passer un ange
et remplit la poche
d'une menue monnaie de jubilations
l'heure où l'on éteint
pour se retrouver avec soi-même
lire dans son dédale
à la bougie du rêve

Dans les yeux de l'enfant
il n'y a que l'absence

Il y a une autre connaissance

Les yeux de l'enfant
ne sont pas des yeux

Ils n'ont pas de larmes
pas plus de cils

Leur éclat glacial
est celui d'un astre insoumis
détaché de la matrice
depuis les origines

when the train slows down
lets an angel pass over
and fills your pockets with
with the small change of joy
the moment when you switch the light off
to be alone with yourself
and explore your labyrinth
by dream's candle

In the child's eyes
is only absence

a different kind of knowledge

The child's eyes
are not eyes

They have no more tears
than they have lashes

Their icy gleam
is that of a rebel star
separated from its matrix
at birth

Hors de la course
à contre-courant
il vogue dans la prison de l'infini
en quête d'une lézarde
d'un trou par où s'échapper
s'éjecter dans l'ailleurs

Là où rien ne se crée
rien ne se transforme

Un au-delà immatériel
où il pourra sans attendre
crever l'abcès de la vie
et retourner à la poussière

L'apocalypse trime
se fait oublier
puis donne de ses nouvelles

Quelle autre fin imaginer ?

Il n'y a pas de fin

Out of the race
against the current
it roams the prison of the infinite
searching for a crack
a hole to crawl through
and project itself
into an elsewhere

A place where nothing is created
nothing is transformed

A non-material beyond
where it might immediately
burst the abscess of life
and return to dust

The apocalypse labors
gets itself forgotten
and then sends a message

What other end can be imagined?

There is no end

Le cauchemar
épouse un cercle parfait

Cela se nomme l'éternité

Un bocal hermétique
qu'aucune magie ne peut ouvrir

The nightmare describes
a perfect circle

It is called eternity

A tightly sealed vessel
that no magic can open

from

POÈMES PÉRISSABLES

PERISHABLE POEMS

(2000)

LE LECTEUR PRESSÉ

Que viens-tu faire ici
lecteur ?
Tu as ouvert sans ménagement
ce livre
et tu remues fébrilement le sable des pages
à la recherche
de je ne sais quel trésor enfoui
Es-tu là pour pleurer
ou pour rire
N'as-tu personne d'autre
à qui parler
Ta vie
est-elle à ce point vide ?
Alors referme vite ce livre
Pose-le loin du réveille-matin
et de la boîte à médicaments
Laisse-le mûrir
au soleil du désir
sur la branche du beau silence

READER IN A HURRY

What are you doing here
reader?
You have opened this book
carelessly
and are sifting frantically through the sand of its pages
in search of
who knows what buried treasure
Are you here to cry
or to laugh
Don't you have anyone else
to talk to
Is your life really
so empty
Well then close this book quickly
Put it far from the alarm clock
and the medicine cabinet
Let it ripen
under the sun of desire
on the branch of beautiful silence

INSÉPARABLES

Pauvre corps
étriqué et mal foutu
Je te remercie de ton hospitalité

Tu pousses la tolérance
jusqu'au vice

J'en profite sans vergogne

Je t'use
et tu m'uses

Inséparables nous sommes
mais pas dupes

INSEPARABLE

Poor body
scrawny and misbegotten
Thank you for your hospitality

You carry tolerance
to the point of vice

I exploit this shamelessly

I use you
and you use me

Inseparable is what we are
but we are not fools

LES IMAGES PÉRIMÉES

Maintenant j'écris
comme l'aveugle voit
La lumière glisse sur mes paupières
et s'évacue par le trou de la page
Les mots font les cent pas dans leur cage
J'entends claquer le fouet du dompteur
et pas de rugissement
Mes images toutes
sont périmées
Je marche
dans le dédale du cœur
sans chien-guide

WORN-OUT IMAGES

I write now
the way the blind man sees
The light slips over my eyelids
and exits via the page's hole
The words pace up and down in their cage
I hear the crack of the lion tamer's whip
but no roar
My images are all
worn out
I walk
in the maze of the heart
with no guide-dog

LE POÈTE ANONYME

Est-ce ma voix
ou celle d'un poète anonyme
venant des siècles obscurs
Quand ai-je vécu
Sur quelle terre
Quelle femme ai-je aimée
De quelle passion
Et puis qui me dit
que je n'étais pas justement une femme
et que je n'ai pas connu d'homme
parce que trop laide
ou n'ayant simplement pas d'attirance
pour les hommes
Me suis-je battu
pour
contre quelque chose
Ai-je eu la foi
des enfants
Suis-je mort jeune
incompris, misérable
ou très vieux, entouré, adulé
héraut d'une tribu se préparant
à conquérir le monde

ANONYMOUS POET

Is this my voice
or that of an anonymous poet
from some dark age
When did I live
And on what earth
What woman did I love
with what passion
And who is to say
I was not in fact a woman
and knew no man
being too ugly
or merely feeling no attraction
to men
Did I fight
for
against something
Did I believe in God
Did I have children
Did I die young
misunderstood, impoverished
or very old, well surrounded, revered
herald of a tribe preparing
to conquer the world

Mes œuvres m'ont-elles survécu
Ma langue est-elle morte
avant que d'être écrite
Mais d'abord étais-je aède
ou roi fainéant
prêtre
pleureuse professionnelle
navigateur
djinn ou adamite
savante almée
jouant du luth dans un harem ?
Peut-être n'étais-je
qu'un artisan sellier
n'ayant jamais monté à cheval
et qui chantait
en trimant la sainte journée
pour que le cuir se ramollisse entre ses mains
et rende de la belle ouvrage
qu'enfourcheront les riches

Alors qui étais-je
pour que ma parole se dédouble
et que le malin sosie
qui en tient les rênes
me piège

Did my works survive me
Was my language dead
before being written
Was I once a bard
or a *roi fainéant*
a priest
a professional weeper
a navigator
a jinni or an Adamite
a wise almeh
playing her lute in a harem?
Perhaps I was no more
than an artisan saddler
who had never mounted a horse
but sang
as he slogged through the livelong day
to make the leather soften in his hands
and become a fine object
for rich people to straddle

So who was I
to have what I say split in two
and the wicked double
who holds the reins
trick me

avec cette question qui n'en est pas une :
est-ce ta voix
ou celle d'un poète anonyme
venant des siècles obscurs ?

with this question that is not a question:
Is this your voice
or that of an anonymous poet
from some dark age?

de POÈMES PÉRISSABLES

Je recueille bout par bout
ce qui subsiste en moi
Tessons de colère
lambeaux de passion
escarbilles de joie
Je couds, colle et cautérise
Abracadabra !
Je suis de nouveau debout
Pour quelle autre bataille ?

* * *

Quand le quotidien m'use
je m'abuse
en y mettant mon grain d'ironie
Voici le chat
et voici la souris
Auteur méconnu de dessins animés
je suis

* * *

Quand on n'a plus à offrir
que le mal de vivre

from PERISHABLE POEMS

Bit by bit I gather
what is left in me
Shards of anger
shreds of passion
cinders of joy
I sew, glue, cauterize
Abracadabra!
I am standing up once more
For what new battle?

* * *

When everyday life wears me down
I am wrong
to counter with a grain of irony
Look at the cat
and look at the mouse
An unknown creator of animated films
is what I am

* * *

When you have nothing to offer
save hopelessness and

le ridicule de la douleur
autant se taire

Quelle indécence déjà à se le dire
en croyant toucher
à je ne sais quel art !

* * *

J'ai cru par l'esprit
me libérer de mes prisons
Mais l'esprit lui-même
est une prison
J'ai essayé d'en repousser les parois
J'essaie toujours

* * *

Parfois je vis
Parfois je meurs
Plus près de la blessure
Plus loin des mots

* * *

Le pilleur des rêves
est encore passé
Au rêveur

the absurdity of suffering
you might as well be quiet

How indecent it already is to tell oneself this
in the belief that one is achieving
some sort of art!

* * *

I thought that with my mind
I could escape from my prisons
But the mind itself is a prison
I tried to push back its walls
I am still trying

* * *

Sometimes I live
Sometimes I die
Closer to the wound
Further from words

* * *

The pillager of dreams
came by again
For the dreamer

il n'a laissé
qu'un goût de sable
dans la bouche

* * *

Laver son cœur
le faire sécher
le repasser
le suspendre sur un cintre
Ne pas le replacer tout de suite
dans sa cage
Attendre
la clé charnelle de la vision
l'impossible retour
le dénouement de l'éternité

* * *

Je vis
la peur au ventre
Peur de quoi ?
De l'apocalypse annoncée
et péniblement reportée
Du tarissement de l'amour
de l'écriture

456

he has left only
a taste of sand
in the mouth

* * *

Wash your heart
dry it
iron it
put it on a hanger
Do not return it right away
to its cage
Wait for
the fleshly key of vision
the impossible return
the dénouement of eternity

* * *

I live
with fear in my belly
Fear of what?
Of the apocalypse announced
and put off so arduously
Of the tarrying of the love
of writing

Du bourreau que j'ai cru oublier
et qui ne m'a pas encore oublié
De commettre quelque ignominie
D'attraper la maladie de la soumission
Ou de mourir par hasard
écrasé comme un chien ?

* * *

Si tu veux
ne pas être trop déçu
prépare-toi
à la déception

* * *

La tristesse
n'est pas mon métier
Mais comme elle est rare
la joie pure !

* * *

Où est l'amour
qui devine en toi la noire tempête
et l'arrête
d'un simple souffle d'entre ses lèvres ?

Of the executioner I thought I had forgotten
who has not yet forgotten me
Of committing some ignominy
Of contracting the sickness of submission
Or of dying by chance
like a dog run over in the street?

* * *

If you don't want
to be too disappointed
get ready
for disappointment

* * *

Sadness
is not my occupation
But pure joy
is so very rare!

* * *

Where is the love
that discerns the dark storm within you
and halts it
with a simple breath from its lips?

Où est l'ami
qui t'appelle
juste pour te dire bonjour ?

Où est le pays
qui ne te réclame pas
chaque année
le prix de ta naissance ?

* * *

Des tonnes de livres que j'ai lues
j'ai presque tout oublié
Suis-je devenu
un homme cultivé ?

* * *

Les athées
jurent leurs grands dieux
Les croyants
pestent contre les leurs

* * *

De cette feuille
dite vierge

Where is the friend who
calls you
just to say hello?

Where is the country
that does not demand
payment for your birth
every year?

* * *

Of the tons of books I have read
I have forgotten almost all
Have I become
a cultured man?

* * *

Atheists
swear by all the gods
Believers
curse theirs

* * *

From this leaf
supposedly virgin

que sortira-t-il
Un bouton de seringa
ou une fleur carnivore ?

C'est moi qui tremble

* * *

Je n'ai pas entendu
la sentence
Et on me donne déjà
la dernière cigarette

* * *

Ils ont tout de l'homme
et ce ne sont pas des hommes
Regardez-les faire
ce qu'aucune bête
n'a jamais pu faire
Ils sont là
tapis en nous
qui nous prétendons hommes

* * *

what will emerge
A seringa bud
or a carnivorous flower?

It is I who tremble

* * *

I have not heard
the sentence
And already they are giving me
my last cigarette

* * *

They have everything of man
but are not men
Look at them doing
what no beast
has ever been able to do
They are there
crouched within us
we who claim to be men

* * *

Depuis qu'il n'y a plus rien à dire
tout a été de nouveau dit
Et tourne manivelle !

* * *

Au lieu
d'égorger un mouton
pour la naissance d'un enfant
pourquoi ne pas planter un arbre ?

* * *

On tombe amoureux
d'une passante
Puis vite
l'amour passe

* * *

Serrer la main d'une femme
n'est jamais innocent

* * *

Attablé. Je me vois passer sur le trottoir d'en face. Une sacoche
à la main, l'habit un peu large, le dos légèrement voûté, la tête

Ever since there was nothing more to say
everything has been said again
so crank it out!

* * *

Instead
of slaughtering a sheep
at the birth of a child
why not plant a tree?

* * *

You fall in love
with a passerby
Then quickly
love is gone

* * *

Shaking a woman's hand
is never innocent

* * *

Seated at a table. I see myself passing by on the sidewalk opposite.
A bag in my hand, a coat rather too large, back slightly hunched, hair

franchement grise, le pas saccadé de quelqu'un qui sait où il va, ou du moins veut donner cette impression, le regard perçant des grands distraits, le vague sourire en coin de celui à qui on ne la fait pas.

Tel que, le passant ne m'inspire ni sympathie ni antipathie. Je ne fais rien pour lui signaler ma présence.

Je n'ai pas envie qu'on vienne troubler ma solitude.

* * *

Souvenir lointain
Le bonheur m'a réveillé
Pour la première fois
j'avais connu l'amour
J'en vibrais encore
des pieds à la tête
J'avais quinze ans
et je me sentais immortel

Un autre souvenir
Seul
entre quatre murs
Malgré la pénombre de rigueur
je pressens l'aube

distinctly gray, the gait jerky like that of someone who knows where he is going or at least wants to give that impression, the piercing gaze of the most absentminded, and the vague sideways smile of a man not about to be fooled.

As such, the passerby arouses neither sympathy nor antipathy in me. I do nothing to signal my presence.

I don't want anyone to disturb my solitude.

* * *

A distant memory
Happiness awoke me
For the first time
I had known love
I was still trembling
from head to toe
I was fifteen
and felt immortal

Another memory
Alone
between four walls
Despite the usual half-darkness
I sense the coming of dawn

L'esprit de l'aimée est là
plus ardent que sa chair
Ce poème muet
jamais je n'ai pu l'égaler

Me réveiller auprès de toi
t'apporter le café
écouter ensemble la radio
accueillir ta tête sur mon épaule
te masser les doigts
L'amour simple
comme bonjour

Tu es là
Tout n'est pas perdu

Devant toi
j'ai honte de mon désespoir

The spirit of my beloved is there
more ardent than her flesh
A mute poem
I have never been able to equal

Wake next to you
bring you coffee
listen to the radio together
welcome your head on my shoulder
stroke your fingers
Love as simple
as good morning

You are here
All is not lost

In front of you
I am ashamed of my despair

from

L'AUTOMNE PROMET

FALL HOLDS PROMISE

(2003)

de L'AUTOMNE PROMET

[...]
Ai-je choisi
de naître sur cette fracture
de la terre humaine
au temps de la disette
de la poussée des peuples
en quête de dignité ?
Comme si le fétu de paille
pouvait élire la tempête
qui va le soulever
jusqu'à l'œil du soleil
ou l'enfouir dans une grotte !
Enigme de la naissance
encore plus opaque que celle de la mort
Avec cette différence
que nous avons toute la vie pour la sonder
la tourner et la retourner
nous en émerveiller ou la maudire
Et puis surtout
vient le moment où il faut décider
d'un enfantement plus ardu
celui par lequel
nous donnons naissance à nous-mêmes

from FALL HOLDS PROMISE

[. . .]
Did I choose
to be born on this rift
in the human earth
at this time of a lapse
in the pressure of peoples
in search of dignity?
As though a wisp of straw
could choose the storm
that will carry it up
into the eye of the sun
or plunge it into a cave!
Riddle of birth
even more obscure than the riddle of death
Except for the fact
that we have a lifetime to ponder it
to turn it this way and that
to marvel at it or curse it
And then above all
comes the moment
when a harder labor
must be chosen
the one whereby
we give birth to ourselves

De cette naissance au moins
j'ai la conscience
J'en éprouve encore les contractions
J'en tiens les mots
qui à leur tour m'ont tenu
Je connais bien la droiture de ces mots
leur délicatesse
et leur férule
leur métier abstrait-concret
sur lequel on doit chaque matin
remettre l'ouvrage
leurs sillons sitôt semés
qu'il faut derechef creuser
Je les connais bien
ces mots farouches
altiers
ne se donnant qu'à celui
qui éperdument
se donne

Le don
ce maître mot
ce sésame

Of that birth at least
I am aware
I can still feel the contractions
I possess the words
that once in their turn possessed me
I well know the rightness of those words
their delicacy
and their ferule
their loom both abstract and concrete
which you must set up afresh
every morning
their furrows that no sooner sown
you must plough up again
I know them well
those untamed words
haughty words
given only to those
who give themselves
with abandon

Gift
that master word
that open-sesame

[. . .]

Chambre noire
Puis des picotements de lumière
Un léger vrombissement
(Est-ce le moteur de l'Histoire
qui tourne au ralenti ?)
Une aile
ou plutôt son mouvement
au fond de la rétine
Dernière image imprimée
d'une vie antérieure
ou prémices d'une nouvelle
qui ne tardera pas à se révéler ?
Tel un chasseur aguerri
je suis aux aguets
et ne ressens nulle angoisse
Je jubile même
de ce que j'estime être
une prometteuse dégustation
Je devine le verre
qu'une main diaphane
aux doigts effilés de pianiste
va me remplir
Verre pour verre

[. . .]
A pitch-dark room
then tiny points of light
A slight hum
(The motor of History
slowing down?)
A wing
or rather its motion
deep in the retina
The last image imprinted
in an earlier life
or the foreshadowing of a new one
about to reveal itself?
Like a seasoned hunter
I am on the qui vive
and feel no anxiety
I am even jubilant
at what I feel is
a promising taste
I picture the glass
that a diaphanous hand
will fill for me
with the trimmed nails of a pianist
Glass after glass

autant que ça soit un bon bordeaux
qui ait du nez
du corps
et une robe seyante
Re-salut à toi Abou Nouwas
prince de la roture
chantre des délices
soi-disant interdites
Salut à vous
frères en arak et poésie
disséminés en vos exils intègres
chenus et fringants
levant rituellement vos coupes
à la jeunesse et au pays bafoué
que vous portez en vous
telle une écharde ignée

Peut-être faudrait-il plus d'un verre
pour que l'image se bonifie
et faisant fi du chaos
s'agrippe à la racine des mots
Pour que son onde de choc
me traverse
exalte mon souffle
et sorte par ma bouche

so long as it is a good bordeaux
with nose
body
and a pleasing robe
Hey there again Abu Nuwas
prince of the common people
bard of so-called
forbidden delights
Hey there
brothers in arak and poetry
scattered in your complete exiles
gray-haired and frisky
raising your cups
in ritual toasts
to youth and to the humiliated country
that you carry in your hearts
like a burning splinter

Perhaps it would take more than one glass
to enhance the image
for it to defy chaos
and lay hold of words by the roots
For its shockwave
to run through me
strengthening my breath
and coming out of my mouth

Inspiré je serais alors
me gardant de vaticiner
Allons !
Poésie n'est pas prophétie
Au départ
c'est juste une façon
d'accorder les instruments de l'âme
de taquiner les cordes du mystère
de laisser entendre tels frôlements
tels balbutiements
telle tombée de rosée
au cœur de la désolation
telle saute de vent messager
de l'éveil
de laisser soupçonner
telle ligne de fuite et de trouvaille
telles épousailles souterraines
telle résurgence de facultés en déshérence

Voici les fruits inattendus
de l'automne
De la mère des voluptés
voici les seins lourds
leur lait giclant dru
mâtiné de sang

I would then be inspired
and take care not to predict
Come on!
Poetry is not prophecy
To begin with
it is just a way
to tune the instruments of the soul
to tweak the chords of the enigma
to give voice to their rustlings
stutterings
a dewfall
in the midst of desolation
a puff of wind
harbinger of awakening
and to sow the idea
of some route to escape and discovery
some subterranean marriage
some revival of disinherited abilities

Such are the unexpected fruits
of autumn
Here are the heavy breasts
of the mother of voluptuousness
their milk spurting thick and fast
mingled with blood

Bois
ô assoiffé
et une fois repu
considère ton privilège
L'image incarnée
que tu as devant toi
touche à l'essence
L'arbre de l'intime perception
s'est élevé
étendu
ramifié
au point d'épouser entièrement
ta vie
C'est le moment ou jamais
de ramasser les dés
et de nous la rejouer
cette vie
en usant de ta main heureuse
verte
calligraphe sans calame
artisane de frissons
Ta main jubilatoire

Drink
oh you who thirst
and once your thirst
is slaked
consider your privilege
The image incarnate
now before you
gets to the quick
The tree of inner perception
has grown
spread
branched out
to completely envelop
your life
Now or never is the time
to gather up the dice
and replay that life
for us
using your lucky hand
your green thumb
that calligrapher without a writing brush
that artisan of frissons
Your jubilant hand

Voyons
n'hésite plus
Laisse les esprits chagrins
à leur visage fermé
leur tête vissée
de pantins macabres
leurs doutes alimentés
par le doute du doute et re-doute
Et ne sois surtout pas objectif
économe de tes moyens
Sois imprudent
irraisonné
éloquent blasphémateur
Fulminant pour fulminant
porte à incandescence les manques
exacerbe
les superbes raisons de vivre
hisse
la bannière de beauté
déclare-la ta guerre d'amour
gagne-la

Come along
no more hesitating
Leave embittered souls behind
to their pinched faces
and stiff necks
macabre marionettes
their doubts nourished
by doubts about doubt and doubt yet again
And above all do not be objective
or sparing with your talents
Be reckless
irrational
an eloquent blasphemer
Fulminating for the sake of it
raise your needs to fever pitch
sharpen
the superb reasons for living
hoist
the banner of beauty
declare it, your war of love
and win it

[...]

Bourrasque de ce matin
soulignant d'un trait rouge
ma dernière envolée lyrique
Quelle est cette tempête adverse
qui m'abuse
en me donnant le sein
et au bout de chaque cycle
s'ingénie
à différer mon sevrage ?
Et c'est miracle
si le périple se poursuit
si rien de vital
ne s'est rompu
dans cette course d'obstacles
à la fameuse lueur
du bout du tunnel

Le tunnel
le revoici
long, long
sur une autre terre
où l'on ne peut même pas
enterrer ses morts

[...]
This morning's squall
drawing a red line
beneath my latest lyrical flight
What is this ill wind
that torments me
by giving me the breast
and at the end of each feeding
contrives
to postpone my weaning?
Indeed it is a miracle
if the cycle proceeds
and nothing vital
is broken
in this obstacle race
to the famous light
at the end of the tunnel

The tunnel
just look at it
long, so long
in another land
where your dead
cannot even be buried

Je t'ai nommée
Palestine !

Je pense à vous
mes amis de là-bas
dont j'ai traduit les poèmes
« Je vous appelle
et serre vos mains »
puis je me sens tout bête
Qu'ai-je à dire
que vous ne diriez
non pas mieux
mais avec une autre matière des mots :
le blanc insondable de la terreur
le noir indélébile du sang
le pourpre du rêve violé
le gris vénéneux des décombres
le jaune dément de la chair brûlée
le vert du torrent injuste des larmes
le bleu ivre des malédictions ?

Je pense à vous mes amis
à nos rires homériques
lors de rares récréations

Let me name you:
Palestine!

I think of you
my friends over there
whose poems I have translated
"I call you
and shake your hands"
then I feel quite foolish
What can I have to say
that you would not say
not better
but with words of a different substance:
the bottomless white of terror
the indelible black of blood
the purple of violated dreams
the poisonous gray of ruins
the crazed yellow of burnt flesh
the green of the unjust flood of tears
the drunken blue of curses?

I think of you my friends
of our homeric laughter
in the rare moments of leisure

dispensées par l'exil
à nos joutes savantes
pour célébrer le vin français
et la femme stupéfiante
équitablement partagée
dans nos pittoresques délires
de machos repentis
Je pense à votre arabe cristallin
que j'ai appris
par amour de vous
à ce passeport surréaliste
qui est le vôtre
que j'ai jadis demandé
et que vous ne m'avez pas encore accordé
Je pense à vos enfants
presque tous musiciens
nourris de fierté
les yeux brillant du plus vif éclat
qu'il m'ait été donné d'attester
Je pense à vos mères
interdisant le jardinage aux hommes
gardiennes du thym
et du secret du savon de Naplouse
Je pense à vos pères

granted by our exile
of our expert jousting
in homage to French wine
and the gorgeous woman
so equally shared
in our picturesque fantasies
of recovering macho men
I think of your sparkling Arabic
which I learnt
through love of you
and of that surrealist passport
which is yours
and which I once asked you for
and which you have still not given me
I think of your children
almost all musicians
nourished by pride
their eyes gleaming as bright as can be
something I was privileged to witness
I think of your mothers
forbidding their men to garden
guardians of thyme
and the secret of the soap of Nablus
I think of your fathers

au visage sculpté
dans le roc du mont des Oliviers
Je pense à Jérusalem
quand le peintre ami
qui en est natif
crut la voir un jour en ma compagnie
du haut des Mérinides à Fès
Je pense à vous
manquant d'eau, de pain
et plus terrible
à vos bibliothèques éventrées
à vos manuscrits foulés aux pieds
Je pense à vous
vous éclairant avec la fragile bougie
de l'espoir
car vous n'avez pas « trahi vos poèmes »
Je pense à vous Ahmad, Fadwa
Ghassane, Ibrahim, Izzat, Jamal
Khayri, Lyana, Mahmoud, Mohammed
Mourid, Nida, Rachad, Sahar
Samih, Walid, Yahia
J'ouvre vos livres
en caresse les dédicaces
finement calligraphiées

their faces hewn from the rock
of the Mount of Olives
I think of Jerusalem
as my painter friend
a native
thought he could see it one day alongside me
from the top of the hill of the Merinids in Fez
I think of you
deprived of water, of bread
and more terrible still
your ransacked libraries
your manuscripts
trampled underfoot
I think of you
lit by the weak candle
of hope
for you have never "betrayed your poems"
I think of you Ahmad, Fadwa
Ghassane, Ibrahim, Izzat, Jamal
Khayri, Lyana, Mahmud, Mohammed
Mourid, Nida, Rachad, Sahar
Samih, Walid, Yahia
I open your books
stroke your dedications
your fine handwriting

et pense
à votre incomparable urbanité
« Je vous appelle
et serre vos mains »

and think
of your incomparable urbanity
"I call you
and shake your hands"*

* The quoted words are taken from a poem by the Palestinian Tawfiq Zayyad.

[...]

Le tunnel
que voici
long, long
Quelle est cette époque
qui nous broie
dans son camion à ordures
Quelle est cette planète
qui nous ferme au nez
toutes ses portes
et ne nous laisse
comme voie de sortie
que celle où il faut apporter la preuve
du désespoir absolu ?
O nuit
toi de nouveau
rare refuge
pour les désemparés
Et pour l'œil
pâturage unique
Peut-être y a-t-il
sur une de tes étoiles
un esprit pur
un témoin juste
qui nous regarde

[. . .]
The tunnel here
is long, so long
What is this age
that crushes us
in its garbage truck
What is this planet
that slams its every door
in our face
and leaves us
no exit
except the one where you must offer proof
of absolute despair?
Oh night
you again
rare refuge
for the distressed
And unique pasture
for the eye
Might there be
on one of your stars
a pure spirit
a fair witness
watching us

et souffre de ne pas pouvoir
lever son petit doigt
Peut-être n'y a-t-il rien
et que ce silence sidéral
obéit lui aussi
à l'abjecte loi de l'indifférence
Comment en être sûr ?
O nuit
donne quelque chose
ne serait-ce qu'un brin d'illusion
ce succédané de l'espoir
ne serait-ce qu'un rai
identifiable à une promesse
même la plus vague
ne serait-ce qu'un souffle
même le plus ténu
qui ranime un peu les cendres de l'âme
Mais de grâce
épargne-nous la pitié
Tout, sauf cela

Je pense à vous
mes amis de là-bas
et brusquement
je ne sais plus ce que penser veut dire

and suffering from an inability
to lift a little finger
But perhaps there is nothing
and the interstellar silence
also obeys
the abject law of indifference
How can we be sure?
Oh night
give us something
if only a twig of illusion
that substitute for hope
if only a ray
identifiable as even the vaguest
of promises
if only a breath of air
no matter how tenuous
to slightly rekindle the ashes of the soul
But for mercy's sake
spare us pity
Anything but that

I think of you
my friends over there
and suddenly
I no longer know what thinking means

ce qu'écrire veut dire
La douleur a pris les rênes
et fouette à mort
la monture du corps
Les parois du tunnel se rapprochent
J'étouffe de votre étouffement
Je me protège la tête
comme j'ai vu tant de fois
le faire vos enfants
Je crie
pour ne pas nous voir
enterrés vivants
Je tremble
comme tout être intègre
au moment de la vérité
Je crois un instant
et apostasie au suivant
Je crache sur la table des lois
et appelle à mon secours
l'apocalypse
Je rampe à l'aveuglette
sous les décombres
de la défunte humanité
et parfois
ô délice

what writing means
Pain has seized the reins
and is flogging to death
the mount that is the body
The walls of the tunnel are closing in
I am suffocating from your suffocation
I protect my head
as I have so often
seen your children do
I cry out
so as not to see us
buried alive
I tremble
like every whole being
at the moment of truth
I believe for an instant
and reject my faith the next
I spit on the tablets of the law
and call the apocalypse
to my rescue
I crawl blindly
through the ruins
of an extinct humanity
and sometimes
oh delight

je doute ferme de mon existence
D'un battement de paupières
j'annule tout
D'abord ma condition de ver de terre
ensuite la Genèse
le jour des Comptes
en passant par le purgatoire
Sans état d'âme
j'efface cette caricature
et sur le métier remets l'ouvrage
l'Œuvre disait-on
Je sens monter en moi
la parole sans égale
et je ne suis l'émissaire de personne
Je ne dis pas à la lumière
sois
mais s'il te plaît
Je ne dis pas à la justice
frappe
mais sois juste
Je ne dis pas à la beauté
couche-toi
mais rayonne
tel un soleil libre
de toute obligation

I firmly doubt my existence
With the blink of an eye
I cancel out everything
First my condition as an earthworm
then Genesis
and the Day of Reckoning
by way of Purgatory
Without qualms
I erase these caricatures
and put the whole thing back on the stocks
the whole Work as they used to say
I feel peerless words
arising in me
and I am the emissary of no one
I do not say to light
Be
but if you please
I do not say to justice
strike
but be just
I do not say to beauty
lie down
but shine
like a sun free
of all constraint

Je ne m'adresse pas
à des tribus ou à des peuples
mais à ceux-là seuls
qui souffrent de la souffrance des autres
et ne s'en vantent pas

Je délire de votre délire
ô mes amis
pardonnez-moi
Le tunnel est encore là
long, long
J'y suis tant que vous y serez
car moi non plus
je n'ai pas « trahi mes poèmes »
« Je vous appelle
et serre vos mains »

I do not address
tribes or peoples
but only those who suffer from
the sufferings of others
and do not boast of it

My raving is your raving
oh my friends
forgive me
The tunnel is still here
long, so long
I am in it so long as you are
for I have not "betrayed my poems" either
"I call you
and shake your hands"

[. . .]

Voici du corps
la danse sacrée
Venez derviches
nos seigneurs en l'occurrence
De la danse
vous connaissez les arcanes
De la musique
vous tenez les plus belles traductions
Vos bras
sont les piliers du sanctuaire
et vos mains
des baguettes magiques
dont nous suivons les indications à la lettre
De vos pieds aériens
foulez donc le ciel ferme
Volez autour de nous
et touchez-nous de vos ailes
Apprenez-nous
la perte
l'abandon
et de l'ivresse
la conscience aiguë
Soyez indulgents
envers nos gestes maladroits

[...]

Here is the sacred dance
of the body
Come dervishes
our lords as it happens
Of the dance you know the mysteries
Of the music
you have the finest renderings
Your arms
are the pillars of the sanctuary
and your hands
the magic wands
whose direction we follow to the letter
So with your airborne feet
tread the firmament
Fly around us
and touch us with your wings
Teach us
loss
abandonment
and the sharp perception
of drunkenness
Be indulgent
toward our clumsy gestures

nos vociférations
nos âmes plates comme nos pieds
nos désirs courts comme notre vue
nos membres empêtrés dans la glu
du quotidien équarrissant nos rêves
nos épanchements d'humanoïdes mal dégrossis
nos larmes faciles
tant l'éternité nous est étrangère

Venez
nos seigneurs
Vous les serviteurs du Pôle
Offrez-nous de la parole
l'épaisseur du silence
Faites descendre en nous
l'esprit des mots
et leur terreau de racines
Mettez-nous sur la voie
vous les habitués de la Voie
et ne vous étonnez pas
de cette humble demande
Croyants nous sommes
même si Dieu n'y est pour rien
Grands brûlés de la vie
nous le sommes par amour

our vociferations
our souls as flat as our feet
our desires as short as our sight
our limbs stuck fast in the mire
of a daily life that slaughters our dreams
our primitive humanoid outpourings
our tears too ready
so foreign is eternity to us

Come
our lords
Come, servants of the Poles of Knowledge
Offer us the solid silence
of speech
Have the spirit of words
and their tangle of roots
come down into us
Show us the way
you who are familiar with the Way
and do not be surprised by this humble request
Believers we are
even if God has nothing to do with it
Badly burned victims of life
for the sake of love

L'ordalie
nous connaissons
car nés sur les marches de l'Empire
dans les contrées du manque
et de l'espérance abrégée
grandis
tant bien que mal
sous la chape des interdits
sous la férule conjuguée du ciel
et de ses lieutenants sur terre
marqués au fer rouge pour un oui
et surtout pour un non
jetés aux oubliettes
pour le moindre clin d'œil
à la beauté aux yeux bandés
appelée
nous le savons par ouï-dire : Justice

Venez nos seigneurs
Emportez-nous vers cette terre
où la danse
si elle ne nourrit pas son homme
le transfigure
lui donne la grâce
des êtres

Trial by ordeal
we know about
for we were born
on the borders of the Empire
in countries of want
of hope cut short
and grew up
as best we could
sealed in by prohibitions
under the joint strap of heaven
and heaven's lieutenants on earth
branded with a hot iron for a yes
and most of all for a no
flung into dungeons
for the slightest wink
at the blindfolded beauty
called
as we know by hearsay: Justice

Come our lords
Carry us to that land
where dance
though it may not keep a man fed
transfigures him
invests him with the grace

libérés des besoins immédiats
le rend beau de l'intérieur
troublant de l'extérieur
ressemblant étrangement
à la terre
que voilà
que voici
gagnée sur le chaos
D'un seul geste
sculptée dans le tourbillon
Toujours disponible
sachant partager le peu du rare
noblesse des humbles oblige

of beings
delivered from immediate need
making him beautiful within
troubling without
strangely reminiscent
of the earth
there
and here
won back from chaos
Sculpted with a single gesture
within the whirlwind
Ever serviceable
ever willing to share what little they have
noblesse (of the poor) *oblige*

[. . .]

Du pays qui a cru m'éloigner
je voudrais enfin vous entretenir
sans lui faire
ou me faire violence
En parler « sereinement »
comme après l'amour
quand les caresses apaisent
expriment la reconnaissance
couronnent le don
et signent la promesse

Plus que de la naissance
et de la mort
la plus grande énigme
n'est-elle pas celle
de l'amour ?

La plus grande
ou la plus belle ?

Assurément la plus féconde
car l'homme
y est pour quelque chose
Il en est le tenant

[...]

About the country that believed it had exiled me
I would like to speak to you at last
without doing it
or doing myself violence
To speak about it "calmly"
as after lovemaking
when the caresses slow down
conveying gratitude
crowning a gift
and signing a pledge

More even than birth
or death
surely the greatest enigma
is love?

The greatest
or the most beautiful?

Certainly the most fertile
because man
has something to do with it
He is the long
and the short of it

et l'aboutissant
la racine
et la frondaison
la cime
et l'abîme
le maître d'œuvre inspiré
et l'édifice imprévisible

Rien ni personne
ne vous impose d'aimer

La fatalité ?
En la matière, elle doit composer
avec la liberté

Et puis l'amour
est la seule force salvatrice

Donc j'aime
sans retenue

Oriental je suis
et le demeure

A prendre
ou à laisser

the root
and the flower
the summit
and the depths
the inspired master architect
and the unpredictable edifice

Nothing and no one
obliges you to love

Fate?
In this realm, fate must
compromise with freedom

And then love
is the only force for salvation

So I love
without restraint

Oriental I am
and remain

Take it
or leave it

[. . .]
Ces carnets s'achèvent
je le sens

Que ne suis-je musicien
et virtuose
pour interpréter le finale
naturellement au violoncelle
et par ma voix travaillée
déployer le chant tremblé
que voici :
Homme de l'entre-deux
qu'as-tu à chercher
le pays et la demeure
Ne vois-tu pas qu'en toi
c'est l'humanité qui se cherche
et tente l'impossible ?

Homme de l'entre-deux
sais-tu que tu es né
dans le continent que tu as découvert
Que l'amour t'a fait grandir
avant que la poésie
ne te restitue ton enfance ?

[. . .]

These notes are coming to an end
I can feel it

Why am I not a musician
a virtuoso
able to perform the finale
on the cello naturally
and with a trained voice
sing the following words tremolando:
Oh man of betwixt and between
what makes you seek
country and home
Can't you see
that it is in you
the humanity that seeks itself
and strives for the impossible?

Oh man of betwixt and between
do you know that you were born
on the continent that you discovered
That love made you grow up
before poetry
gave you back your childhood?

Homme de l'entre-deux
ta voile
ce sont les voiles qui se dressent encore
sur ton itinéraire
Appartenir dis-tu ?
Tu ne t'appartiens même pas
à toi-même

Homme de l'entre-deux
accepte enfin de te réjouir
de ta liberté de parole
et de mouvement
Les miracles se fêtent
surtout quand ils s'accomplissent
au détriment des tyrans

Et maintenant
quelle autre promesse
veux-tu arracher à l'automne
Juste l'énergie pour le livre suivant ?
Soit
Adjugé
et bon vent !

Oh man of betwixt and between
your ship
is all the ships that still await
along your route
Belong you say?
You do not belong
even to yourself

Oh man of betwixt and between
allow yourself to rejoice at last
in your freedom of speech
and of movement
Miracles are to be celebrated
especially when they happen
to the detriment of tyrants

And now
what other promise
do you want to extract from the fall
Just enough energy for the next book?
Very well
Granted
and fair winds!

from

LES FRUITS DU CORPS

THE FRUITS OF THE BODY

(2003)

de LES FRUITS DU CORPS

Ma chair désaccordée
De tes doigts de saphir
tu tournes les pages
de la partition
Tu chantes juste
L'harmonie me gagne
Je sculpte l'instant
avant qu'il ne soit trop tard

* * *

Les lèvres en fleurs
abeilles gourmandes
gonflées de suc
De la fleur
ou de l'abeille
qui butine l'autre ?

* * *

Des genoux aussi lustrés
refléteraient la lune
en sa naissance

from THE FRUITS OF THE BODY

My flesh is off-key
With your sapphire fingers
you turn the pages of the composition
You sing in tune
Then the harmony takes hold of me
I chisel out the moment
before it is too late

* * *

Lips in flower
gluttonous bees
bursting with nectar
Is it from the flower
or from the bee
that we others gather the honey?

* * *

Such lustrous knees
might reflect
the waxing moon

Ils décrètent
la fin du ramadan
alors qu'il vient d'être annoncé

* * *

Le lit constellé
vogue par à-coups
Partant du nombril
la Grande Ourse
et juste au-dessus de la hanche
l'étoile du berger

* * *

Je n'imagine rien
Je n'invente rien
Je crois sur-le-champ
Je vois et touche
l'objet de ma croyance
ce divin pubis

* * *

Vasque renversée
païenne à souhait

But they decree
the end of Ramadan
as soon as it is declared

* * *

The star-frecked bed
roams by fits and starts
Beginning at the navel
the Great Bear
with just above the hip
the evening star

—

* * *

I imagine nothing
I invent nothing
I believe on the spot
I see and touch
the object of my faith
that divine Mount of Venus

* * *

Inverted bowl
pagan to perfection

J'hésite entre les dunes
et le fil de soie
qui les relie
J'hésite
entre les deux grottes magiques

* * *

Comme un lierre fou
je m'enroule
autour de tes branches
Ton écorce s'attendrit
et s'ouvre
Goutte à goutte
je reçois ta sève
Un moment
et je commence à bourgeonner

* * *

Je te couvre
et de toi m'enveloppe
Lumière ou pas
je t'éclaire
et tu m'éclaires

I hesitate between its dunes
and the silk thread
that links them
I hesitate
between the two magic caverns

* * *

Like crazy ivy
I wind myself
around your branches
Your bark softens
and opens up
Drop by drop
I receive your sap
In a moment
I begin to bud

* * *

I cover you
and wrap you around me
Light on or off
I illuminate you
and you me

* * *

Au fond des iris
lestes et radieux
on dirait la vulve
réjouie de sa soif

* * *

Cris de la douleur d'aimer
Acte de reconnaissance
ou appel à la prière ?

* * *

Tu te recouvres
pour retenir la vague
le courant chaud qui l'a portée
Je voudrais être l'enfant
le tien ou le mien
blotti contre toi

* * *

Gazelle inattendue
Tu n'es pas sortie
entre chien et loup

* * *

The depths of your irises
lively and radiant
like the vulva
reveling in its thirst

* * *

Cries of love's pain
An act of acknowledgment
or a call to prayer?

* * *

You cover yourself
to hold back the wave
the warm current that brought it
I want to be an infant
yours or mine
snuggled up against you

* * *

Surprise gazelle
You did not spring
at twilight

d'une rivière
Tu ne m'as pas fait miroiter
une fontaine remplie d'or
Je n'ai pas vu
tes sabots de chèvre
Disons-le
tu es tombée du ciel

* * *

Le désir
ne se déclare
ni ne se commente
Il brûle
et se propage
ou meurt
en silence

* * *

Tu me donnes la main
ce qui s'appelle donner
Et tu sais jusqu'où
ira la mienne
Elle entreprendra d'abord
la nuque satinée

from a river
You did not have me picture
a spring full of gold
I did not see you
with cloven hooves
Let's say it
you fell from heaven

* * *

Desire
does not announce
or comment upon itself
It burns
and spreads
or dies
in silence

* * *

You give me your hand
in the strongest sense
And you know how far
mine will go
First it will take on
the velvet nape of your neck

Descendra pour s'égarer
entre monts et vaux
Puis mettra le cap
sur la perle flottante
bivouac de tes délices

* * *

Quand je prends
l'initiative
je ne fais que t'obéir
Alors dicte-moi
Tu sais que je suis
un bon scribe

* * *

Me lasser
moi
Rechigner à la divine besogne ?
Je suis un forçat
qui en redemande

* * *

Je ne me suis jamais incliné
devant quelque puissant que ce soit

descend and wander
up hill and down dale
then set its cap
for the floating pearl
abode of your raptures

* * *

In taking
the initiative
I merely obey you
So dictate to me
You know I am
a fine scribe

* * *

Me, grow tired
balk at the sacred task?
I am a forced laborer
who asks for more

* * *

I have never bowed
before any power

Devant toi
si
ô ma souveraine

* * *

Nous avons tout le temps
pour peindre cette toile
et nous en revêtir
Sculpter cette idole
et la manger
Ecrire ce poème
et le brûler

* * *

L'as-tu remarqué ?
Ce faisant
nos mains veulent attraper
serrer quelque chose
Quoi ?
La crinière de l'instant
la poignée du paradis
ou l'âme de l'autre ?
Ce faisant
nous sommes comme un noyé

Before you
I do
oh my queen

* * *

We have plenty of time
to paint this canvas ·
and wear it
To sculpt this idol
and eat it
Write this poem
and burn it

* * *

Have you noticed?
In doing this
our hands try to grab
and hang on to something
What?
The mane of the moment
the hand of paradise
or the soul of the other?
In doing this
we are like the drowning man

qui s'agrippe à un autre noyé
pour échapper aux sauveteurs

* * *

Sans ablutions
je fais ma prière
tout nu
Et m'est avis
que le ciel apprécie

* * *

A n'importe quel âge
en amour
on est tous
des débutants

* * *

Nous sommes le poème :
subtil, cru
doux, ravageur
Son encre humaine :
sueurs
salive

538

who clings to another drowning man
to avoid the rescuers

* * *

Without ablutions
I say my prayers
stark naked
and I have realized
that heaven appreciates it

* * *

At any age
we are all beginners
at love

* * *

We are the poem:
subtle, crude
gentle, predatory
We are its human ink:
sweat
saliva

larmes
eau vive
Et nous sommes
son parfum naturel

* * *

Dans les fruits du corps
tout est bon
La peau
le jus
la chair
Même les noyaux
sont délicieux

* * *

Celui qui n'a jamais
goûté à l'interdit
qu'il me jette
la première pomme

* * *

Misérables hypocrites
qui montez au lit
du pied droit

tears
spring water
We are also
its natural scent

* * *

In the fruits of the body
all is good
The skin
the juice
the flesh
Even the pits
are delicious

* * *

Let anyone who has never
tasted forbidden fruit
cast the first apple
at me

* * *

Wretched hypocrites
who get into bed right foot first

et invoquez le nom de Dieu
avant de copuler
De la porte
donnant sur le plaisir
vous ne connaîtrez
que le trou aveugle
de la serrure

* * *

Quand les théologiens
enturbannés ou non
se mêlent de sexe
cela
me coupe l'appétit

* * *

Je peine à lire
les traités d'érotologie
La gymnastique m'ennuie

Si l'amour
n'était pas
création

invoking the name of God
before you copulate
Of the door
that opens to pleasure
you will never know
anything but the blocked
keyhole

* * *

When theologians
beturbaned or not
meddle with sex
it kills my appetite

* * *

I have trouble reading
manuals of erotology
Gymnastics leave me cold

If love
were not
a creation

œuvre personnelle
j'aurais déserté son école

* * *

Portrait de femme
avec enfant
Il a six ans
peut-être sept
Et il lui va
à merveille

* * *

Mes enfants
croient peut-être
que je n'ai pas de sexe
Moi
je n'ai jamais douté du leur

* * *

J'arrose consciencieusement
mes plantes
leur parle
et les caresse

a personal work
I would have left its school

* * *

Portrait of woman
with child
He is six
maybe seven
And he suits her
marvelously well

* * *

My children
may believe
that I have no sex
For my part
I have never had doubts about theirs

* * *

I water my plants
conscientiously
talk to them
caress them

Leur met de la musique arabe
du jazz
du tango revisité
par le Cuarteto Cedrón
une chanson de Cesária Évora
ou d'Amália Rodrigues
Autant d'attentions
qui valent déclaration
Autre déviance dira-t-on
J'assume

* * *

Quand tout milite
en faveur du désir
et qu'à l'évidence
le corps à corps s'impose
la vertu devient
un peu vile

* * *

Que restera-t-il de la collision
Après l'embrasement
que lira-t-on dans les cendres ?
La chair

Play them Arab music
jazz
tango as revisited
by the Cuarteto Cedrón
a song by Cesária Évora
or Amália Rodrigues
So much attention
calls for justification
A sort of perversion some might say
I accept that

* * *

When everything defends the cause
of desire
and hand-to-hand combat
is clearly unavoidable
virtue becomes
rather vile

* * *

What will remain of the clash
After the conflagration
what will be read in the ashes?
Flesh

s'est détachée de la chair
Arbre déraciné
l'homme gît
auprès de la femme

* * *

Ta mousse
reconnaît mon arbre
Mon arbre
se perd dans ta forêt
Ta forêt soutient mon ciel
Mon ciel te restitue tes étoiles
Tes étoiles chutent dans mon océan
Mon océan berce ta barque
Ta barque atteint ma rive
Ma rive est ton pays
Ton pays me subjugue
et j'en oublie le mien

* * *

Dans le rêve prolifère
tu en as pris des audaces
et j'en ai pris
Ton corps s'est multiplié

has been stripped from flesh
An uprooted tree
the man lies
alongside the woman

* * *

Your moss
recognizes my tree
My tree
gets lost in your forest
Your forest supports my sky
My sky gives you back your stars
Your stars fall into my ocean
My ocean cradles your boat
Your boat reaches my shore
My shore is your country
Your country subdues me
and I forget mine

* * *

In the prolific dream
you showed boldness
and so did I
Your body extended itself

le mien aussi
Nous avons battu des ailes
Nous nous sommes éloignés
de la terre
Et dans la dernière lueur
de conscience
nous avons su que nous traversions
le mur de la mort
Un fou rire
nous a réveillés

* * *

Faste
cette nuit à Berlin
où nous avons goûté
à des fruits inconnus
où nous avons détruit
un autre mur
Le lendemain
nous avions rajeuni
de dix ans
Sur la photo
prise ce jour-là
nous avions la beauté
de deux animaux fabuleux

so did mine
We flapped our wings
We flew away
from the earth
And in the last glimmer
of consciousness
we realized that we were crossing
the wall of death
Wild laughter
awoke us

* * *

How glorious
that night in Berlin
when we tasted
fruits unknown
when we demolished
another wall
The next morning
we had shed
ten years
In the photo
taken that day
we had the beauty
of two fabulous animals

Lieux inattendus
qui avez abrité nos furtives amours
vous souvient-il ?
Nous ne faisions que passer
lorsque le harpon du désir
s'incrustait dans les reins
Nos cœurs battaient
nos lèvres tremblaient
et nos yeux imploraient votre secours
Qu'il fasse jour ou nuit
vous nous ouvriez vos bras
protégiez des regards indiscrets
vous couvriez de vos ramages
le concert de nos halètements
Lieux bénis entre tous
veuillez accepter l'hommage
de vos amants reconnaissants

* * *

Récite avec moi :
O amour
jardin de la Création
résiste à toutes les malfaisances

* * *

Oh surprising places
that harbored our furtive love
do you remember?
We were merely passing
when the arrow of desire
lodged itself in our loins
Our hearts would be beating fast
our lips trembling
and our eyes imploring your help
Night or day
you opened your arms to us
screened us from prying glances
and covered the concert of our breathing
with your twittering
Places blessed above all others
pray accept the homage
of these grateful lovers

* * *

Recite with me:
Oh love
garden of Creation
resist all maleficence

Protège-nous
de l'insignifiance
du dessèchement
des pouvoirs mal acquis
Ne nous refuse pas ton asile
quand du cœur
les frontières rétrécissent
Guide-nous dans tes allées
vers la source où les corps
acquièrent
la juste beauté des âmes
Donne-nous la force
de ne pas mépriser nos faiblesses
Etends sur nous
la mansuétude de tes palmes
à l'heure cynique
de l'éclipse

Protect us
from insignificance
from desiccation
from powers usurped
Do not refuse us your shelter
when the frontiers of the heart
shrink
Guide us down your paths
to that source where bodies
acquire
the deserved beauty of souls
Give us the strength
not to despise our weaknesses
Spread the gentleness
of your palms over us
in the cynical hour
of the eclipse

from

ÉCRIS LA VIE

WRITE LIFE

(2005)

RUSES DE VIVANT

Ce bout de route
devant moi
plus proche de la nuit
la vraie
la véridique
l'incontournable
Je ralentis le pas
Je fais semblant
d'admirer le paysage
Ruse de vivant

J'y crois
et n'y crois pas
L'arrêt en si bon chemin
quand la lumière enfin
est en visite
pas au chevet
mais au berceau de l'être

Faire provision de cette lumière
la porter à la bouche
de l'enfance
de l'adolescence

RUSES OF THE LIVING

There's a short way
ahead of me
as night comes on
the true
real
ineluctable night
I slow my steps
I pretend
to admire the view
Ruse of the living

I believe
and don't believe
This halt on so good a road
when at last the light
is visiting
not the bedside
but the cradle of being

Store some of that light
put it in the mouth
of childhood
of adolescence

de l'âge mûr
En garder un peu
pour l'instant où les yeux
bêtement ouverts
seront refermés
par la plus douce
des mains amies

Surtout
ne pas se retourner
Il n'y a pas de nuit
qu'on ne puisse affronter
Il n'y a pas de ténèbres
sans ligne d'horizon

Quitter
ne sera pas
la première déchirure
ni le premier scandale
Est-ce vraiment
l'ultime exil ?

Je me dis
qu'il faut être prévoyant
Je ferai donc à temps
mon humble valise

of maturity
Save a little
for the moment when eyes
foolishly opened
are closed
by the gentlest
of friendly hands

Above all
do not turn around
There is no night
that you cannot face
No darkness
without a horizon

Leaving
will not be
the first rift
nor the first outrage
Is this really
the ultimate exile?

I realize
one must be prepared
So I will pack my simple bag
in good time

Un ou deux livres
mon numéro matricule
le foulard jaune
de la prophétesse de mes jours
une fiole
des senteurs de Fès
un zeste d'orange amère
un caillou
ramassé à Jérusalem
et ce que l'aimée
à mon insu
y aura glissé

Ah si la sérénité
pouvait être au rendez-vous
Quitter alors
serait
un acte de générosité

Je me retourne vers toi
peur immémoriale
Sur ton visage lisse
je découvre comme un reflet
du sourire inexplicable
qui m'a toujours accompagné

One or two books
identification card
the yellow scarf
of the prophetess of my life
a phial
of the scents of Fez
a bitter-orange zest
a pebble
picked up in Jerusalem
and whatever my beloved
unbeknownst to me
has slipped in

Oh if only serenity
could be at the rendezvous
Leaving would then be
an act
of generosity

I turn back to you
oh immemorial fear
On your smooth face
I find a kind of reflection
of the inexplicable smile
that has always kept me company

De te sentir ainsi percée
tes traits se durcissent
J'en suis rassuré

Cela dit
c'est de persister qu'il s'agit
Ne pas oublier
le feuillage ayant cette vertu
les astres inexplorés
qui naviguent à vue
sur les flots de l'éternité
Protéger de ses poèmes nus
la flamme de la petite bougie
Supporter la brûlure
de ses larmes
et savoir à temps
la passer au suivant

Brûler de l'intérieur
ou sur un bûcher
L'offrande est la même
même s'il y a questions
et Question

At feeling yourself thus exposed
your expression hardens
This reassures me

Which said
the point is to persist
Never to forget
the foliage has this virtue
and the unexplored celestial bodies
that navigate by eye
on the seas of eternity
To protect
the flame of the little candle
of one's naked poems
To put up with the burning
of one's tears
and know in good time
how to pass it on to the next

To be burnt from within
or at the stake
The sacrifice is the same
even if there are questions
and the Question

Le terme
le commencement
dans le cœur des hommes
cette libre patrie
où nous n'aurons plus besoin
pour nous désigner
que d'un seul nom
où notre filet de voix
sera audible dans les galaxies
où la Promesse
aura des accents de serment

Dépêchons !
La vie n'attend pas

Même innocents
du sang de notre prochain
il nous arrive
de tuer
la vie en nous
Plusieurs fois
plutôt qu'une

Le voile
qui nous recouvre les yeux

The end
the beginning
in the human heart
that free home country
where we shall no longer need
to designate ourselves
with more than one name
where our reed of a voice
will be audible across the galaxies
where the Promise
will be more like an oath

Hurry!
Life does not wait

Innocent as we may be
of spilling our neighbor's blood
we happen
to kill
the life in ourselves
Several times
not just once

The veil
that covers our eyes

et le cœur
Les barricades
que nous dressons
autour du corps suspect
La lame froide
que nous opposons au désir
Les mots
que nous achetons et vendons
au marché florissant du mensonge
Les visions
que nous étouffons dans le berceau
La sainte folie
que nous enfermons derrière les barreaux
La panique
que nous inspirent les hérésies
La surdité
élevée au rang d'art consommé
La religion
largement partagée
de l'indifférence

Bien des messagers
frapperont encore à notre porte
Y aura-t-il quelqu'un
dans la maison ?

and our heart
The barricades
we erect
about a suspect body
The cold blade
we oppose to desire
The words
we buy and sell
on the flourishing market of lies
The visions
we strangle at birth
The sacred madness
we lock behind bars
The panic
that heresies inspire in us
The deafness of which
we are passed masters
The widely shared
religion
of indifference

Many a messenger
will still knock at our door
Will there be anyone
in the house?

Dites-moi
vers quel néant
coule le fleuve de la vie
C'est quand
la dernière fois
que vous vous y êtes baignés ?

Tell me
into what void
the river of life flows
When
was the last time
you bathed in it?

LOIN DE BAGDAD

Bruit de bottes
Ismaël
a repris la place du bélier
Dieu a changé d'avis
et les larmes d'Abraham
n'y pourront rien
Les équarrisseurs sont arrivés !

Perdus nous sommes
atterrés
tels ces dromadaires
en plein désert d'Irak
regardant passer
une caravane de blindés

Que l'eau
s'achète et se vende
passe
Seulement voilà
elle sert maintenant
à monnayer les consciences

FAR FROM BAGHDAD

Sound of boots
Ishmael
has taken the place of the Ram
God has changed his mind
and the tears of Abraham
can do nothing about it
The slaughterers are here!

We are lost
as dumbstruck as
those dromedaries
in the middle of the Iraq desert
to see a passing caravan of armored cars

That water
should be bought and sold
so be it
But now
it is also used
to buy off consciences

Après les pilleurs de tombes
voici les pilleurs de musées
Admirez le progrès !

La statue a été décapitée
Ce n'était qu'une masse
de bronze ou d'acier
Mais dans la tête des hommes
rien n'a changé
Le tyran est mort
vive le tyran !

La liberté s'arrache
avons-nous tous répété
comme des perroquets
Finie la rengaine
Sachez-le
la liberté s'octroie

« Si je ne te tue pas, je te fais une faveur », dit un vieil adage marocain. Il y a de ces traits de sagesse qui donnent froid dans le dos.

« On ne prête qu'aux riches », dit l'adage français. Adapté en arabe populaire, il donnerait ceci : « Rajouter de la graisse dans le cul d'un mouton déjà engraissé. » As-tu bien jubilé, ô traducteur !

After tomb plunder
now we have museum plunder
Some progress!

The statue has been beheaded
It was just a lump
of bronze or steel
But in the minds of men
nothing has changed
The tyrant is dead
Long live the tyrant!

Freedom must be seized
as we used to repeat
parrot-like
But the song is over
Be it known
that freedom is granted

"If I don't kill you, I'll be doing you a favor," goes an old Moroccan
saying. There are some words of wisdom that send chills down the
spine.

"You lend money only to the rich," according to a French expression.
The rough equivalent in vernacular Arabic would involve "stuffing
grease up the ass of a fatted sheep." Does that tickle you, oh
translator?

On ne parle que de la prohibition des armes de destruction massive.
Et les armes de destruction partielle, qu'en fait-on ?

Au vu du sang humain répandu à profusion chaque jour, je m'étonne
que l'une de ces multinationales n'ait pas eu l'idée d'en tirer une
nouvelle source d'énergie.

Les charniers mis au jour
filmés
sous toutes les coutures
Étrange butin de guerre

Près d'un véhicule carbonisé
on piétine les cadavres
le sourire aux lèvres
Même dans la haine
on atteint le grotesque

Y aurait-il des assassins plus nobles que d'autres ?

Tant de poètes se sont arrêtés ici
devant d'autres ruines
après d'autres ravages
Mais eux au moins
n'avaient qu'une idée en tête
improviser de nouveaux chants d'amour

All they talk about is banning weapons of mass destruction. What about weapons of partial destruction?

Considering the quantity of human blood spilt so profusely every day, it's a wonder that one or other of those multinationals has not thought of turning it into a new energy source.

Mass graves uncovered
and filmed
from every angle
Strange booty

By a burnt-out vehicle
they are trampling on corpses
with smiles on their lips
Even hatred
can produce the grotesque

Could some killers be nobler than others?

So many poets stopped at this point
before other ruins
after other depredations
But for their part at least
they had but one idea in mind
the improvisation of new love songs

Pour chaque femme
qui met
ou remet le voile
ce sont dix ans
de progrès
qui partent en fumée

Bassorah
Il y a trente ans
Le plus corsé des araks
coulait à flots
Les poètes rassemblés fraternisaient
riaient jusqu'aux étoiles
croulaient sous les visions
L'arak est traître !

Quelque part ici
la Sagesse
a eu sa maison
Aristote a été sauvé de l'oubli
Shéhérazade a conçu
la mère des récits
L'esprit a soufflé
à en perdre haleine
avant de succomber

Each woman
who starts or resumes
wearing the veil
equals
ten years
of progress
gone up in smoke

In Basra
Thirty years back
The most potent arak
flowed freely
Poets gathered and fraternized
laughed up a storm
collapsed under the spell of their visions
Arak! that traitor!

Somewhere around here
Wisdom
once dwelt
Aristotle was saved from oblivion
Scheherazade conceived
the mother of all tales
The spirit breathed
until it was out of breath

suffoqué par la pollution
de la « mère des batailles »

Un peuple ne peut avoir raison de son oppresseur que s'il lui est
supérieur, moralement

Un berceau de l'humanité
s'accorde-t-on à dire
Qu'on ne s'étonne pas dans ce cas
comme dans d'autres
que les prédateurs soient recrutés
au berceau

Mais on dirait
que l'opprimé n'a qu'une hâte
prendre la place de l'oppresseur
et sévir à son tour
contre le premier venu
ou sinon
contre lui-même

Malgré sa haute perspicacité, le grand Ibn Khaldoun n'a pas saisi ce
fondement tordu de l'Histoire universelle

before being overwhelmed
suffocated by the pollution
of the "mother of all battles"

A people cannot overcome its oppressor unless it is superior to him,
morally

A cradle of humanity
as everyone agrees
Why be surprised then
that here as elsewhere
predators are recruited
in the cradle?

But it is as though
the oppressed
can hardly wait
to take the place of the oppressor
and come down hard in their turn
on the nearest to hand
or for that matter
on themselves

His great perspicacity notwithstanding, the great Ibn Khaldoun
failed to grasp this distorted foundation of universal History

Quand la morale est tirée
il faut la boire jusqu'à la lie

Voir l'indicible et mourir

Dans le boyau de la nuit
un cri monte
Vers où ?
Les sept cieux
aspirés par le trou noir
ont rejoint la file
des désemparés

Once morality is drawn
it must be drunk to the dregs

See the unspeakable and die

In the bowels of the night
a cry goes up
Where to?
The seven heavens
sucked into a black hole
have joined the line
of the downtrodden

GENS DE MADRID, PARDON!

¡Ay qué día tan triste en Madrid!
Qu'on se le dise
la terre n'a pas tremblé ce jour-là
Nul astéroïde vagabond
ne s'est écrasé sur la Bourse
Pas de nouvelle marée noire
et la précédente allait bientôt
être traitée dans les urnes
La télévision aboyait, miaulait, caquetait
stridulait, croassait, brayait, blablatait
Les footballeurs s'étaient mis au vert
Les taureaux paissaient
Les écrivains faisaient la grasse matinée
Le moustachu polissait son discours d'adieu
Le serial killer
s'était donné un temps de réflexion
et Dieu le père ou la mère
était comme à l'accoutumée
aux abonnés absents

Qu'on se le dise
le temps s'est brusquement figé

PEOPLE OF MADRID, PARDON!*

¡Ay qué día tan triste en Madrid!
Make no mistake
the earth did not quake that day
No stray asteroid
crashed into the Stock Market
No new black tide rose
and the latest one would soon
be dealt with at the polls
The television barked, mewed, clucked
chirped, croaked, brayed, blathered
The footballers were taking a break
The bulls were at pasture
The writers were sleeping in
The man with the mustache was polishing up his farewell speech
A serial killer
was giving himself time to think things over
and God the Father or the Mother
was absent as per usual
at roll call

Make no mistake
time suddenly froze

* First published in May 2004 in the daily *Aujourd'hui le Maroc*, this poem was a response to the train bombings in Madrid on 11 March 2004.

puis il y eut cette sonnerie anodine
perdue parmi la cacophonie des sonneries
Quelques secondes
et la digue de la raison a cédé
la chaîne de l'espèce humaine s'est rompue
Ay qué día tan triste en Madrid !

Les héritiers obligés que nous sommes
de toutes les andalousies
de toutes les lumières
De tous les génocides
de toutes les ténèbres
Hébétés
ridicules
Comme des rats
pris au piège de l'impuissance
Pour la millième fois
cherchant à comprendre
alors qu'on a cru avoir compris
la dernière fois
Crevant les yeux
le gouffre insondable du mal
Alors plongeons-y
ne serait-ce que pour éprouver
une infime parcelle du calvaire

then came the first unremarkable siren
swiftly drowned in a cacophony of sirens
A few seconds
and the dike of reason gave way
the chain of humanity snapped
¡Ay qué día tan triste en Madrid!

Heirs that we are willy-nilly
of all the Andalusias
all the enlightenments
All the genocides
all the darkness
Bewildered
ridiculous
Like rats
trapped by their powerlessness
For the thousandth time
trying to understand
what we thought we had understood
the last time
With the bottomless pit of evil
staring us in the face
So let us plunge into it
if only to experience
a tiny part of the calvary

des nouveaux arrivants
au bal masqué de l'horreur
là où la chair et l'âme sont fourguées
dans le crématorium d'un cercle de l'enfer
que nul texte inimitable
ne nous a signalé

Messieurs les assassins
vous pouvez pavoiser
Spéculateurs émérites, vous avez acquis à vil prix le champ
incommensurable des misères, des injustices, de l'humiliation, du
désespoir, et vous l'avez amplement fructifié.
La technologie des satans abhorrés n'a plus de secrets pour vous.
Vous êtes passés maîtres dans l'art de tirer les ficelles de la haine pour
repérer, désigner, traquer, coincer et régler son compte au premier
quidam conscient ou inconscient du risque de simplement exister.
Qu'il mange, qu'il soit debout ou couché, qu'il fasse sa prière, qu'il
remue des idées dans sa tête ou se rende à son travail la tête vide, qu'il
caresse la joue de son enfant ou cueille une fleur, qu'il écoute une
musique lui rappelant la terre de ses origines ou la rencontre qui a
changé le cours de sa vie, qu'il écrive un poème ou remplisse sa feuille
d'impôts, qu'il parle au téléphone avec un plombier ou à sa mère
alitée dans un hôpital, qu'il lise un livre de Gabriel García Márquez
ou un prospectus de pizzeria, qu'il s'ébroue sous la douche ou
s'ennuie aux toilettes, le caleçon coincé entre les genoux, qu'il ouvre

of the new arrivals
at horror's bal masqué
where flesh and spirit are tossed
onto the funeral pyre of a circle of hell
that no peerless text
ever warned us about

Esteemed assassins
you can put your flags out
Seasoned speculators that you are, you have snapped up at a
knockdown price and amply exploited the measureless tract of woe,
injustice, humiliation, and despair.
The technology of your despised Satans has no secrets for you.
You are passed masters in the art of pulling the strings of hate and
spotting, targeting, tracking, cornering, and doing for the first comer
conscious or not of the risks he runs merely by existing.
And this, whether he is eating, standing or lying down, saying his
prayers, mulling ideas in his head or on his way to work with head
empty, stroking his child's cheek or picking a flower, listening to
music that reminds him of his native land or an encounter that
changed the course of his life, writing a poem or filling out a tax
return, talking on the phone to a plumber or to his mother lying
in a hospital bed, reading a book by Gabriel García Márquez or a
pizzeria menu, splashing about in the shower or feeling irritable on
the toilet with his underpants stuck between his knees, opening his

son cœur à son voisin dans le bus ou baisse les yeux devant le regard insistant de son vis-à-vis, qu'il empoigne sa valise avant de monter dans un train ou coure dans les couloirs kafkaïens d'un hôtel de luxe ou de merde, qu'il vienne d'apprendre que son hépatite C ne lui laisse que quelques mois à vivre ou tâte sa poche pour s'assurer que son portefeuille est bien là, qu'il se gratte les couilles ou tape du poing sur la table, qu'il aime la compagnie des chiens ou celle des chats, qu'il soit déjà homme, femme, ou encore à cet âge béni où l'ange n'a pas vraiment de sexe et surtout pas d'ailes.

Toutes les marionnettes se valent. Il suffit de ne pas être couché dans une tombe pour être le premier servi.

O doux enfant
est-ce pour cela que tu criais
à t'écorcher les poumons
au moment de naître ?

Messieurs les assassins
On dit que vous faites bien fonctionner vos méninges. Alors, puis-je vous poser une question simple :
C'est quoi pour vous un être humain ?
Pourquoi ce silence ? Répondez-moi !
Ah je devine votre rictus méprisant et j'imagine la bulle que vous laissez échapper par inadvertance de vos lèvres blêmes. J'y vois un petit insecte sur lequel s'abat un poing velu, et en guise de commentaire cette exclamation : Ça lui apprendra !

heart to the person next to him on the bus or lowering his eyes under the insistent stare of the person opposite, picking up his suitcase before boarding a train or running through the Kafkaesque corridors of a posh hotel or a shitty one, coping with the news that his hepatitis C gives him only a few months to live or patting his pocket to make sure his wallet is still there, scratching his balls or banging his fist on the table, whether he prefers the company of cats to the company of dogs or vice versa, and whether he is already a man, or a woman, or still at that blessed age when angels don't really have any sex and certainly no wings.

Any puppet will do. Anyone not lying in their grave can be first served.

O sweet child
is that why you howled
at the top of your lungs
at the moment of birth?

Esteemed assassins
They say you know how to use your gray cells. So let me ask you a simple question:
Just what is a human being for you?
Why this silence? Answer me!
Ah, I can just imagine your scornful snort and the bubble of air spontaneously popping from your bloodless lips. I visualize a little bug squashed by a hairy fist, and by way of sole commentary an interjected "That'll teach it!"

C'est vrai, et je continue à sonder vos pensées, que cet insecte nuisible a été enfanté par l'être qui vous donne des sueurs froides et que vous vous évertuez à avilir en appliquant à la lettre le principe de précaution : j'ai nommé la femme, pardonnez-moi l'expression. Je devine votre peur et votre dégoût, l'horreur que vous inspire l'avènement de la vie quand, après les ahanements et les cris de la parturiente, la tête visqueuse de l'enfant se libère du conduit immonde que vous avez été bien obligés de labourer et, comble de la déveine, d'ensemencer. Vous ne vous pardonnerez jamais d'être passés par là. C'est pourquoi la mort est votre unique passion. Pour elle vous rougissez, pâlissez. Votre cœur palpite. Vous défaillez. Et quand vous l'avez célébrée, vous vous voyez frappant à la porte de je ne sais quel Éden où des délices perverses vous ont été promises.

Ay qué día tan triste en Madrid !
Qu'on se le dise
C'est à Rabat, Alger, Le Caire, Bagdad
qu'on devrait le plus se lamenter
de ne pas savoir que penser
de ne pas savoir que dire
de ne pas savoir que faire
Les héritiers obligés que nous sommes
d'un âge d'or livré aux pleureuses
De tant de rêves avortés
de tant d'avanies

True, and I am continuing to read your minds, this noxious insect was born of a being who puts you into a cold sweat and whom you incessantly strive to vilify by applying the precautionary principle to the letter: I refer to woman, if you'll pardon the phrase. I can imagine what fear and disgust, what horror the advent of life fills you with when the panting and screams of the laboring mother are followed by the emergence of the infant's slimy head from the putrid furrow that you were obliged to plough and even, worst luck of all, to seed. You will never forgive yourselves for going there. Which is why death is your only passion. For death you blush, for death you go pale. Your heart beats faster. You swoon. And when you have celebrated it, you see yourselves knocking at the door of who knows what Eden where perverse delights have been promised you.

¡Ay qué día tan triste en Madrid!
Make no mistake
It is in Rabat, Algiers, Cairo, Baghdad
that the lamentation should be loudest
over not knowing what to think
not knowing what to say
not knowing what to do
Heirs that we are willy-nilly
to a golden age abandoned now to professional mourners
To so many miscarried dreams
so many extortions

de tant de tyrannies
Hébétés
ridicules
rongés de l'intérieur
par la bête immonde
que nous avons pris l'habitude
de renvoyer d'un coup de pied
à la figure de l'Autre
Responsables ? Coupables ?
Victimes tout aussi bien
des bourreaux que nous excrétons
comme le foie sécrète la bile
Cycliquement écrasés, annihilés
par les potentats que nous exécrons et adorons
parfois luttant
avec la force de l'espoir et du désespoir
pour que nos descendants
puissent croire peut-être un jour
qu'avant la mort
il y a ce qu'une vieille rumeur nomme
vie :
un fleuve maternel
où il fait bon se baigner
de jour
de nuit

so many tyrannies
Bewildered
ridiculous
gnawed within
by the foul beast
that we have become accustomed
to kick back into
the face of the Other
Responsible? Guilty?
Just as much victims
of the executioners whom we excrete
like the liver secreting bile
Cyclically crushed, annihilated
by potentates that we despise and adore
sometimes struggling
with the strength of hope and despair
so that our descendants
might perhaps believe some day
that before death
something exists that an old legend calls
life:
a maternal river
where it is good to bathe
by day
by night

En toutes saisons belles
et prometteuses
Seul miracle
sans trucage

Gens de Madrid
que vos morts reposent en paix
De la graine sacrée de la vie
déposée en eux
aucun n'a démérité
Comme tout un chacun, ils ont abrité le souffle qui anime l'Univers
et la Création. Chaque atome de leur corps a vibré et tourné autour
du soleil intérieur qui a illuminé leur chemin. Leur voyage fut le
nôtre, et notre voyage sera dorénavant le leur. Nous continuerons à
rêver dans leurs rêves, à nous écorcher l'âme dans leurs écorchures, à
nous interroger dans leurs interrogations, à caresser la lumière dans
leurs caresses, à nous émerveiller dans leurs émerveillements. Nous
continuerons même à faiblir de leurs faiblesses, à nous enfermer dans
leurs enfermements. Nous ne négligerons ni les œillères ni les petites
lâchetés. Nous prendrons à notre compte leur part d'intolérance, de
bêtise et d'indifférence car nous ne sommes que leurs frères et sœurs
humains, rien qu'humains. Mais nous tâcherons de résister encore
mieux dans leur résistance, nous alimenterons le feu vacillant de
notre mémoire avec le charbon cuisant de leur mémoire.

In every fine season
full of promise
The only miracle
that is not faked

People of Madrid
may your dead rest in peace
The sacred seed of life
sown in them
was undeserved by none
Just like anyone else, they harbored the breath that quickens the
Universe and all Creation. Every atom of their bodies vibrated and
revolved about the inner sun that lit their way. Their journey was our
journey, and our journey shall henceforth be theirs. We shall carry
on dreaming their dreams, lacerating our souls with their lacerations,
questioning ourselves with their questions, caressing the light with
their touch, marvel as they marveled. We shall even continue to
weaken from their weaknesses, to retreat into their retreats. We shall
neglect neither their blinkers nor their small acts of cowardice. We
shall assume their portion of intolerance, stupidity or indifference
because we are merely their human brothers and sisters, no more and
no less than human. But we shall seek to resist even better through
their resistance, and to feed the wavering flames of our memory with
the hot coals of theirs.

Gens de Madrid
puisque personne n'a pensé
à vous demander pardon
c'est moi qui le ferai
Moi ! Qui est moi ? Mon nom ne vous dira rien
Pourquoi je le fais ? Peu importe
Le cri précède la parole
qui parfois précède la pensée
Et puis le cœur a ses raisons
que l'esprit parfois ignore

Alors pardon, gens de Madrid
Pardon de ces nuits à venir
blanches ou grises
où l'être cher
reviendra en fantôme menaçant
vous reprocher de lui avoir survécu
Pardon pour la main
qui n'a pas été retrouvée
Pour l'anneau de mariage calciné
la boîte de maquillage ouverte
utilisée au dernier instant
Pardon pour les chaussures intactes
et le soutien-gorge fleurant encore bon
la vanille ou la rose

People of Madrid
since no one has thought
to beg your pardon
it is I who shall do so
I? Who is I? My name will mean nothing to you
Why do I do it? No matter
The cry precedes speech
which sometimes precedes thought
And then the heart has its reasons
that the mind at times knows nothing of

And so pardon, people of Madrid
Pardon for those nights ahead
white or gray
when a loved one
comes back as a threatening ghost
to rebuke you for having survived
Pardon for the hand
that was never found
For the scorched wedding ring
for the open makeup compact
used at the last instant
Pardon for the shoes still intact
and the bra still fragrant
with the scent of vanilla or rose

Pardon pour les amants au cœur d'androgyne
coupé en deux
Pour le rire électrocuté des enfants
Pardon pour les mères de la future place
du 11-Mars
Pardon pour le silence de mes frères
pour ne pas dire leur indifférence
Pardon pour ce que certains d'entre eux
pensent tout bas
Pardon de ne pas avoir fait plus et mieux
contre le loup qui décime
ma propre bergerie
Pardon de ne pas avoir appris suffisamment
votre langue
pour m'adresser à vous dans le meilleur castillan
Pardon à Lorca, Machado, Hernández
de ne pas les avoir fait lire à mes enfants
Pardon pour les lacunes et les incantations
Pour les yeux secs de la compassion
Pardon du peu que les mots peuvent
disent à moitié
et souvent ne savent pas
mais s'il vous plaît
pardon

Pardon for the androgynous lovers
sliced in two
For the electrocuted laughter of the children
Pardon for the Mothers
of the future
Plaza del 11 de Marzo
Pardon for the silence of my brothers
not to say their indifference
Pardon for what some among them
think but do not say
Pardon for not doing more and better
against the wolf ravaging
my own sheepfold
Pardon for not having learnt your language
and addressed you in perfect Castilian
Pardon to Lorca, Machado, Hernández
for not having my children read them
Pardon for the absences and the mantras
For the dry-eyed compassion
Pardon for how little words can do
or can only half-say
and often fail to grasp
but if you please
I beg your pardon

RÊVES

Dans mon réduit
je me suis amusé à ranger
mes idées
à faire le tri dans mes rêves
En voici quelques-uns
que j'ai d'abord hésité à garder :

Jouer à la roulette en compagnie de Dostoïevski

Aimer sans que le désir y soit pour quelque chose

Me réveiller un jour parlant toutes les langues du monde

Avoir des ailes, pas pour voler, juste comme parure

Voir G. W. Bush traduit devant un tribunal international de justice

Libérer les arbres de leur immobilité

Écrire un premier livre

DREAMS

In my den
I entertained myself by arranging
my ideas
and sorting out my dreams
Here are a few dreams
that at first I was disinclined to keep:

Playing roulette with Dostoevsky

Loving without desire having any part in it

Waking up one day able to speak every language in the world

Having wings, not to fly with, but merely as an adornment

Seeing George W. Bush brought up before an international court of
justice

Freeing trees from their immobility

Writing my first book

Acquérir une toque d'invisibilité

Faire une apparition au mariage de mon arrière-arrière-petite-fille
ou petit-fils

Découvrir la source du mal

Jouer à la perfection de la cithare

Rester assis seul dans le désert sept jours et sept nuits durant

Boire, ce qui s'appelle boire, sans fumer

Serrer la main de Nazim Hikmet

Pêcher à la ligne les poèmes des peuples disparus

Faire pousser un magnolia dans le jardin de la maison que je n'ai pas
eu

Attendre à la porte de l'école la dernière de mes filles nées et la
raccompagner à la maison

Traduire *Dieu et moi* de Jacqueline Harpman et en faire un best-seller
dans le monde musulman

Acquiring a toque of invisibility

Making an appearance at the wedding of my great-great-granddaughter or grandson

Discovering the root of evil

Playing the zither to perfection

Sitting alone in the desert for seven days and seven nights

Drinking, really drinking, without smoking

Shaking the hand of Nazim Hikmet

Angling for the poems of extinct peoples

Growing a magnolia in the garden of the house I never had

Waiting at the school entrance for my lastborn daughter and walking her home

Translating Jacqueline Harpman's *Dieu et moi* (God and Me) and making it into a bestseller in the Moslem world

Dire à ma mère, de son vivant : Je t'aime

Extraire les balles qui ont troué le corps de Che Guevara, refermer ses blessures, lui caresser le front et lui murmurer en toute confiance : Lève-toi et marche !

Persuader Sisyphe qu'il a été victime d'une erreur judiciaire

Faire aboyer le mot chien (n'en déplaise au poète ami)

Saying to my mother, still alive: I love you

Extracting the bullets that riddled the body of Che Guevara, closing his wounds, stroking his brow, and murmuring to him with complete confidence: Arise and walk!

Convincing Sisyphus that he was the victim of a miscarriage of justice

Making the word dog bark (with all due respect to our friend the poet)

CE MONDE N'EST PAS LE MIEN

Ce monde n'est pas le mien
et je n'ai pas d'autre monde
Je ne dispute à personne son royaume
Je ne convoite
que ce qui a été délaissé
par les convoitises :
un arpent de terre en jachère
un mouchoir de ciel
imbibé de lavande
un filet d'eau
plus pour le plaisir des yeux
que pour la soif
un fruit resté seul sur l'arbre
des livres hors commerce
usés à force d'être lus
des amitiés pour le simple repos du cœur
une étoile complice pour les confidences
en cas de douleur
des miettes pour attirer
les hirondelles de la vision
un bâton solide de pèlerin
pour entreprendre

THIS WORLD IS NOT MINE

This world is not mine
and I have no other
I contest no one's realm
I covet
only that which covetousness
has passed over:
an acre of fallow land
a handkerchief of sky
infused with lavender
a trickle of water
more for the eye's pleasure
than to slake the thirst
a piece of fruit
the last left on the tree
collector's editions of books
tattered from use
friendships built on the heart alone
a comforting star as confidant
in times of suffering
crumbs to attract
the swallows of vision
a pilgrim's stout staff
to set out

encore et toujours
le seul voyage qui en vaille la peine
celui au centre de l'homme

ever and always
on the only worthwhile journey
the journey to the center of man

POURQUOI CETTE FEUILLE?

À un détail près
le monde n'a pas changé
en si peu de temps
À un détail près
ce matin est une réplique
grisaille à l'appui
du précédent
À un détail près
le poids écrasant la poitrine
ne s'est pas allégé d'un iota
À un détail près
l'on se sent toujours vivant
un peu plus
un peu moins
Le même équilibre
fragile ou non
À un détail près
celui de cette petite question entêtante :
Pourquoi cette feuille
ni plus jaune ni plus verte que les autres
est-elle tombée de l'arbre ?

WHY THAT LEAF?

Except for one little thing
the world has not changed
in such a short time
Except for one little thing
this morning is a replica
complete with grayness
of yesterday morning
Except for one little thing
the crushing weight on my chest
has not eased one iota
Except for one little thing
you still feel alive
a bit more
or a bit less
The same balance
perhaps delicate, perhaps not
Except for one little thing
one nagging little question:
Why did that leaf
neither yellower nor greener than the others
fall off the tree?

ÉCRIS LA VIE

Es-tu prêt à aimer
sans connaître le fin mot de l'histoire
sans demander le nom
la provenance et la destination ?
Aimer en baissant les yeux
sans dévorer la main que tu serres
sans feux ni contre-feux
de désirs et d'outrages
Aimer de près
et encore plus de loin
Aimer comme respirer
sans défense ni gilet de sauvetage
dans la fournaise des purifications
et la tempête des passions inavouables
Es-tu prêt à vivre
de cet amour-là
d'eau fraîche
et de ta plume d'oiseau ordinaire
brûlant au feu de l'utopie
dont on ne sait
s'il restera des cendres ?

* * *

WRITE LIFE

Are you ready to love
without knowing the whole story
without asking for name
origin and destination?
To love with eyes lowered
without devouring the hand you are clasping
without the fire and return fire
of desires and violations
To love up close
even more from afar
To love as you breathe
without defense or life-jacket
in the furnace of purification
and the storm of unmentionable passions
Are you ready to live
from that kind of love
from plain water
and from your ordinary quill
burning in the fire of utopia
about which we do not know
if it will leave any ashes?

* * *

Que tu écrives ou non
tu es là
fidèle à l'attente qui guère ne déçoit
D'elle
tu peux dire que tu as épuisé
les postures et les significations
tu en as rempli à ras bord
toutes tes jarres
Quand la bise viendra
tu auras largement de quoi te sustenter
et secourir à l'occasion
tes prochains par trop imprévoyants
L'attente
est ta grande école
Sur un tableau noir
on peut lire
« Les classes fermeront bientôt »
L'inscription ne date pas d'aujourd'hui
Elle remonte à ta préhistoire
Pourtant tu es encore là
que tu écrives ou non
fidèle à l'attente qui guère ne déçoit

* * *

Whether you write or not
you are here
loyal to the waiting that rarely disappoints
From that wait
you can say that you have drained
all positions and meanings
and filled all your pitchers to the brim with them
When the icy winds blow
you will have plenty with which to sustain yourself
and rescue if need be
your too heedless friends
The waiting
is your university
On a blackboard
are the words
"Classes will close shortly"
This inscription does not date from today
It goes back to your prehistory
And yet you are still here
whether you write or not
loyal to the waiting that rarely disappoints

* * *

D'humus et de lave tu es pétri
et davantage de la matière noire
n'ayant toujours pas dit son nom
L'esprit qui a soufflé sur ta glaise
n'est autre que le tien
hérité de tous ceux qui se sont frottés
à la roue féroce de l'histoire
pourfendeurs de l'ordre vénal
guetteurs de l'évidence de l'aube
semeurs de l'éveil
Ceci est ton office
que tu ne peux résigner
puisque la vie
daigne encore te rendre visite
et parfois
privilège insigne
te mettre dans la confidence

* * *

Les dés sont jetés
Malgré toutes tes contorsions
tu n'as pas de prise sur la mort
Alors
écris la vie !

You are molded from humus and lava
even more from a dark matter
whose name you have not yet uttered
The spirit breathed into your clay
is none other than your own
inherited from all who have come up against
the ferocious wheel of history
shatterers of the venal order
watchers for signs of the dawn
sowers of awakening
Such is your post
from which you cannot resign
because life
still deigns to visit you
and on occasion
as a special privilege
let you into the secret

* * *

The die is cast
For all your contortions
you have no say over death
So
write life!

ton calame d'encre et de sang
ton royaume sans sujets ni maître
ta patrie sans terre
ta seule croyance hors religion
tes yeux et ta langue
ta richesse et ton dénuement
ta face éclairée et ton ombre
ta génitrice et ta progéniture
ta perdition et ton salut
ta croix d'infamie et ton diadème
ton lupanar et ton temple
ton désert et ton oasis
ta science et ton ignorance
ta boussole et ton dédale
ton jeu de marelle et ta cité idéale
ta règle et ton exception
ta peau de chagrin et ton éternité
ta blessure et ta drogue

Écris la vie
ainsi nommée
qualifiée
et reconnue

pen it in ink and blood
your realm with no subjects and no masters
your country with no land
your only belief non-religious
your eyes and your tongue
your wealth and your poverty
your illuminated face and your shadow
your progenitress and your progeny
your doom and your salvation
your cross of infamy and your diadem
your whorehouse and your temple
your desert and your oasis
your knowledge and your ignorance
your compass and your maze
your game of hopscotch and your ideal city
your rule and your exception
your *peau de chagrin* and your eternal life
your wound and your remedy

Write life
so named
described
and acknowledged

from

MON CHER DOUBLE

MY DEAR DOUBLE

(2007)

MON CHER DOUBLE

Mon double
une vieille connaissance
que je fréquente avec modération
C'est un sans-gêne
qui joue de ma timidité
et sait mettre à profit
mes distractions
Il est l'ombre
qui me suit ou me précède
en singeant ma démarche
Il s'immisce jusque dans mes rêves
et parle couramment
la langue de mes démons
Malgré notre grande intimité
il me reste étranger
Je ne le hais ni ne l'aime
car après tout
il est mon double
la preuve par défaut
de mon existence

* * *

MY DEAR DOUBLE

My double
an old acquaintance
whom I visit with moderation
He is a shameless fellow
who plays on my shyness
and has the knack of profiting
from my distractedness
He is the shadow
who follows or precedes me
aping my walk
He even winkles his way into my dreams
and speaks the language of my demons
fluently
Despite our close intimacy
he is still a stranger to me
I neither hate nor love him
for after all
he is my double
the proof by default
of my existence

* * *

Parfois
je le trouve assis à ma place
et n'ose pas lui dire
de se lever
Je le reconnais à l'odeur particulière
de mes phalanges
quand je suis souffrant
Son inconstance charnelle
me trouble
et j'en suis un peu jaloux
Comme il n'y a qu'un siège
dans la chambre
je reste debout
J'imagine qu'il travaille pour moi
à sa façon
Il peint sur la lumière
pour m'indiquer
comment je dois m'y prendre
avec les mots
et si je m'avise d'ouvrir la bouche
aussitôt il disparaît

* * *

Occasionally
I find him sitting in my place
and dare not tell him
to get up
I recognize him by the particular odor
of my fingers
when I am ill
His bodily changeability
bothers me
and I am a little jealous of it
As there is only one seat
in the room
I remain standing
I fancy he works for me
in his own way
He paints the light
to show me
how I should handle words
and if I decide to open my mouth
he vanishes

* * *

Au moment
où je découvre un pays
il en arpente un autre
et m'envoie des messages désobligeants
Ce qui m'émerveille
le laisse de marbre
La langue à laquelle je m'initie
n'atteint pas la cheville
de celle qu'il bredouille
Le plat national
que je m'apprête à déguster
sans préjugé
manque toujours du piquant
ou de l'onctueux dont il raffole
et de la beauté
qui me renverse au passage
il cherche et trouve immanquablement
le vice caché
Voilà pourquoi je limite
depuis quelque temps
mes voyages

* * *

Whenever
I discover a new country
he swaggers through another
and sends me disobliging messages
Whatever fills me with awe
leaves him cold
The language I try to speak
cannot hold a candle
to the one he stumbles along in
The national dish
that I am ready to try
with an open mind
always lacks the spice
or the unctuousness that so delights him
and in the beauty
that astounds me as I pass
he unfailingly seeks and finds
the hidden flaws
Which is why
for some time now
I travel so much less

* * *

Lui se prétend argentin
alors que j'ai du mal
à m'estimer français
Plus marocain que lui tu meurs
quand je me complais
dans ma sauvage liberté
d'apatride
Il argumente
en faveur de la crémation
et moi je suis loin
d'avoir réglé
le casse-tête d'une terre
de sépulture
Il cherche à s'inscrire
à des cours de tango
sans égard
pour ma colonne vertébrale
largement foutue
C'est peu de dire
qu'il m'épuise

* * *

He claims to be an Argentine
whereas I struggle
to consider myself French
There is no one on earth more Moroccan than him
when I revel
in the wild freedom
of the ex-pat
He argues
for cremation
while I am far
from settling
the thorny question
of a burial site
He wants to sign up
for tango lessons
with not a thought
for my largely ruined
spinal column
It is putting it mildly to say
he exhausts me

* * *

J'aurais bien aimé
à mon âge respectable
cultiver tranquillement mon jardin
caresser les feuilles de mon bambou
et les lustrer une à une
me faire l'abeille de mes roses
et les butiner à satiété
enfoncer mes bras dans la terre
et attendre patiemment qu'ils repoussent
en deux magnolias
tendre ainsi mes branches
pour recueillir la rosée du firmament
abriter les oiseaux migrateurs
ou les enfants
qui auraient lu et apprécié
Le Baron perché
Non
rien à faire
quand j'entends les ricanements
de celui qui s'acharne
à planter autour de moi
une haie
de miroirs déformants

* * *

I would have loved
at my venerable age
to cultivate my garden quietly
caress the leaves of my bamboo
and polish them one by one
turn into the bee on my roses
and gather my fill of pollen
plunge my arms into the earth
and wait patiently for them
to grow into two magnolias
spread my branches
to catch the dew of the heavens
and shelter migrating birds
or children
who have read and loved
The Baron in the Trees
But no
there is nothing for it
I can hear the sniggers
of the one who is bent on
surrounding me with a palisade
of distorting mirrors

* * *

Un jour
m'inspirant de l'histoire d'Abraham
en service commandé
je m'apprête à égorger l'intrus
en espérant
cela va sans dire
l'intervention divine
sous forme de bélier
ou à défaut
de dindon
Ne voyant rien venir
et en désespoir de cause
je me résous
à retourner l'arme contre moi
Quelle arme ?
Je ne vois entre mes doigts
qu'un stylo Bic ordinaire
et j'enrage en découvrant
qu'il vient de rendre l'âme

* * *

One day
inspired by the story of Abraham
on his official assignment
I got ready
to cut the intruder's throat
hoping
needless to say
for divine intervention
in the shape of a ram
or failing that
of a turkey
Seeing no such thing
and at my wit's end
I resolved to turn my weapon on myself
But what weapon?
All I could see between my fingers
was an ordinary ballpoint
and I fumed on discovering
that it had just given up the ghost

* * *

Il y a des jours bénis
où je me repose de lui
Qu'il soit là ou non
j'arrive à l'expulser
de ma bulle de protection
Quel bonheur !
Mes douleurs
me laissent un répit
la sangsue des questions
relâche sa pression
la faucheuse
passe son chemin
sans me fusiller du regard
l'infini devient habitable
et la maison de l'âme
assez vaste pour accueillir la procession
de mes visiteurs désemparés
Maître de ma propre durée
je ne cours plus après l'harmonie
je me sens antérieur à elle

* * *

There are blessed days
when I get a rest from him
Whether he is there or not
I manage to eject him
from my protective bubble
What joy!
My pain
grants me some respite
the bloodsucking questions
relax their pressure
the reaper
goes on by
without looking daggers at me
the infinite becomes inhabitable
and the house of the soul
vast enough to host the procession
of my visitors in distress
Master of my own span
I no longer chase after harmony
I feel sure that I precede it

* * *

Mais il ou elle
revient
En affirmant cela
je m'avance peut-être
Est-il, est-elle réellement
le, la même
Qu'en sais-je ?
De ses multiples manifestations
j'essaie en vain de déceler l'essence
et me contente d'en capter
le message subliminal
souvent trivial d'ailleurs :
Cesse de fumer
Soigne ta manie de l'ordre
Fais attention à ne pas te tacher
quand tu manges
Arrête de regarder la télévision
Décide-toi à acheter
les œuvres complètes de Paganini
Ne cherche pas le chat noir
dans la chambre noire
surtout si le chat n'existe pas

* * *

But then he or she
comes back
In saying that
perhaps I am going too fast
Is he, or she, really
the same
What do I know?
From his or her many manifestations
I try in vain to discern an essence
and am satisfied simply to capture
the subliminal message
which by the way is often banal:
Give up smoking
Curb your obsessive orderliness
Try not to stain your clothes
when you are eating
Stop watching television
Make up your mind to buy
Paganini's complete works
Do not go looking for a black cat
in a dark room
especially if the cat does not exist

* * *

Avec lui
je perds mon humour
qui paraît-il
réjouit mes amis
Fustiger la bêtise
la sienne y comprise
et tous les jours que diable fait
n'est donné
qu'à une poignée d'élus
Pourtant
et c'est là que réside mon orgueil
je pense que ma candidature
n'est pas usurpée
J'ai découvert cette propension
sur le tard
et suis navré de la voir réduite
à la portion congrue
à cause d'une ombre
fantasmée si ça se trouve
Alors que faire ?
comme disait le camarade Lénine

* * *

With him
I lose the sense of humor
which supposedly
delights my friends
To castigate stupidity
one's own included
and to do so every day the devil sends
is given only
to a select few
All the same
and this is what I am proud of
I feel that my claim to be among them
is not bogus
I discovered this propensity
late in the day
and am irked to see it reduced
to a bare minimum
on account of a shadow
more than likely a fantasy
So what is to be done?
as Comrade Lenin used to say

* * *

Cultiver mon unicité ?
Cela ne me ressemble pas
Consulter ?
Rien à faire
Me mettre en chasse de mes sosies
les attraper au filet tel un négrier
et les enfermer dans une cale ?
Non
je n'ai pas cette agressivité
Écrire des petits poèmes
sur les fleurs et les papillons
ou d'autres bien blancs et potelés
pour célébrer le nombril de la langue ?
Très peu pour moi
quand les cornes du taureau
m'écorchent les mains
et que le souffle de la bête
me brûle le visage
Autant crier à mon double
en agitant devant lui la muleta :
Toro
viens chercher !

* * *

Cultivate my uniqueness?
Not like me
Seek advice?
Hopeless
Start hunting down my doubles
Catch them in a net like a slave trader
and throw them into a ship's hold?
No
I am not aggressive enough
Write little poems
about flowers and butterflies
or others nice and white and chubby
in celebration of the language's navel?
Hardly does for me
when the bull's horns
are ripping my hands
and the beast's breath
is burning my face
I might as well challenge my double
waving the muleta in front of him:
Toro!
Come and get it!

* * *

En triant mes papiers
je découvre d'étranges brouillons
surchargés de notes et variantes
des réflexions du genre :
à approfondir, dégraisser
chercher l'antonyme
des titres de livres en projet
certains soulignés trois fois
d'autres marqués en marge d'une croix
des quatrains auxquels il manque
un vers ou deux
des indications de scène
pour le tableau orphelin
d'un drame immature
ce qui s'apparente à des citations
sans mention du nom de l'auteur
des dessins naïfs rappelant les images
des manuels scolaires
de l'époque du Protectorat
Dans ce fatras
la similitude avec mon écriture
est frappante
Je reconnais ma manie de la datation
et de la précision du lieu
De là à en admettre la paternité

As I sort my papers
I come across strange drafts
laden with notes and variants
comments such as:
go deeper, clean up
find antonym
titles of projected books
some triply underlined
others marked by a cross in the margin
quatrains lacking
a line or two of verse
stage directions
for the orphan outline
of an undeveloped play
what seem like quotations
with no author attribution
naïve drawings reminiscent of pictures
in the school textbooks
of Protectorate times
In all this jumble
the resemblance to my handwriting
is striking
I recognize my mania for noting
date and place
From this to acknowledging paternity

il y a un pas
qu'honnêtement je ne saurais franchir
Seul un test ADN
pourrait confondre l'imposteur
et me sortir
inchaallah
de cet embarras

* * *

is but a short step
that frankly I cannot take
Only a DNA test
could expose the impostor
and free me
inshallah
from my embarrassment

* * *

Il croit m'accabler
en me faisant remarquer
que j'ai le cul entre deux chaises
et la tête dans les nuages
aujourd'hui lourdement pollués
que la langue de l'Autre
qui me sert à m'exprimer
ne sera jamais ma patrie
que mon lecteur supposé naturel
m'ignore royalement
que la marge où je me tiens
fièrement
achèvera d'engloutir mes écrits
que puisque je ne revendique
aucune ascendance littéraire
je n'aurai pas non plus de postérité
que mon exil conjugué à tous les temps
et ma prétendue ubiquité
ne sont, si on commence à gratter
que des figures rhétoriques de l'absence
que le corps que j'habite
n'est qu'une chambre de bonne
sous-louée
que le nomade dans l'âme
que je pense être devenu

He thinks he can wear me down
by pointing out
that I am between two stools
and have my head in clouds
these days thoroughly polluted
that the language of the Other
which I use to express myself
will never be my homeland
that my supposedly natural reader
has never heard of me
that the margins where I dwell
proudly
will eventually swallow up my writings
that since I claim
no literary forebears
I shall have no posterity either
that my exile conjugated in all tenses
and my alleged universality
are if you scratch the surface
nothing but rhetorical expressions of absence
that the body I inhabit
is nothing but a subleased
maid's garret
that the nomad at heart
I think I have become

n'est qu'un sédentaire
un peu trop imaginatif
que l'obscurantisme
contre lequel je m'obstine
à envoyer des fusées éclairantes
finira par l'emporter
que les amours
que j'ai élevées au rang de foi
sont comme toutes les choses humaines
périssables elles aussi
que le miracle de la vie
que j'ai eu à cœur de célébrer
n'est pour ceux qui se battent
pour la survie
qu'un cauchemar à passer
que le rire que je promène
dans les artères, les autoroutes
de la bêtise
est l'envers dissimulé
du désespoir qui me ronge
Bref que j'ai passé ma vie
à guerroyer contre les moulins à vent
et que mes certitudes
ne sont que naïvetés avérées

is just a rather too imaginative
sedentary soul
that the obscurantism
against which I persist
in sending up flares
will end up routing
that the loves
I have made into matters of faith
are just as evanescent
as all things human
that the miracle of life
which I have so striven to celebrate
is for those who fight
for survival
merely a nightmare to survive
that the laughter I trot
down the arteries, the superhighways
of stupidity
is but the mask
of the despair that tears me apart
In short that I have spent my life
warring against windmills
and that my certainties
are demonstrably naïve

À l'alter ego
qui pense m'ouvrir ainsi les yeux
et me ramener à la dure réalité
je ne dirai pas
merci

* * *

To this alter ego
thinking thus to open my eyes
and bring me back to harsh reality
I will not say
thank you

* * *

Suivant les conseils d'un philosophe
– nommer, c'est faire exister –
j'ai cherché à lui trouver un nom
en écartant d'abord
la liste des sobriquets
dont on m'a affublé depuis l'enfance
et jusque sur le tard
ensuite les qualificatifs
où la rumeur publique
a cru m'enfermer
enfin mes propres trouvailles
quand il m'est arrivé
de tomber dans le panneau de Narcisse
Tenant à être objectif
et voulant l'originalité à tout prix
que pouvais-je inventer ?
À défaut d'un prodige de mon imagination
c'est un conte populaire
qui vient à ma rescousse
Oublié depuis des décennies
le nom du petit héros
de cette saga bourrée de facéties
me revient
et semble s'imposer :

Following the advice of a philosopher
– to name is to cause to exist –
I tried to find a name for him
first eliminating
all the nicknames
I was saddled with from childhood
and even much later
and then all the monikers
that public chatter
had seen fit to
imprison me in
and lastly my own inventions
when I happened to fall
into the trap of Narcissus
Wanting to be objective
and original at all costs
what could I come up with?
Absent a miracle from my imagination
a folktale is what
came to my rescue
Forgotten for decades
the name of the little hero
of a saga peppered with jokes
came back to me
and seemed perfect:

« Entendeur »
ou mieux
« Écouteur de la rosée »

* * *

"Hearer"
or better
"Listener to the Dew"

* * *

Le problème que j'ai avec la société
et jusqu'à mon entourage
c'est que je prends tout mon temps
et élève au rang d'art la distraction
J'abandonne volontiers la course
aux gagneurs
aux accumulateurs et autres tueurs
À la voie royale
des apprentis dominateurs
je préfère le sentier, la lisière
là où les oiseaux ne chantent pas encore
en service commandé
et l'herbe intelligente pousse à vue d'œil
là où l'errant a une chance
de rencontrer son frère
et qui sait son peuple
là où l'on sent son cœur battre
et que les questions essentielles affleurent

Saura-t-on un jour
que le vrai centre
se situe dans la marge ?

* * *

The problem I have with society
and even with my entourage
is that I take my time
and raise distractions to the level of an art
I readily leave the race
to winners
to accumulators and other kinds of killers
To the royal road
of apprentice tyrants
I prefer the byway, the fringe
where the birds do not yet sing on command
and the grass grows intelligently within eyeshot
where the wanderer has a chance
of running into his brother
and maybe even his people
where you can hear your heartbeat
and fundamental questions come up

Will we realize some day
that the real center
is in the margin?

* * *

Ce qui me vexe particulièrement
c'est le peu d'intérêt qu'il accorde
à un chantier nouveau que j'ai ouvert
et qui consiste rien de moins
à féminiser la langue
Le pouvoir masculin pourrait, je crois
y laisser d'autres plumes
Quoi
le jeu n'en vaut-il pas la chandelle
alors que le beau parler s'étiole
la grammaire fout le camp
et que tant de foyers ardents
se sont éteints dans les langues ?
Son scepticisme me laisse pantois
On dirait qu'il ne me lit pas
ou ne retient
dans la diversité délibérée
de mes écrits
que ce qui l'arrange

* * *

What particularly riles me
is the scant interest he shows
in a new undertaking of mine
which consists in nothing less
than the feminizing of language
Male power would not, I feel
survive this unscathed
How can he say
the game is not worth the candle
when speaking skills are fading
grammar is down the toilet
and so many blazing fires
in our languages have gone out
His skepticism staggers me
It is as if he does not read me
or retains
from the intentional diversity
of my writings
only what suits him

* * *

J'ai escaladé vaillamment
le demi-siècle dernier
et je dévale d'un pas alerte
le suivant
Combien de marches reste-t-il
avant le saut dans le vide ?
Dans ce puits enténébré
je préfère jeter, le moment venu
une torche plutôt qu'un caillou
lancer un rire dont je suis sûr
que les parois renverront l'écho
Mais tant que je sentirai le dur
sous mes pieds
je continuerai à offrir mes yeux
au soleil ami
qui, je le sais
dévale lui aussi sa pente
même si chacune de ses marches se compte
en millions d'années

À l'administration suspicieuse
qui me la réclame
j'ai l'honneur de joindre, ci-dessus
mon attestation de vie !

* * *

I bravely scaled
the last half-century
and at a brisk pace
I am now climbing down
the next
How many more steps
before the leap into the void?
Into that gloomy well, come the moment
I would rather cast
a flaming torch than a pebble
or produce a laugh certain
that the walls would send back its echo
But so long as I feel solid ground
under my feet
I shall continue to raise my eyes
to my friend the sun
who I know
is also heading downward
even if each of his steps
takes millions of years

To a suspicious administration
who ask me for it
I have the honor of attaching, below
my life certificate!

* * *

Est-il temps de se quitter ?
Je ne dirais pas non
Ma jubilation risque de retomber
et je devrais scruter de nouveau
la scène inchangée
de ce qu'il me faudra fustiger
à en être meurtri
Le règne de barbarie
ne connaît pas le chômage
Son taux de croissance
dépasse celui de la Chine
Pitié !
Dans le royaume des désemparés
l'on pleure au moins et l'on rit
On se ridiculise pour s'estimer un peu
On se fait mal pour se faire du bien
On crève les baudruches
avant de penser à sculpter
on prend d'assaut la prison du langage
pour libérer les mots proscrits
et autour des rêves menacés par les fauves
on entretient le feu
La rencontre
ne passe pas par pertes et profits
Elle déstabilise, illumine

Is it time to part company?
I would not say no
My elation is liable to diminish
and I ought to re-examine
the unchanged prospect
of what I need to lambast
at the risk of injuring myself
The reign of barbarism
knows nothing of unemployment
Its growth rate
outstrips China's
Preserve us!
In the land of the downtrodden
there are at least tears and laughter
People make fun of themselves for a little self-respect
They hurt themselves to feel better
They deflate windbags
sooner than create anything
they besiege the prison of language
to free forbidden words
and keep fires burning
around dreams threatened by wild animals
Meeting
is not governed by profit and loss
It unsettles, illuminates

et donne raison à notre soif de vérité
La vie et la mort se rapprochent
de celles qui se manifestent dans la nature
Le ciel et la terre nous observent
parce que nous les observons
Dans le royaume des désemparés
l'on veille de jour et de nuit
telles des vigies
revenues des miracles
mais qui gardent les yeux rivés
sur l'horizon
de la bonne espérance

and justifies our thirst for truth
Life and death
closely resemble
their manifestations in nature
Heaven and earth watch us
because we watch them
In the land of the distressed
we keep watch day and night
like lookouts
no longer believing in miracles
but still keeping our eyes riveted
to the horizon
of good hope

ÉPILOGUE

Je constate
au bout de ma confession
que je ne lui tiens pas tant rigueur
de m'avoir malmené
Plus
je suis obligé de lui reconnaître
des vertus décapantes
et quelque perspicacité
car qu'étais-je avant de le fréquenter
et que serais-je devenu ?
Notre corps à corps
a donné de l'animation à ma vie
m'a révélé
des énergies insoupçonnées
Et si je ne sais pas
ce qu'il en est pour lui
de mon côté
même s'il m'en coûte
je dois avouer
que je suis
un schizophrène heureux
Presque

EPILOGUE

I realize
at the end of this confession
that I do not bear him such a grudge
for abusing me
What is more
I am forced to grant him
cleansing virtues
and a measure of perspicacity
for what was I before I had to do with him
and what would I have become?
Our hand-to-hand fighting
has helped animate my life
and shown me
my unsuspected powers
And though I don't know
how it is for him
for my part
though it pains me to do so
I have to admit
that I am
a happy schizophrenic
Almost

from

TRIBULATIONS D'UN RÊVEUR ATTITRÉ
TRIBULATIONS OF A CERTIFIED DREAMER
(2008)

LES ÉPAULES ET LE FARDEAU

La terre
plate ou ronde
Quelle différence ?
si l'on doit immanquablement
revenir sur ses pas
et ne trouver
que ponts écroulés
carcasses de maisons
où le corbeau a fait son nid
jardins et tombes profanés
arche en béton au mât de laquelle
pend le même drapeau en berne
et pas âme qui vive
pour narrer sans en rajouter
le millième épisode
de cette piètre apocalypse

* * *

La bête humaine-inhumaine
de plus en plus intelligente
usant encore
de vieilles ruses éventées

BACK AND BURDEN

The earth
flat or round
What's the difference?
if we are inevitably bound
to retrace our steps
and find only
crumbling bridges
ruined houses
where crows have nested
gardens and tombs defiled
a concrete archway from whose flagpole
the same flag dangles at half-staff
and not a living soul
to give an unadorned account
of the thousandth episode
in this wretched apocalypse

* * *

The human/inhuman beast
ever more intelligent
still using
such stale old tricks

telle cette voie unique
du salut
où des bulldozers tracent aujourd'hui
l'autoroute d'une civilisation
aussi sommaire
que le hamburger
qui lui sert de mascotte
Et les peuples asservis
de se bousculer au portillon
en parfaite connaissance
et désespoir de cause

* * *

Comme si l'on pouvait choisir
dans l'éventail de l'horreur
couvrant la planète
La raison vacille
mais il faut se reprendre
S'indigner
dénoncer
certes
Pour autant
serons-nous quittes ?

as this sole path
to salvation
with bulldozers today breaking ground
for the superhighway of a civilization
as artless
as the hamburger
that it takes for its totem
And oppressed peoples
clamoring at the entry barrier
in full awareness
and complete desperation

* * *

As if there was any choice
in the spectrum of horror
that covers the planet
Reason wavers
but we must pull ourselves together
Protest
denounce
of course
But will even that
be enough?

La colère se refroidit
tandis que d'autres brasiers
se présentent
à la permanence de l'horreur

* * *

À l'heure du dîner
les images annoncées comme insoutenables
On détourne les yeux
ne sachant plus ce qui distingue
la décence de l'indécence
et quand on regarde
la ligne est tout aussi mince
entre lâcheté et courage
À la fin du repas
il arrive qu'on se demande
si l'on n'a pas mangé
la chair de son prochain
plus précisément
celle de ses propres enfants
Le match de foot
ou le film en prime time
vient à point nommé
balayer ces petits soucis

Rage cools
while other blazes
offer to reinforce
the permanence of the horror

* * *

At the dinner hour
come images described as unbearable
We turn our eyes away
no longer knowing how to tell
the decent from the indecent
and when we inspect
the dividing line
between cowardice and courage
it is just as narrow
With the meal over
we sometimes wonder
if we haven't just eaten
the flesh of our fellows
or more accurately
that of our own children
The football match
or the prime-time movie
comes right on time
to dispel these minor concerns

*　*　*

L'enfer est bien achalandé
mais ses rayons d'approvisionnement
sont vides
sauf de caméras
de plus en plus sophistiquées
Les visites sont commentées
par des savants portant uniforme
et couvre-chefs ethnicolor
« Au nom de Dieu », proclame l'un
« Ce qu'il faut savoir », avertit l'autre
et tous d'entonner le même cri de guerre
« Arrière Satan ! »
L'enfer moderne
possède un sacré avantage
sur les précédents
Il est tourné en studio

*　*　*

Contrairement à tous les messages
rabâchés
sur la compassion, la justice
l'espérance, l'amour
la colère du ciel s'abat en priorité

Hell has plenty of customers
but its shelves are bare
except for
more and more sophisticated
cameras
Guided tours are led
by experts in uniform
and ethnicolor headgear
"In the name of God," declares one
"What you need to know," warns another
And all of them raise the same war cry
"Get thee behind me Satan!"
Modern hell
has a darned good advantage
over its predecessors
It is shot in the studio

* * *

In contrast to all the messages
churned out
on compassion, justice
hope, or love
the bolts of heaven

– soit dit en passant –
sur les condamnés de l'existence
les désemparés
sans dents et sans épaules
Et les malentendants du cœur
les borgnes de l'esprit
les fossoyeurs aux dents longues
au visage entièrement refait
d'aboyer à la face des survivants
et jusqu'à l'oreille des trépassés :
Expiez vos péchés !

* * *

À force de sévices
le récipient de la mémoire
risque de déborder
et l'on ne sait d'ailleurs
si le fond en est étanche
Faut-il réchauffer à feu doux
ou laisser refroidir ?
La soupe du crime
naturellement abondante

(lest we forget)
come down first and foremost
on life's afflicted
the downtrodden
those with no teeth or no muscle
While it is the tone-deaf of heart
the blind of spirit
and the wolfish gravediggers
with their completely made-over faces
who bellow right at the survivors
and even into the ears of the departed:
Atone for your sins!

* * *

The tide of brutality
tends to make the
the vessel of memory
overflow
nor can we be sure by the way
that the bottom is watertight
Should we heat the contents on a low flame
or let them cool down?
The soup of corruption
is of course more abundant

est plus largement distribuée
que la soupe populaire
Elle reste souvent sur l'estomac
et provoque des nausées
mais ses vapeurs engourdissent
cycliquement
les consciences

* * *

La liste ne saurait être exhaustive
Il y a les enfants jetés en pâture
aux charognards du sexe et de la guerre
le chantage à la famine
le négoce du désespoir
le trafic d'organes de la pensée
le blanchiment des idées sales
Il y a le rapt des rebelles
ayant levé la main sur le Temple
l'écrasement du moindre bourgeon
qui a eu l'idée d'éclore
en souvenir de la défunte espérance
Il y a le crime parfait
l'immunité de la Force
adoubée et acclamée à la Bourse

and more widely distributed
than that served in soup kitchens
It can settle on the stomach
and provoke nausea
and periodically
the steam alone
numbs consciousness

* * *

The list cannot be exhaustive
There are children tossed as feed
to the vultures of sex and war
blackmail by starvation
trade in despair
organ trafficking of the mind
laundering of foul ideas
There is the abduction of rebels
who have waved a fist at the Temple
and the crushing of the tiniest bud
that takes a notion to open
in memory of now defunct hopes
There is the perfect crime
the impunity of brute force
anointed and acclaimed by the stock market

Il y a les verres qu'on entrechoque
les propos graveleux
et le rire des vainqueurs
à deux pas des charniers

* * *

La connaissance ne pardonne pas
Elle te ronge
De quoi serais-tu coupable ?
D'un quelconque oubli
ou de surenchère
De te sentir brûler avec les mots
que tu as mis sur l'innommable
et de rester vissé sur ton siège
en sirotant ton café ?
Ose le dire :
même innocent du mal
tu en es l'otage
Peut-on pacifier le cœur des bourreaux
changer d'humanité ?
Personne n'a la réponse
La rédemption, la Rédemption
murmures-tu
cette équation insoluble

There are the clinked glasses
the smutty chatter
and the laughter of the victors
just two steps from the mass graves

* * *

Knowledge does not forgive
It gnaws at you
What might you be guilty of?
Some small thing overlooked
or overdone?
Of feeling fired up by the words
you have applied to the unspeakable
while remaining stuck to your chair
sipping your coffee?
Dare to say it:
even if you are innocent
you are hostage to evil
Can the heart of the torturer be placated
can humanity be changed?
No one has the answer
redemption, you mutter, Redemption
but the equation cannot be solved

* * *

Du droit de t'insurger tu useras
quoi qu'il advienne
Du devoir de discerner
dévoiler
lacérer
chaque visage de l'abjection
tu t'acquitteras
à visage découvert
De la graine de lumière
dispensée à ton espèce
chue dans tes entrailles
tu te feras gardien et vestale
À ces conditions préalables
tu mériteras ton vrai nom
homme de parole
ou poète si l'on veut

* * *

Ce n'est pas une affaire d'épaules
ni de biceps
que le fardeau du monde
Ceux qui viennent à le porter
sont souvent les plus frêles

* * *

Whatever happens
you will make use of the right to rise up
Barefaced you will fulfil your duty
to discern
unmask
and savage
every aspect of abjection
You will make yourself
the guardian and vestal
of the seeds of enlightenment
bestowed on your race
and lodged in your gut
By meeting these requirements
you will earn your true name
man of his word
or poet if you prefer

* * *

The burden of the world
is not a matter of broad shoulders
or biceps
Those who end up bearing it
are often the frailest

Eux aussi sont sujets à la peur
au doute
au découragement
et en arrivent parfois à maudire
l'Idée ou le Rêve splendides
qui les ont exposés
au feu de la géhenne
Mais s'ils plient
ils ne rompent pas
et quand par malheur fréquent
on les coupe et mutile
ces roseaux humains
savent que leurs corps lardés
par la traîtrise
deviendront autant de flûtes
que des bergers de l'éveil emboucheront
pour capter
et convoyer jusqu'aux étoiles
la symphonie de la résistance

They too are subject to fear
to doubt
to demoralization
and sometimes fall to cursing
the glittering Idea or Dream
that has exposed them
to the fires of Gehenna
Yet if they bend
they do not break
and when as often happens
they have the misfortune
to be cut and mutilated
these human reeds
know that their bodies pierced
by treachery
will become so many flutes
which shepherds of the awakening
will put to their lips
to capture
and carry up to the stars
the symphony of resistance

LA HALTE DE LA CONFIDENCE

La fiction du désert, élaborée à l'extrême, étonnamment indigente. Ta nudité est plus flagrante car tu l'as cultivée au détriment des images, et surtout de l'orgueil. Maintenant, il n'y a plus que le linceul, non cousu, qui pourra la recouvrir. Cette proximité du terme devrait te donner le courage, somme toute modeste, de celui qui n'a rien à perdre. Tutoyer enfin le sphinx, regarder dans les yeux la Gorgone tapie entre ses ailes, dire haut et fort ton incompatibilité avec les croyances auxquelles on t'a condamné depuis que tu es tombé du ventre de ta mère. Te purifier d'avance au bûcher dont tu es le bois et la flamme.

Devant toi, le désert muet, sans autre message que celui de sa nudité.

* * *

Après les paroles, les écrits s'en vont, eux aussi. La halte s'impose, et tu sais que, si telle est ta volonté, tu vas « presque quitter la condition humaine », renoncer au partage, te résoudre à la solitude extrême. Même l'amour, dans son acception la plus rare, ne te sera pas d'un grand secours. Dans les profondeurs non élucidées de l'esprit, il y a comme un trou noir qui aspirera les quelques lumières que tu as cru faire sur le monde et que tu as naïvement élevées au rang de visions.

Devant toi, la ligne mince, tracée à l'encre invisible.

Aurais-tu peur ?

A HALT TO DISCLOSURE

The fiction of the desert, developed to the extreme, amazingly impoverished. Your nakedness is all the more flagrant in that you have cultivated it at the expense of images, and above all at the expense of pride. Now only your shroud, unsown, can cover it. This closeness of the end should give you the courage, as modest as it may be, of someone who has nothing to lose. The courage to address the Sphinx in familiar tones, to look the Gorgon, crouched between its wings, straight in the eye and say loudly and clearly how at odds you are with the beliefs to which you have been subjected since you tumbled from your mother's womb. To purify yourself in advance for the pyre of which you are at once the wood and the flames.

Before you, the mute desert, its sole message its nakedness.

* * *

After the spoken word, writing too departs. It is time to call a halt, and you know that if you so wish you will shortly "almost quit the human condition," give up sharing, and embrace extreme solitude. Even love, in its rarest form, will be of little help to you. In the unexplained depths of the mind is a sort of black hole which will suck in the few rays of light that you thought you had shed on the world and that you so naively promoted to the rank of visions.

Ahead of you, a thin line drawn in invisible ink.

Could you be afraid?

Nuit après nuit, tu scrutes les étoiles. Leur beauté n'est pas le sujet. Les nommer te paraît dérisoire. La distance qui t'en sépare ? Un détail. Tu cherches plutôt à établir avec elles un lien, disons physique. Peu à peu, ton corps se libère de la pesanteur. Ses formes, ses aspérités et sa consistance se dissolvent pour ne laisser place qu'à la conscience organique que tu en as. Il en résulte une extrême concentration allant de pair avec une expansion prodigieuse. Les battements de ton cœur deviennent audibles. Heureusement que tu es seul ! Ils s'élèvent en une colonne d'harmonies naviguant à la vitesse de la lumière. À cette colonne, tu adhères. Tu sais qu'au bout de sa trajectoire elle va rejoindre d'autres battements, une autre colonne d'harmonies venant de ce que l'on appelle communément l'infini. De celui-ci, chaque étoile accrochée là-haut n'est qu'une halte semblable à la tienne. Pour l'heure, tu te réjouis à l'idée de cette correspondance heureuse.

Du moins sa promesse.

* * *

Le fil est si ténu, mais tu en tiens le bout. Il ne s'agit pas d'entreprendre le fameux voyage sans retour, d'accéder à la strate de l'éther où se révèlent enfin le Visage, et tout aussitôt la Balance. Tu as cessé d'être dans cette attente dès que tu as refermé, de tes mains sales, le Livre. Dès lors, ta pensée a été « souillée ». Plus d'ailes

*   *   *

Night after night you scrutinize the stars. Their beauty is not the question. Naming them seems trivial. Their great distance from you? A detail. What you want is to establish a link with them, a physical link so to speak. Little by little your body is freed of weight. Its forms, rough and smooth, dissolve, leaving only the organic consciousness that you have of them. The result is an extreme concentration coupled with an extraordinary expansion. Your heartbeats become audible. Luckily you are alone! They rise as a column of harmonies traveling at the speed of light. To this column you attach yourself. You know that at the end of its journey it will join other heartbeats, another column of harmonies coming from what is usually called infinity. From that point every star hanging up there is merely a halt just like yours.
On the moment, you delight in the idea of this happy correspondence.

Or at least the promise of it.

*   *   *

The thread is so slender, but you hold the end of it. It is not a question of embarking on the famous journey of no return, of reaching that level of the ether where the Face of God is finally revealed, immediately followed by the Scales. You stopped waiting

tutélaires. Plus d'allégeance. Et le risque pour règle d'or. La liberté au prix fort ! Tu n'attends ni châtiment ni récompense, et l'idée d'une vie éternelle t'ennuie à l'extrême. Pâle est la prophétie au regard de l'intuition. De celle-ci, le fil est tout aussi ténu, mais tu en tiens le bout.

Surtout, ne lâche pas prise !

* * *

La mer s'est recouverte du voile opaque de la nuit. Sa respiration d'amante inassouvie te parvient, portée par une brise hors saison. À peine revenu sur terre, le corps criblé d'étoiles, tu es aux prises avec une autre captation. Assurément, la vie d'ici-bas ne t'a pas quitté, elle qui t'a révélé que l'écoute, le regard et l'odorat sont autant de catégories du désir. De celui-ci d'ailleurs, la vie n'est-elle pas une simple émanation ? Bien avant l'acte de tes géniteurs, tu as donc été désiré. Façon inédite de poser la question des origines.

Ainsi, la mer t'a parlé dans son rêve décousu.

* * *

for this when, with your dirty hands, you closed the Book. From then on your thought was "soiled." No more tutelary wings. No more allegiance. And risk as the golden rule. Freedom at the highest price. You expect neither punishment nor reward, and the notion of eternal life you find utterly boring. Prophecy pales in comparison with intuition. The thread there is just as slender, but you hold the end of it.

Whatever you do, don't let go!

* * *

The sea is cloaked by night's opaque veil. Its breathing, like an unsatisfied lover's, reaches you on an unseasonable breeze. Hardly back on earth, your body riddled by stars, you find yourself locked in struggle with another seduction. Decidedly, life here below has not left you, the life which taught you that hearing, sight and smell are just so many categories of desire. Of which, moreover, is life not simply an emanation? Well before the act of your procreators, you were therefore desired. A new way of looking at the question of origins.

So the sea has spoken to you in its disjointed dream.

* * *

Quelque part au pays de l'intime. La cahute se transforme en une vraie maison avec des escaliers lumineux qui débouchent sur une terrasse donnant sur la mer. Un luxe, à l'évidence. Pourtant, tu te sens toujours démuni, ou du moins prêt à renoncer sans hésitation à ce que l'on assimile de près ou de loin au confort. L'âme de moine que tu as contractée dans ta cellule s'est enrichie de l'esprit de dérision. Le renoncement peut s'effectuer dans la joie. « Nudité, ô ma demeure ! » lances-tu en direction des vagues. J'aurai hanté ce promontoire, non pour jouir des merveilleux couchers du soleil et guetter le rayon vert, mais pour m'assurer de mon propre éveil, préméditer ce mouvement de la pensée n'appartenant qu'à l'homme et grâce auquel on parvient à lire derrière les lignes du ciel, soulever la mer afin qu'elle submerge le miroir des étoiles et recueillir dans la paume, ne serait-ce qu'une fraction de seconde, l'infini de soi et de l'univers.

Sans quoi la réconciliation avec la vie, donc la mort, demeure illusoire.

* * *

De nouveau la nuit. Elle a avancé, comme on dit. Autour de toi, le calme s'installe et te gagne. La voix d'un muezzin s'élève, à contretemps. Ce n'est ni la dernière prière du soir ni celle de l'aube. L'appel t'est-il adressé en personne, réponse incorruptible

Somewhere in the land of private life. The hut has turned into a real house with shining stairs that lead onto a balcony overlooking the sea. Luxurious, obviously. All the same, you still feel deprived, or at any rate quite ready to give up those things normally more or less identified with the comforts of life. The monkish soul acquired in your cell has been enriched by a taste for mockery. Renunciation can be achieved in the midst of joy. "Oh nakedness, my dwelling-place," you cry to the waves. I shall have haunted this promontory not to revel in the glorious sunsets or to look out for the green ray, but rather to reassure myself of my own wakefulness and to meditate in advance on that movement of thought which is man's alone and which makes it possible to see beyond the profile of heaven, to raise the sea until it submerges the mirror of the stars, and to gather into one's palm, if only for the fraction of a second, the infinity of the self and the universe.

Without which any reconciliation with life, and hence death, must remain illusory.

* * *

Night once more. It has deepened, as we say. Around you, calm sets in and sweeps over you. The cry of a muezzin rings out, incongruous at this hour. It can be neither for the last prayers of the day nor for those of the dawn. Is the call addressed to

à tes cogitations blasphématoires ? Curieusement, cette voix, assez fruste, te procure un certain plaisir. Soucieux de sa dignité, tu lui as ouvert ta poitrine. Là, tu n'es en guerre contre personne, et la guerre intestine que tu livres à tes limites ne viole que ta seule conscience. À ce stade de la halte, tous les dogmes, y compris ceux que tu as fréquentés, se sont évanouis. Ta mémoire en a évacué la trace pour ouvrir sur un autre chemin de la connaissance.

La chandelle, compagne obligée de ton soliloque, vient de rendre l'âme.

Comme elle a été vaillante et belle !

* * *

Tu as quitté la terrasse, la maison, le pays. L'Andalousie t'a ouvert les bras. Tu es entré, sans te déchausser, dans la mosquée de Cordoue. Devant le mihrab central, tu es resté figé à contempler le Christ écartelé tournant le dos à la direction de La Mecque. Un touriste japonais est venu te disputer ta rêverie. Ta compagne, pourtant munie d'une caméra dernier cri, n'a pas jugé bon d'immortaliser la scène. Heureusement, sinon comment aurais-tu pu l'évoquer à l'instant, en regardant simplement par la fenêtre

you personally, an unbendable response to your blasphemous ruminations? Oddly, this voice, rather rough-hewn, gives you a certain pleasure. Respectful of its dignity, you have opened your heart to it. At present you are at war with no one, while the inner war you are waging with your limitations ravages only your own conscience. At this stage in your halt, all dogmas, including those with which you have sympathized, have vanished. Your memory has erased all trace of them and opened up another way to knowledge.

The candle, inevitable companion to your soliloquy, has just given up the ghost.

How brave and beautiful it was!

* * *

Now you have left the balcony, the house, the country. Andalusia has opened her arms to you. You have entered the Great Mosque of Cordoba without removing your shoes. Before the central mihrab you stood stock still contemplating the Christ on the cross with your back to Mecca. A Japanese tourist came up and interrupted your revery. Your female companion, though equipped with an ultra-modern camera, felt it best not to immortalize the scene. Thank goodness, for otherwise how would you have been able to evoke it now simply by looking out of the window to make sure

pour t'assurer que l'arbre est toujours là, confident muet de la ronde effrénée des saisons de l'âme ?

De la terre ou de toi, qui a vraiment tourné ?

* * *

Finalement, le vocable qui rend le mieux compte de ta situation dans la condition humaine appartient à la langue arabe. *Gharib* : être de l'exil, étranger aux autres, souvent à lui-même, déserteur du sens commun, sculpteur de l'écart, habitant de la marge, coutumier des absences, jardinier des confins de solitude.

Un rêveur de plus, alors !

that the tree is still there, mute confidant to the unbridled round of the seasons of the soul?

As between the earth and you, which has actually turned?

* * *

Finally, the word that best sums up your situation with respect to the human condition is an Arabic one. *Gharib*: a being of exile, stranger to others, often to himself, deserter of common sense, sculptor of separation, inhabitant of the margins, habitué of absences, gardener of the borders of solitude.

In short, another dreamer!

from

ZONE DE TURBULENCES

AREA OF TURBULENCE

(2012)

L'HABITACLE DU VIDE

Avant de reconnaître humblement
la défaite du corps
un dernier verre
à la santé des mots
qui ont fait leurs preuves
Compagnons d'infortune
confidents amusés
des quelques joies volées à la tire
Les mots
braves et indulgents
et maintenant perplexes
face
à ce qui se nomme
– joliment faut-il dire –
l'inconnu

Cette nuit avalant le jour
avec un peu d'eau
comme un cachet d'aspirine
La meute dehors, dedans
ne s'est pas calmée
Du sang, du sang ! réclame-t-elle

THE DWELLING-PLACE OF THE VOID

Before humbly acknowledging
the defeat of the body
a last glass
to the health of words
which have proved themselves
Companions in misfortune
confidants amused
at a few pilfered pleasures
Words
courageous and indulgent
and perplexed now
when confronted by
what is known
(prettily it must be said)
as the unknown

Night swallowing day
with a little water
like an aspirin
The pack outside, and inside
has not settled down
Blood! Blood! is its cry

Quel sang ?
Doucement
les yeux du témoin
se referment
sur l'image au ralenti
de la curée
Doucement
ils s'ouvrent de l'autre côté
de la lumière
et se posent en un coin aveugle
de ce qui se nomme
faute de mieux
l'éternité

Dans l'attente sans appel
les témoins du corps
s'éteignent l'un après l'autre
Le toucher en premier
puis l'odorat
L'ouïe ne capte plus
que la vibration du son
à sa naissance
Le regard se fragmente
et s'effrite

What blood?
Gently
the witness's eyes
close
on the slow-motion image
of the fleshing of the hounds
Gently they open again
on the far side
of the light
and come to rest on a blind corner
of what is known
for want of a better name
as eternity

During the inevitable wait
the body's witnesses
are extinguished one by one
First the sense of touch
then smell
The hearing now catches
only the vibration of sound
at its source
Sight splits
and crumbles

N'en subsiste que l'irradiation
d'une tête d'épingle
inaltérée
au fond des iris

L'obscurité se teinte
de couleurs inconnues
bruissant comme des feuilles
caressées par le vent
ou la main d'un jardinier lyrique
Derrière la toile de fond
un pinceau invisible s'active
Noir sur noir
il esquisse des formes abstraites
où la géométrie est absente
puis des silhouettes humanoïdes
sans bras
ni jambes
Un tableau assez réaliste
auquel on pourrait donner pour titre
« L'habitacle du vide »

Le lieu
si tant est qu'on puisse
le désigner ainsi
atteste une présence

All that remains is an unimpaired
pinhead gleam
deep in the irises

The obscurity is tinged
by unknown colors
rustling like leaves
caressed by the wind
or the hand of a lyrical gardener
Behind the backdrop
an invisible brush is at work
Black on black
it sketches abstract shapes
without geometry
then humanoid silhouettes
without arms
or legs
A fairly realist picture
which might well be entitled
"The Dwelling-Place of the Void"

The place
if indeed it may be
so designated
attests to a presence

Est-ce l'âme des croyances anciennes
La mémoire de ce qui dans la matière
ne cesse de tourner autour
du plus petit soleil imaginable
inimaginable
Le reliquat d'une conscience
naguère obstinée
incapable de concevoir
la disparition pure et simple
L'esprit que parfois l'on prête
à l'arbre ou à la roche
Le souffle
de l'incandescence originelle
toujours à l'œuvre
et dans les siècles des siècles ?

Ce ne serait
que la petite mort
Une galerie de rêves
faisant office de miroirs
où se projettent
des gestes décomposés
par une caméra experte
des fragments de visages
juxtaposés dans un désordre

Is it the soul of ancient beliefs
The memory of what in matter
continually circles
the smallest sun imaginable
or unimaginable
The remnant of a consciousness
once obstinately
unable to conceive of
disappearance pure and simple
The spirit that we sometimes attribute
to trees or rocks
The breath
of primal incandescence
still at work
for ever and ever?

It would be
only a little death
A gallery of dreams
serving as mirrors
onto which are projected
actions dissected
by expert camerawork
and fragments of faces
juxtaposed in a disorder

se voulant insondable
où viennent ricocher
en guise de commentaire
les échos de quelques vocables rares
dont l'usage s'est perdu
depuis des lustres

Le plus étrange
ou plutôt le pire
c'est que sous pareil climat
le rire semble inconcevable
et le sens du ridicule avec
À n'en pas douter
on touche là
à l'irréparable

La peur
l'archaïque
devient lisse
Il y a juste
cette vieille et bonne tristesse
qui fait des siennes
avec des larmes
probablement sèches
la restitution brève

712

meant to be unintelligible
and onto which
by way of commentary
echoes ricochet of a few rare words
long since
fallen out of use

The oddest thing
or rather the worst
is that under these circumstances
laughter seems inconceivable
and along with it any sense of the ridiculous
No doubt about it
we are very close here
to the irreparable

Fear
archaic fear
softens up
There is just
that good old sadness
up to its tricks
with tears
probably dry-eyed
that brief revival

de la douceur des êtres
devant lesquels on s'est prosterné
en pensée
parfois en vrai
Il y a juste
ce trouble de la nostalgie
qui habite au-delà des humains
même les pierres

Il y a cette question
ni grave ni légère
que le spectacle du corps étendu
presque inerte
pose à la conscience :
mais pourquoi
en ce moment encore
la souffrance ?
Et de la murmurer
a un effet de baume
C'est comme un lien ultime
avec l'espérance
que l'on prend soin
de ne pas rompre

of the sweetness of beings
before whom we prostrated ourselves
in our thoughts
sometimes in reality
There is just
that troubling nostalgia
that dwells
beyond humans
even in stones

There is the question
neither serious nor trivial
that the spectacle of the body laid out
almost inert
poses to consciousness:
but why
even now
does suffering continue?
And murmuring it
serves as balm
It is like a very last link
to the hope
that we are at pains
not to lose

Ce moment-ci
daté
inscrit
dans l'événement premier
quand un caillou acéré
un couteau
des ciseaux
ont tranché le cordon
la pure merveille
Dès lors
être
devenir soi
revient toujours à tuer
sa génitrice
et s'acheminer
délibérément
vers « l'habitacle du vide »

Circulez
il n'y a rien à voir !
Laissez l'intrus
délirer encore un peu
ressasser ses prétendues visions
avouer

This moment
dated
graven
upon the primal event
when
a sharpened stone
a knife
scissors
cut the cord
a sheer wonder
From that moment on
being
becoming oneself
always comes down to killing
one's progenitress
and heading
deliberately
for "the dwelling-place of the void"

Move along
nothing to see here!
Let the intruder
rave on for a while
chew over his supposed visions
confide

à l'interlocuteur imaginaire de son choix
ses doutes
ses remords
ses zones d'ombre
jouer la petite musique de son invention
pour soulager ses peines
Laissez-le
réciter sa prière silencieuse
se préparer à l'oubli
Et si, contrairement aux usages
il tient à garder les yeux ouverts
respectez cette autre bizarrerie
Sortez
en fermant derrière vous
la porte du sanctuaire

to the interlocutor of his choice
his doubts
his regrets
his areas of confusion
and play the little tune of his own invention
that relieves his suffering
Let him
recite his silent prayer
prepare himself for oblivion
And if, contrary to usual practice
he insists on keeping his eyes open
respect this additional idiosyncrasy
Leave
and close the sanctuary door
behind you

de LE LIVRE

Ô jardinier de l'âme
as-tu prévu
un carré de terre humaine
où planter encore quelques rêves ?
As-tu sélectionné les graines
ensoleillé les outils
consulté le vol des oiseaux
observé les astres, les visages
les cailloux et les vagues ?
L'amour t'a-t-il parlé ces jours-ci
dans sa langue étrangère ?
As-tu allumé une autre bougie
pour blesser la nuit dans son orgueil ?
Mais parle
si tu es toujours là
Dis-moi au moins :
qu'as-tu mangé et qu'as-tu bu ?

Nous sommes encore vivants
pour quelque temps
même si le corps se vide de la sève
antérieure au sang
À peine savons-nous reconnaître

from THE BOOK

Oh gardener of the soul
have you thought of
a plot of human earth
to plant a few more dreams in?
Have you selected the seeds
sunned the tools
consulted the flight of birds
observed stars, faces
stones, waves?
Has love spoken to you recently
in its foreign tongue?
Have you lit another candle
to wound the night in its pride?
But speak
if you are still there
Tell me at least
what have you eaten and what have you drunk?

We are still alive
for a while
even if the body is losing all its sap
its blood will be next
We can barely recognize

les caresses émanant du mystère
et nos yeux
bientôt n'auront plus d'île
où déposer leurs offrandes
au pied de l'arbre de la vision !
Que nous arrive-t-il
Est-ce la mort
qui a fixé de nouvelles règles
Dites plutôt
qu'avons-nous fait ?

Le poète
et la roue des questions
A-t-il failli lui aussi ?
Il s'est battu
tant que le monde avait une assise
et le berger une étoile
Il a hurlé avec les fous
et arboré le sourire de l'éveillé
Il a tendu la main
jusqu'à ce qu'on la lui coupe
De sa marge
il observe maintenant les broyeurs
succédant aux broyeurs
Jusqu'à quand ?

the caresses of the mystery
and our eyes
will soon have no isle
upon which to place their offerings
at the foot of the tree of vision!
What is happening to us
Is it death
that has laid down new rules
But tell us rather
what have we done?

The poet
and the wheel of questions
Has he too failed?
He fought
as long as the world had a foundation
and the shepherd a star
He screamed with the mad
and displayed the smile of the enlightened
He held out his hand
until they cut it off
Now from his margin
he watches destroyers
follow upon destroyers
For how long?

Il erre dans l'infini
entre quatre murs
Pourtant
l'idée de se faire la belle
ne l'a jamais effleuré
Il a meublé de bric et de broc
l'étrange demeure
Sur les parois
il a accroché quelques images pieuses
de la femme aimée jusqu'à plus soif
des enfants conçus en plein soleil de l'utopie
du père et de la mère
installés, dans leur bulle d'éternité
sur un trône de lumière
des amis disparus sans dire ouf
du pays qui l'a blessé à mort
sans qu'il lui en tienne rigueur
Ne sachant s'il avance ou recule
il arpente, la tête haute
cette geôle à ciel ouvert
se sustente à heure fixe
pour ne pas dépérir
et fume sans vergogne

He roams infinity
between four walls
All the same
the thought of breaking out
has never occurred to him
He has furnished his strange abode
with bric-à-brac
On the walls
he has stuck a few worshipful pictures
of the woman loved beyond all measure
of children conceived in the bright sunshine of utopia
of the father and the mother
seated in their bubble of eternity
on a throne of light
of friends vanished without a word
of the country that mortally wounded him
though he bears it no grudge
Unable to tell if he is going forwards or backwards
he paces his open-air jail
head held high
eats regularly
so as not to starve
and smokes shamelessly

Dans ses poumons
l'air se raréfie
comme partout ailleurs
Son souffle
naguère ample et brûlant
le lâche au milieu de l'ascension
Sa colère
ravage plus ses artères
que l'objet de sa colère
Sur le métier imperturbable du temps
la trame de ses désirs s'effiloche
Il n'a plus que l'énergie
de flanquer un coup de pied
à la projection
de sa dépouille

Des idées noires
il en a toujours eu
mais pas comme celles-ci
Il en a honte
Sa culpabilité
provient on croirait
d'une malformation originelle de l'être
ajoutée à celle du monde

In his lungs
the air is getting scarce
as it is everywhere else
His breath
formerly generous and warm
stalls halfway up his windpipe
His anger
wreaks more havoc on his arteries
than on its target
On time's imperturbable loom
the weft of his desires is threadbare
He has strength enough
only to deliver a good kick
to his imagined
corpse

Dark thoughts
he has always had
but not like these
Of these he is ashamed
His feelings of guilt
come seemingly
from a basic defect of his being
added to the world's

comme si le péché des péchés
était celui
de naître

La vie
méritait-elle semblables outrages ?
Oh que non
pour qui l'aurait goûtée un tant soit peu
Et que dire des chantres inconditionnels
qu'elle était en droit d'attendre ?
À leur place
il n'y eut que des prophètes attardés
flétrissant les plaisirs d'ici-bas
multipliant les promesses pour l'au-delà
traçant les voies du martyre
Les chantres, eux, souvent
désertaient l'arène
et de la symphonie pérenne
du monde des vivants
ne tendaient l'oreille
qu'au chant du cygne

Ce miracle en nous
que nous scrutons de loin en loin
élus frivoles

as though the sin of sins
were the sin
of being born

Did life deserve
such violation?
Certainly not
for those who have had the slightest taste of it
And what of the fervent minstrels
that life was entitled to expect?
In their stead
came only curmudgeonly prophets
castigating the pleasures of the here below
heaping up promises about the beyond
pointing the way to martyrdom
The minstrels for their part
often abandoned the field
and in the perennial symphony
of the world of the living
harkened
solely to swansongs

This miracle within us
to which we pay heed but rarely
privileged but frivolous as we are

si peu reconnaissants
d'une arche vaillante
qui défonce l'obscur
le non-sens
la banquise de l'amnésie
et à la demande, fait halte
pour que chacun aille en quête
de son havre
sa moitié perdue
son soleil intérieur
Ce miracle en nous
qui s'en émerveille encore
et le bénit chaque jour
dans ses prières ?

Il en va de même de son creuset
et sa forge
cette planète nôtre
unique jusqu'à plus ample informé
fenêtre orpheline
éclairant l'univers
les pages noircies du livre inachevé
des origines
agneau du genre prétendu humain
devenu expert en boucheries

so loath to acknowledge
the valiant ark
that breaks through the shadows
the nonsense
the frozen wastes of amnesia
and on request calls a halt
for each to go in search
of their haven
their lost half
their inner sun
This miracle within us
who is still awed by it
and blesses it every day
in their prayers?

The same goes for its crucible
and forge
this planet of ours
unique until further notice
orphan window
illuminating the universe
the blackened pages of the unfinished book
of the origins
lamb of the allegedly human race
now expert in butchery

et messes noires
Qui s'émerveille encore de ce prodige
et pour sa part affirme :
De vivre en son sein
ou juste à ses pieds
quel privilège !

De la résurrection comme métaphore
que retenir ?
Il faudrait renverser du temps
la logique primaire
découvrir l'espace d'une genèse
dont ne nous est parvenue
qu'une vague rumeur
artère après artère
remonter le fil d'une mémoire
tissée à même la chair
et son antique glaise
De là
se pencher sur le berceau de l'esprit
opérant sa fission
repenser le feu, l'eau
la lave, les métaux, les fibres

and black masses
Who still marvels at this wonder
and declares:
What an honor
to live within it
or just at its feet!

What to retain
from the resurrection as metaphor?
One would have to reverse
the basic logic of time
discover the site of a genesis
about which no more than a vague rumor
has reached us
track back
artery by artery
the thread of a memory
woven into the very flesh
and its ancient clay
From there
study the cradle of the mind
and its divisive action
reconceive fire, water
lava, metals, fibers

puis bourgeonner, fleurir
articuler patiemment le langage
ouvrir enfin les yeux
sur l'aube inédite
qui verra se lever dans toute sa gloire
le soleil du poème

then patiently
bud, flower
articulate language
and open one's eyes at last
on the unprecedented dawn
that will herald the rise
in all its glory
of the sun of the poem

[…]

J'ai été donc moi aussi
un enfant
J'ai senti
ses premières sensations
J'ai été dans son incompréhension
du monde des adultes :
violence
hypocrisie
hystérie
J'ai pleuré de ses larmes
pour un oui ou pour un non
J'ai été dans son émerveillement
par les contes de la grand-mère
ou de l'oncle
J'ai été emporté par son sommeil
si profond
si paisible
et me suis réveillé dans son réveil
sans amertume dans la bouche
J'ai appris goulûment
ses premières expressions
et fredonné ses comptines
J'ai joué le plus sérieusement du monde
à ses jeux

[…]

So I too was once
a child
I felt
a child's first sensations
I knew his bewilderment
at the grown-up world:
violence
hypocrisy
hysteria
I cried his tears
over a yes or a no
I experienced his awe
at a grandmother's tales
or an uncle's
I fell into his sleep
so deep
so peaceful
and woke up in his awakening
with no bitter taste in my mouth
I greedily learnt
his first words
and lilted his counting-rhymes
I played his games
with utter gravity

et eu son irrésistible tentation
de tricher
J'ai ri à gorge déployée
de son rire cristallin
sans une once de cruauté
J'ai scruté avec ses yeux
les animaux
les plantes
les cailloux
et les ai dotés sans hésiter
d'une âme
Je leur ai parlé
avec des mots de son invention
et ils m'ont répondu
sans se faire prier
J'ai regardé, médusé
passer les cortèges funèbres
et parfois je les ai suivis
pour me donner de l'importance
Avec lui
j'ai ressenti la vraie faim
la vraie soif
le besoin impérieux du petit chien
d'être caressé
J'ai prié

and suffered his irresistible temptation
to cheat
I laughed uproariously
with his crystalline laughter
and not an ounce of cruelty
With his eyes I examined
animals
plants
stones
and unhesitatingly
assigned them souls
I spoke to them
with words of his invention
to which they replied
without being asked twice
I watched in fascination
as funeral processions passed
and sometimes to look important
I joined them
With him
I knew real hunger
real thirst
the little dog's imperious need
to be petted
I prayed

comme on le lui avait appris
sans rien comprendre
J'ai cru aux fantômes
aux djinns bienfaisants et malfaisants
au ciel qui tombe sur la tête
à la marque d'infamie qui apparaît sur le front
en cas de péché
aux signes avant-coureurs
de la fin du monde
J'ai eu une peur bleue du tonnerre
des serpents
des scorpions
et par-dessus tout
de la malédiction jetée sur sa tête
par le père
et surtout la mère
J'ai menti pour me tirer d'affaire
et bravé – déjà ! –
quelques interdits
Je me suis délecté de son inconscience
et j'ai gardé sur mes lèvres
son sourire de Joconde
Longtemps
longtemps après
j'ai fait tout ce qui était en mon pouvoir

as he had been taught to pray
understanding none of it
I believed in ghosts
in djinns good and bad
in a sky that could fall on your head
in the mark of shame that appeared
on your forehead if you sinned
in prophetic signs
of the end of the world
I had his unholy dread of thunder
snakes
scorpions
and most of all
the curse brought down on his head
by the father
or especially by the mother
I lied to get myself out of hot water
and broke – already! –
a few rules
I basked in his unconsciousness
and kept his Giaconda's smile
on my lips
For the longest time
afterwards
I did everything I could

pour ne pas démériter de lui
Et maintenant
de son éloignement irrémédiable
je reste inconsolable

Je me vois
sur la plus haute branche
de l'arbre qui me fait face
Je suis l'oiseau immobile
absorbé par le spectacle
du soleil levant
J'ai de lui les ailes
le bec
le regard perçant
le petit cœur
battant plus vite que le mien
Il ne faut surtout pas que je bouge
que j'aie l'idée saugrenue
de m'envoler
Je voudrais tant
rester encore un peu oiseau
juste le temps
de n'avoir nul besoin de parler
écrire, penser
d'oublier en somme que je suis
homme

not to dishonor him
And now
with his departure irreversible
I am inconsolable

I see myself on the highest bough
of the tree across the way
I am the motionless bird
absorbed by the spectacle
of the rising sun
I have that bird's wings
its beak
piercing gaze
little heart
beating faster than mine
Above all I must not move
take a wild notion
to fly away
I would like so very much
to be a bird for a little longer
just long enough
with no need to speak
write, think
and forget in short that I am
man

[…]

Faute d'inspiration
ma complainte touche à sa fin
en même temps que le monde
auquel j'ai appartenu
Je ne sais
si dans le vacarme sidéral
mon mince filet de voix
aura quelque chance d'être entendu
si ce que j'ai tenu à consigner
pour mémoire, dirions-nous
retiendra l'attention
d'un chercheur un peu fou
d'une âme sensible
ayant eu vent de cet art archaïque
que nous autres humains
appelions poésie
et considérions encore
du moins dans certaines de nos contrées
comme le maître des arts
le guide des égarés
dans le dédale de l'esprit
les cercles de l'enfer du monde
dans la jungle et l'océan sans rivages

[…]
For want of inspiration
my complaint is coming to an end
at the same time as the world
to which I belonged
I do not know
whether in the cosmic hullabaloo
my thin reed of a voice
will have any chance of being heard
whether what I sought to register
as a report, so to speak
will catch the attention
of some slightly crazy researcher
with a sensitive soul
who has heard tell of the ancient art
that we humans used to call poetry
and still viewed
at least in some of our countries
as the greatest of the arts
the guide of those lost
in the maze of the mind
in the world's circles of hell
in the jungle and the boundless ocean

de cette singulière aventure
que nous avons vécue

Peu importe
j'aurai fait
dans le sillage
de mes prédécesseurs émérites
mon devoir d'homme
J'aurai essayé
de déchiffrer les hiéroglyphes
de l'avers
et l'envers
de l'humain
J'aurai égratigné
avec les moyens du bord
la férule de l'oubli

J'aurai gravé sur l'éther
des voix
des cantilènes
des cris
des bribes d'histoire
des dates sans commentaire
des mots d'adieu
repris à des stèles funéraires

of the singular adventure
that we have lived

No matter
I shall have fulfilled
in the wake
of my venerable predecessors
my duty as a man
I shall have tried
to decipher the hieroglyphs
of the obverse
and the reverse
of the human
With the means to hand
I shall have scratched the surface
of the iron rule of forgetfulness

In the ether I shall have registered
voices
melodies
cries
snatches of stories
dates without comment
words of farewell
borrowed from tombstones

des chemins d'exil
des bateaux de retour
des nervures d'arbres
des silhouettes d'oiseaux
des corps de femmes
des traces de pas
des cours de fleuves
des dessins d'enfants
une main coupée
un cœur nu
un lever de soleil
que j'ai imaginé le premier
sur terre
une étoile
que j'ai souvent visitée
dans mes rêves éveillés
un homme debout
les pieds fermes
la tête haute
et dans ses yeux où perle une larme
subitement agrandis à la dimension du ciel
j'aurai gravé en pointillé
la flèche de l'infini

roads of exile
boats of return
latticework of trees
silhouettes of birds
women's bodies
footprints
river courses
children's drawings
a hand cut off
a heart bared
a sunrise
that I fancied
was the first on earth
a star
that I often visited
in my waking dreams
a man standing
firm-footed
head high
and in his eyes where a teardrop is forming
eyes suddenly widened to the scale of the sky
I shall have drawn a dotted line
the arrow of infinity

J'aurai marqué
cette page
et refermé
le livre

I shall have marked
this page
and closed
the book

from

LA SAISON MANQUANTE,
suivi de AMOUR-JACARANDA

THE MISSING SEASON,
followed by JACARANDA MY LOVE

(2014)

SENSATION

À l'instant où ils s'ouvrent
les yeux
créent la lumière
Autant d'yeux
autant de lumières

À l'instant où elle éclot
la conscience
crée le monde
puis l'univers
Autant de consciences
autant de mondes
puis d'univers

Que les yeux se ferment
ou que la conscience s'éteigne
et le Tout disparaît

Ceci
n'est qu'une sensation
Rien qui mérite
d'être gravé dans le marbre
ou « rester dans les bouquins »
Mais c'est ma sensation

SENSATION

The moment they open
the eyes
create light
So many eyes
so much light

The moment it blooms
consciousness
creates the world
then the universe
So much consciousness
so many worlds
then so many universes

If the eyes close
if consciousness is extinguished
the Whole disappears

This
is just a sensation
Nothing that deserves
to be graven in stone
or "written in a book"
But it is my sensation

Je suis là
les yeux entrouverts
accroché au fil
qui coud le jour à la nuit
les voiles du dedans
aux voiles du dehors
les langes aux linceuls

Je ne suis plus là
La cavale des mots
piaffe
bat des ailes
entre les doigts et la page

Sois le bienvenu
cher
si cher inconnu !

I am here
eyes half-open
clinging to the thread
that sews day to night
the veils within
to those without
and swaddling clothes to shrouds

I am no longer here
The cavalcade of words
paws the ground
fails to get moving
between fingers and page

Welcome
dear
so dear stranger!

SUPPOSITIONS

À supposer
une naissance sans douleur
une histoire vierge
L'air
entièrement renouvelé
Les océans nettoyés à fond
L'eau de source
à elle seule prodiguant
nourriture et connaissance
Le feu cultivé
pour obtenir du vin
et l'élixir de l'enfance
Le vent propice
ramenant du large
les harmonies savantes
qui ont présidé à la création
Des animaux libres
portés sur la beauté
veillant sur les espèces rares

À supposer
une nouvelle demeure
pour la langue et l'Idée

PICTURE

Picture
a birth without pain
a history still virgin
Air
completely renewed
Oceans utterly clean
Spring water
singlehandedly bestowing
nourishment and knowledge
Fire cultivated
to make wine
and the elixir of childhood
A favorable wind
from the open sea
bearing the sage harmonies
that presided over creation
Animals free
friends of beauty
and protectors of rare species

Picture
a new home
for language and the Idea

À supposer
ce que tout un chacun désire
au plus profond de lui-même :
une vie de rechange
où l'on choisirait librement
ses géniteurs
son lieu et sa date de naissance
son nom et son sobriquet
sa voix
sa ou ses langues intimes
sa religion si besoin est
ses amours
uniques ou multiples
la couleur de ses idées
ses combats mûrement réfléchis
sa maison avec son arbre tutélaire
son errance et ses pèlerinages
les livres
la musique
la peinture
qui soient à la hauteur
de ses propres talents
et tant qu'à faire
quelques secrets
ne faisant de mal à personne

Picture
what just anybody wants
in their heart of hearts:
a different life
where you can freely choose
your procreators
your place and date of birth
your name and nickname
your voice
your natural tongue or tongues
your religion if need be
your loves
one or many
the cast of your ideas
your long-mulled battles
your house and its guardian tree
your ramblings and pilgrimages
books
music
paintings
on a par
with your own
talents
and while we are at it
a few secrets

comme celui d'un double intime
à qui l'on pourrait se confier
sans risque de se trahir
ou d'être trahi
quelques futilités
pour se distinguer de la masse
comme de rire
de ce qui n'est apparemment pas risible
de pleurer quand l'ambiance est à la fête

À supposer
une vie
que l'on créerait
librement
de A à Z

À supposer
la femme et l'homme
guéris de la peur
de la soumission
n'ayant rien à acheter
rien à vendre
soulagés de la possession
Toujours amoureux
toujours mortels

that harm no one
such as a personal double
to confide in
without risk of betraying yourself
or being betrayed
and a few idiosyncrasies
to mark yourself off from the herd
like laughing
at what does not seem funny
or shedding tears at festive moments

Picture
a life
that we could freely construct
from A to Z

Picture
women and men
cured of the fear
of submission
having nothing to sell
nothing to buy
relieved of possession
Still in love
still mortal

À supposer une vie
sans salles d'attente
après laquelle
il n'y a ni regrets
ni remords
Un conte que l'on se transmet
depuis les commencements
et que chacun meuble
interprète
à sa façon

À supposer
un épisode inédit
de la Genèse
qui verrait surgir
un nouveau continent
où de plus chanceux que nous
connaîtraient enfin
la saison manquante

L'utopie
serait dans son élément
Du rêve à la réalité
il y aurait des délais raisonnables
et à coup sûr
des passerelles

Picture a life
without waiting rooms
a life followed by no regrets
no remorse
A tale handed down
from the beginning
that each of us designs
and interprets
after their own fashion

Picture
an unknown episode of Genesis
describing a new continent
where luckier people than us
would at last experience
the missing season

Utopia
would be in its element
From dream to reality
There would be reasonable delays
and undoubtedly
short cuts

Vivre
ne serait pas de trop
L'on ne dormirait que de l'œil
extérieur au cœur
et l'on ne se sustenterait
que de l'imagination
pure et impure
sans entrée ni accompagnement

L'on rêverait toujours
mais en plus grand
comme d'habiter l'univers entier
sans besoin de s'y transporter
comme de négocier un traité de paix
équitable
avec les éléments déchaînés
de la nature
comme d'introduire
le principe d'amour
dans le préambule
de la Constitution universelle

L'on supprimerait
le nombre adéquat
des souffrances incompréhensibles

Living
would not be futile
We would no longer sleep
by closing eyes
separated from the heart
or get nourishment
save from imagination
pure and impure
without appetizer or accompaniment

We would still dream
but dream bigger
likewise inhabit the whole universe
with no need to travel
likewise negotiate a fair peace treaty
with the unchained
forces of nature
and likewise introduce
the principle of love
into the Preamble
to a Universal Constitution

We would eliminate
the minimum quota
of incomprehensible punishments

pour ne garder que celles
qui alimentent la vigilance
le questionnement
la quête de probables
et d'improbables lumières

L'on prendrait soin
comme de la prunelle de nos yeux
de chaque goutte d'eau
chaque grain de sable
chaque particule de l'air
et encore plus près de nous
du fragile
du balbutiant
de l'éphémère
de ce qui
au fond de l'être
persisterait de la solitude
et de la peur

La mort déchirante
dégradante
ferait place

and keep only those that
increase security
and aid inquiry
and the quest
for probable
and improbable enlightenment

We would lavish care
as on the apple of our eye
on every drop of water
every grain of sand
every molecule of air
and, even closer to us
on all the frail
hesitant
fleeting
remnants in the depths of being
of solitude
and fear

Death
harrowing
degrading
would be replaced

à une disparition discrète
propre
dont tout un chacun
comprendrait les raisons
saluerait l'élégance

À supposer l'inatteignable
à notre portée
et l'instinct puissant
le trait de génie
qui nous feraient tendre la main
non pour le caresser
comme en rêve
mais pour l'empoigner
résolument

À supposer
de notre aventure
l'incroyable
qui repartirait
de plus belle

by a discreet
clean departure
whose reason would be understood
and elegance hailed
by any and everyone

Picture the unattainable
within our reach
and the powerful instinct
the streak of genius
that would make us extend our hand
not to caress it
as in a dream
but to seize it
resolutely

Picture
our adventure
incredibly
resuming
with renewed vigor

AMOUR-JACARANDA

Je me sens maladroit
à parler des femmes
a fortiori de La femme
Je ne peux parler
que d'une femme
Elle seule
– je veux dire toi –
sait
ce qui du féminin m'éblouit
me traverse
me transforme au jour le jour
m'est tantôt plus qu'intime
tantôt insondable
m'incite à écrire
me dresse contre l'oppression
et me rapproche
de l'humanité de mes rêves
Toi seule sais
ce qui nous anime
ce qui nous unit
dans cette bataille sans fin
contre nous-mêmes
hommes et femmes

* * *

JACARANDA MY LOVE

I feel awkward
speaking of women
and especially of Woman
I can speak only
of one woman
She alone
– I mean you –
knows
what dazzles me in the feminine
what runs through me
what transforms me day by day
sometimes beyond intimacy
sometimes incomprehensible
what drives me to write
what makes me rise up against oppression
and takes me closer
to the humanity of my dreams
You alone know
what brings us to life
what joins us together
in this endless battle
against ourselves
men and women

* * *

Tous les jacarandas du pays
en quelque sorte, nous appartiennent
parce que nous sommes
parmi les rares
à les nommer sans hésiter
en nous délectant de la musique
de leur nom
à caresser du regard
leur coiffe en bataille
leurs bras déjetés
leurs jambes malingres
à nous inquiéter de savoir
s'ils vont ou non passer
la mauvaise saison
à guetter
leur incroyable floraison
à éviter de fouler le tapis
mauve tendre
qu'ils s'empressent d'étendre
sous les pieds des passants
et
où que l'on aille
villes ou campagne
à les chercher parmi la foule désordonnée
des arbres

All the jacarandas in the country
belong, in a sense, to us
for we are among the few
to name them without hesitation
delighting in the music of
that name
to run a caressing gaze
over their wild headdress
their lopsided arms
their puny legs
to worry whether they will make it
through the bad season
to watch out
for their incredible flowering
to avoid treading
on the soft mauve carpet
that they are eager to lay
beneath the feet of passersby
and
wherever we may go
in town or country
to seek them amid the jumbled host
of trees

où ils se sentiraient étouffés
perdus
Les jacarandas savent-ils
que notre amour à nous deux
procède
des mêmes attentions ?

Je t'appartiens
Tu m'appartiens, en quelque sorte
comme dans ce poème

* * *

where they must feel smothered
lost
Do the jacarandas know
that this love of yours and mine
is nurtured
by the same attentions?

I belong to you
You belong to me, in a way
just as in this poem

* * *

Bientôt
un demi-siècle
depuis le sacre païen
rocambolesque
de notre union
Chaque fois que j'y pense
j'en suis de nouveau stupéfait
mais pas autant que ceux auxquels
il nous arrive incidemment de révéler
ce qui est loin d'être un secret
Les bras leur en tombent
Ils hésitent entre l'incrédulité
et une admiration un peu forcée
Ils peinent à cacher
la pointe de jalousie
voire un soupçon d'hostilité
comme s'ils cherchaient
dans cette union d'extraterrestres
la faille
le maillon faible
le vice caché
ce qui s'apparenterait
à l'inhumain

Soon
half a century
since the fantastical
pagan sacrament
of our union
Every time I think of it
I am dumbfounded all over again
but not so much as those to whom
we happen to reveal
what is far from a secret
Words fail them
they flounder between incredulity
and a slightly forced admiration
They find it hard to hide
a twinge of jealously
even a trace of hostility
as though they were searching
in this union of extraterrestrials
the flaw
the weak link
the hidden vice
something bordering
on the non-human

Bientôt
un demi-siècle
et pour me paraphraser
je dirai
que nous sommes
à peine nés
à l'amour

* * *

Soon
half a century
and to paraphrase myself
I will say
that we are
scarcely born into the world
of love

* * *

Ton rire
franc
mais plus franc
que ce que la belle expression
laisse entrevoir
C'est toute une composition
une cantate
avec les récitatifs des lèvres
le chœur à l'unisson des dents
l'air entraînant
qui secoue la partition du visage
fait vibrer la poitrine
renverser la tête
et fermer à moitié les yeux
pour que des escarbilles de malice
y crépitent allégrement
Ton rire
ma bouée de sauvetage
l'hymne de ma joie
ma juste rétribution
quand je me mets en frais
d'intelligence

* * *

Your open laugh
more open even
than those fine words
suggest
is a whole composition
a cantata
with the recitatives of your lips
the choir in unison of your teeth
the catchy air
that shakes up the score of your face
makes your bosom tremble
your head fall back
and your eyes half-close
to let dancing sparks of malice
crackle within
Your laugh
my lifebelt
the hymn of my joy
my just reward
when I bend over backwards
to be witty

* * *

Saisissant au mot l'adage marocain :
« Mange selon tes envies
et habille-toi selon l'envie des autres »
je prends plaisir à choisir tes habits
sachant que ce faire confine, pour toi
à la corvée
Tu rechignes à me suivre dans les magasins
où j'ai repéré d'avance
l'ensemble que je trouve à mon goût
le nouveau manteau qui te siérait
encore mieux que le précédent
la couleur du chemisier
qui n'agresserait pas
le teint frais de ta peau
la paire de chaussures
qui tiendrait bien
tes chevilles si fragiles
Parfois
je me trouve être le seul homme
dans les rayons pour femmes
celui de la lingerie fine y compris
un peu penaud
un peu bravache
peut-être un peu voyeur
aux yeux des vendeuses

Taking literally the Moroccan adage:
"Eat according to your wishes
and dress according to the wishes of others"
I love choosing your clothes
fully aware that for you choosing them
is almost like forced labor
You balk at following me into the shops
where I already picked out
an ensemble to my taste
a new coat that will suit you
even better than the last one
a blouse whose color
will not be at odds
with your fresh complexion
a pair of shoes
well able to support
your delicate ankles
Now and again
I find I am the only man
in women's apparel
even in fancy lingerie
a little shamefaced
a little rakish
perhaps something of a voyeur
in the eyes of the saleswomen

mais je n'en ai cure
je pense uniquement à toi
à ta joie proprement enfantine
quand tu essaies un nouvel habit
te soumets avec inquiétude
au jugement du miroir
et trouves malgré tout
qu'il se prononce en ta faveur

* * *

but there is nothing for it
I think only of you
of your truly childish delight
when you try on a new garment
anxiously submit it
to the mirror's judgment
and nevertheless
receive a favorable verdict

* * *

J'apprends, c'est tout frais, que le jacaranda est né au Paraguay, entre les mains savantes des Indiens guarani, peuple de mon ami musicien Raul Barboza, celui qui sait faire parler l'accordéon dans la langue première du père Cosmos et de la mère Terre. Celui qui a su, un soir à Hérouville-Saint-Clair, traduire en *saudade* classique et déchirante mon « Spleen de Casablanca ». Notre arbre a essaimé en Argentine, a traversé l'océan pour prendre ses aises en Afrique du Sud, puis s'est envolé vers la Chine. Plus près de nous, il a trouvé une autre terre d'élection au Portugal. On descend un peu, et où le retrouve-t-on comme dans son élément naturel ? À Fès mon amie, oui à Fès qui lui prête ses murailles pour s'y accouder et rêver tout son saoul. Enfin Rabat, de l'allée des Facultés au quartier du Souissi, où il détrône sans peine le banal palmier.

Est-ce un hasard s'il est venu frapper à la porte de ma ville natale, puis de ma ville d'adoption ? Ne cherchait-il pas, à travers le vaste monde, parmi les humains, quelque confident, un être pouvant se sentir arbre, rire et pleurer arbre, donner ce que donne l'arbre en ne demandant en retour qu'un peu d'eau, de lumière, de temps en temps une caresse ?

Je m'aventure, là, et reconnais mes penchants à l'excès…

I have learnt, only very recently, that the jacaranda was born in Paraguay at the skillful hands of the Guarani Indians, the people of my musician friend Raul Barboza, he who can make the accordion speak the original language of Father Cosmos and Mother Earth. Who was able, one night in Hérouville-Saint-Clair, to translate my "Casablanca Spleen" into a classic, searing *saudade*. Our tree swarmed into Argentina, crossed the ocean to takes its ease in South Africa, then flew over to China. Nearer home, it found another choice residence in Portugal. And, just a little further down, where else do we find it as if in its element? In my beloved Fez – yes, in Fez, which lends it its walls to lean against and dream to its heart's content. And, finally, in Rabat, from Allée des Facultés to the neighborhood of Souissi, where it easily dethrones the banal palm tree.

Can it be sheer chance that the jacaranda knocked at the door of my native city, then at that of my adopted one? Was it not in search, somewhere in the wide world, among humans, of a confidant, a being able to experience himself as a tree, to laugh and weep tree, to give what a tree gives while asking for nothing in return save a little water, a little light, and from time to time a caress?

That is a stretch, however, and I admit I am prone to exaggeration. . .

Mais, sans telle aventure et tels excès, comment aurais-je pu répondre à ton appel, te parler en confiance, d'égal à égal, ô jacaranda!, bel errant, mon frère ?

* * *

On the other hand, without that stretch, without such exaggeration, how would I ever have been able to respond to your call and speak to you in confidence on an equal footing, oh jacaranda, my fine nomad, my brother?

* * *

L'époque nous fut rude
Espoirs insensés
aussitôt fracassés
Un long tunnel
et au bout
un labyrinthe à ciel ouvert :
le maître exil
Telles deux tourterelles
séparées par la tempête
nous avons continué à chanter
inlassablement
et avec le retour de l'éclaircie
nous avons reconstruit
avec mille attentions
notre nid
Nous avons tenu bon
car l'espoir
aussi insensé soit-il
ne nous a jamais quittés
Et voilà qu'aujourd'hui
nous en sommes presque à bénir
l'époque qui nous fut si rude
D'elle
nous avons tout appris
sur notre réelle identité

The time was rough for us
Wild hopes
instantly dashed
A long tunnel
and at the end
an open-air labyrinth:
the mother of exiles
Like two turtle-doves
separated by the storm
we went on singing
tirelessly
and when the clouds cleared
we rebuilt our nest
with inordinate care
We held firm
for hope
no matter how wild
never left us
And here we are today
close to blessing
the time that was so rough for us
From it
we learnt everything
about our real identity

le pourquoi
pour qui
de nos rêves
le sens de l'aventure humaine
son épopée tragique
et l'incroyable de ses réalisations
Bénie soit-elle
de nous avoir fait une petite place
pour en témoigner
et mordre
remordre insolemment
à la vie

the what for
and who for
of our dreams
the meaning of the human adventure
its tragic saga
and incredible achievements
Bless that time
for having given us a little space
to bear witness to it
and bite
and impudently bite again
into life

CHANSON

De la chanson
qui sera nôtre
et peut-être nous survivra
je n'ai dans la tête
ô paradoxe
qu'une ritournelle
un air obsédant !

À quoi me sert d'être poète
un peu magicien
selon la rumeur
dompteur de mots
si je n'arrive pas
à inventer, de cette chanson
les paroles ?

J'ai beau écrire
dans ma tête
puis sur la feuille
sur la page du ciel
et des vagues
sur l'argile
et les arbres

SONG

Of the song
that will be ours
and perhaps outlive us
there is nothing in my head
oh paradox!
but a jingle
a nagging tune

What good is it my being a poet
something of a magician
so it is said
a tamer of words
if I cannot manage
to find words for that song?

What use my writing
in my head
then on paper
on the page of the sky
or the waves
about the soil
and the trees

J'ai beau écrire
sur ma poitrine
et mes ongles
sur la rosée
et le vent
sur la joue de l'enfant
et la bouche de la femme

J'ai beau écrire
sur la robe de la nuit
et les gradins de l'aube
sur la planche invisible
du destin
et le fil tendu
de la mémoire

J'ai beau écrire
dans le ventre de la baleine
sur les arcs-en-ciel
et les étoiles filantes
sur les oiseaux d'acier
les bottes et les armes
qui pleuvent

What use my writing
about my chest
and my nails
about the dew
and the wind
about the cheek of a child
or the mouth of a woman

What use my writing
about the cloak of the night
and the phases of dawn
about the invisible slate
of destiny
and the taut thread
of memory

What use my writing
in the belly of the whale
about rainbows
and shooting stars
about the deluge
of birds of steel
and boots and arms

J'ai beau écrire
sur les miroirs de l'âme
et la flamme des bougies
sur les roses en fin de vie
et l'empreinte des pas
sur l'œil à demi fermé des volcans
et le calme précédant la tempête

J'ai beau écrire
sur la galette
et la peau des olives
entre les mains des déshérités
des oubliés de la vie
sur les injustices courantes
et l'increvable espoir

J'ai beau écrire
sur telles amours
et les nôtres
sur les cœurs qui battent à se rompre
et les yeux qui chavirent
dès que les doigts se touchent
sur la vraie vie qui fait toc toc
à la fenêtre

What use my writing
about the mirrors of the soul
and candle flames
about roses about to die
and footprints
about the half-closed eye of volcanoes
and the calm before the storm

What use my writing
about galettes
and olive skins
in the hands of the disinherited
those left behind by life
about everyday injustices
and hope indestructible

What use my writing
about some love or other
and our own
about hearts beating fit to break
and eyes melting
the instant fingers touch
about real life knock-knocking
at the window

J'ai beau écrire
sur le lit déserté
et les draps tendus de la séparation
sur le tableau peint en noir
et le vase brisé
sur les habits et les livres
abandonnés à la poussière

J'ai beau écrire
sur la grande Histoire
sur le temps et l'infini
sur la fuite des galaxies
le Trou noir
et même sur Dieu
et son compère le Diable

J'ai beau écrire et récrire
ma petite histoire
mais de la chanson qui sera nôtre
et peut-être nous survivra
je n'ai toujours dans la tête
ô paradoxe, qu'une ritournelle
un air obsédant !

What use my writing
about the arid bed
and taut sheets of separation
about the painting all black
and the broken vase
about clothes and books
covered in dust

What use my writing
about grand History
about time and the infinite
about fleeing galaxies
Black Holes
even about God
and his pal the Devil

What use my writing and rewriting
my own little story
when of the song
that will be ours
and perhaps outlive us
there is still nothing in my head
oh paradox!
but a jingle
a nagging tune!

À quoi me sert, bon sang
d'être poète
un peu magicien
selon la rumeur, dompteur de mots
si je n'arrive pas
à inventer, de cette chanson
les paroles ?

What good is it, damn it
my being a poet
something of a magician,
so it is said
a tamer of words
if I cannot manage
to find words for that song?

WRITING AND THE NEW WORLD DISORDER

(1995)

WRITING AND THE NEW WORLD DISORDER

Sometimes a writer, weary of the "interrogations" – be they well or ill intended – to which he is used to submitting, feels the need to frame his own questions, to interrogate himself about what seem to him the reasons or lack thereof for his writing, for his life.

This compulsion does not reflect some narcissistic urge to mislead future commentators, bloodhounds of literary history eager to create lifelike portraits or death masks. It arises instead from simple anger at incomprehension, misinterpretations, reductive readings, or sheer calumny.

Those writers who are most talked about, whose works are most thoroughly dissected, are not necessarily – far from it – the most over-joyed. The most exigent among them fear no examinations as much as those by people who take a mischievous pleasure in describing them as more intelligent and profound than they really are – or for that matter crazier or unhappier.

Of course others bask in the waves of incense released in celebration of their works and take toadying for appropriate and well-merited homage.

Literary cliques flourish like any other mutual admiration society where cronyism rules. Countless literary careers, ephemeral or not, must have been built on such shared deception. The phenomenon has nothing new about it. Why burden our times with every sin? Even if

the commercialization of culture in general – and hence of literature in particular – has now reached a critical point, it is hardly difficult to discern this kind of thing at every period of history when intellectuals were more concerned with their career than with their function, with their fame than with their freedom – at all periods when certainty was so important that it silenced all their questions and anxieties.

But it is not my intention here to talk of others, whether positively or negatively. Nor to strut the stage of formidable "theory." I can speak only from my personal experience, and even there I realize that I am going out on a limb, taking risks, for it involves the quest for a particular truth, one that concerns me first and foremost, and I have always thought that lying to yourself is the worst abomination.

Now that I come to think back on my journey, I realize that I am one of those writers who is obsessed with balance sheets. Balance sheets of themselves, of their writing, of the world. Consequently I have subjected myself regularly to a sort of self-examination, an examination, as it were, of literary health.

Allow me to recall a few of them. One I undertook some ten years ago now in *La Brûlure des interrogations* (The Burn of Questions). Another, in a different mode, from five years later, is to be found in my novel *Les Rides du lion* (The Lion's Wrinkles). A more recent balance sheet was drawn up in 1993 in my collection of poems entitled *L'Étreinte du monde* (The World's Embrace), notably in the long introductory work "Les Écroulements" ("Collapses").

At each of those moments I sought to grasp the whys and where-fores of the development that made me a writer. I sought to grasp how this status allows me or not to stand on my own two feet, to have the strength to keep my eyes open, my hands open, and not to renounce the essence of the values thanks to which I am able to defend the human, care for the injured words dragged through the mud by triumphant lies, go in search of meaning when it vanishes, and, not least, refuse servitude, the stupidity of consensus, and the buying and selling of conscience.

And here I am today feeling disoriented once again, as though all those questions and the answers that I thought I had attempted to provide were already far away, very far away, as though my thirst for interrogation were still unslaked. All it has taken is a few years for new dangers to arise and for a gale of horror and irrationality to blast against the fruit of the tree of knowledge and hope, along with its deepest and most well-protected roots. So here I stand with my few remaining forces murmuring my litany of questions. Why this void in my head once again, this feeling of being on the edge of a glacial desert that must be crossed, this chill in the heart that the supposedly warm sun of my rediscovered country fails to dispel? Why this shadow falling over and obscuring my page, formerly so prodigal with enlightenment and visionary trances? Why am I afraid, I who have always devoted myself to creating courage from any material, even the modeling clay of despair? What has changed in me, around me, to make me stammer

instead of taking words by the horns, or by the mane, and hurling them against injustice and the tenacious reign of barbarism? What has managed to so waylay my writing that I should put my entire experience in parentheses and, in forward or backward flight, choose to abandon it in enemy territory alien both to it and to me, in the tunnel of a purgatory that owes nothing to myth, and where it will be obliged to labor at a second self-birth, to reinvent good and evil, heaven and hell, human and inhuman, and where it must reconquer love – sole, unique love – amid the ruins of a continent laid waste by hatred, money, and power? And what is the origin, in the end, of this intransigence between it – writing – and me, as though we were two wrestlers simultaneously torn apart and bonded together by an implacable love and readying ourselves for a decisive combat – not in order to win or lose but rather to reassure each other that the opponent still exists, complete with their belligerence and fire, their measureless memory, their taste for all that glistens and flames in the eyes, for everything unforeseen written in the lines of the palm, for whatever is murmured between earth and heaven, between the mud and the water, between the bird and the rainbow, for whatever travels from rock to rock and is whispered between trees pretending to be motionless?

I am afraid, as I say, but afraid neither of death, now as familiar to me as this pen stuck to my fingers, nor of the retired torturer whom I have absolved in a rush of compassion, but rather of this state between life and non-life where my protagonist – writing – might slip away and cast doubt on the hour and day of our usual appointment. Though a

very punctual person, even prone to arrive early so as to enjoy waiting, I fear absences and abhor farewells.

So what is this other balance sheet that I am now trying to construct: a crown of thorns where words, my dear accomplices, find it hard to help me glimpse a slim window of clarity?

Can a writer say "I am in pain" or "I no longer know where I am up to?" without seeming ridiculous, without falling into the now cardinal sin of self-pity? No. He must manage to put it some other way, under the cover of the poem or the mask of narrative, and it is best for those who speak in this way to use the third person, not the first. A little decency is called for, surely – a little distance, for goodness sake, to leave the reader to his own emotions!

The thing is, however, that I have decided to ask myself the questions, and I have no wish to convince or convert with intelligent answers. I want to understand in order to assist the one who, within me, still believes that writing has some use, if indeed writing is still even possible.

For me, today just as yesterday, writing cannot be taken for granted. Not that, in order to exist, it must be legitimated. After all, literature is not some privileged realm of virtue. It is a domain much like others, where human contradictions and passions have full rein, with their cavalcade of interests and their stakes: power and seduction, love and hate, jealousy and complicity, generosity and iniquity, truth and error, will to power and magnificent self-dedication. In this vast theater of human consciousness, the writer is not the solid rock that we suppose,

not the ever-wakeful vigil, or the perpetually fertile creator. He is also a being just like you and me whose frail body the winds of History may pick up at any moment and hurl onto the reefs of aphasia and failure.

Let me explain why I want to ask myself about this obsession of mine with taking stock. Does it come from a systematic doubt as to my own literary abilities? Or from a collapse of my belief in the primacy of literature over other ways of apprehending human reality? Am I sometimes assailed by the feeling of being a traitor if I am content to write and merely attempt to interpret the world while leaving to others the task of changing it? Or again, does my concern stem from the equally strange feeling that leads me from time to time to revolt against writing's dictatorship when engaging in it is to the detriment of my other desires, in the first place the desire to live, simply to live, but to do so to the full without having to give an account of myself to the vampiric page and to those lovable cannibals who read it in order to judge my strength, lucidity, or shortcomings? It is hardly a secret that on occasion I have decided to go on writer's strike and have experienced thereby delectable moments of respite. I suppose that other writers must have had the same experience, that at one time or another they have embraced what the Princesse de Clèves murmured when she at last withdrew from the world and relinquished her passions: "It suffices to be."

We might think of Rimbaud here too. Was not his flight to Abyssinia a response to the same logic, the same fright precipitated by

poetry's demoniac character? It could be pointed out that such rever-
sals of attitude are unexceptional. They occur throughout the history
of literature and the turbulent lives of writers. I concur, but with one
reservation: while the problems of literature are recurrent and universal,
their features and their acuteness differ according to the location –
more social and cultural than geographical – where they arise. In the
Western world, especially since the Enlightenment, the act of writing is
a natural one. Writers have acquired a function and a position implying
that the exercise of their craft as they understand it is part of the fabric
of society's needs. Books and the other vectors of cultural expression
are acknowledged as values in themselves. The evolution of society is
no longer conceivable without them, so writers no longer need question
the worth of their activity and the standing of their role. At moments of
great social and political tension, of course, notably during the tragedies
of the recent great wars, some writers formed doubts as to the meaning
and usefulness of their means of expression. Others, eager to combat
the horror and inhumanity, did not hesitate to overestimate their task
and its prerogatives. But such times of fluctuation or deviation are
after all circumscribed and do not significantly alter the character of
the writerly function.

For a writer of the South or of the periphery the situation is quite
different. Writing there cannot be taken for granted. Often it takes on
a transgressive character. It amounts to a violation of the law of silence
imposed by the tyrannies in power and by the social consensus, be it

moral, religious, or patriotic in nature. What is more, writing is not a normal activity in societies still dominated by oral traditions and prey to illiteracy.

The marginality of writers in that context is thus first objective and then subjective. The writer's function is ill defined and inevitably becomes the object of a struggle governed by an unequal balance of forces. A large portion of the population still does not perceive books as a necessity, much less a source of intellectual and spiritual benefit. The status of writers in such societies is thus hypothetical.

And nor does writing have the same meaning. To its customary tribulations are added others which threaten its very foundations, not to mention, of course, the question of its intelligibility and real impact. And the cruelest cut of all is perhaps the one that affects the very heart of literary practice – assuming we wish to conceive of that as the most uncompromising possible practice of freedom.

When writers of the South reject exile – or do not have the luxury of that option – and must therefore write from the periphery, they know, unless they are deceiving themselves, that they will have in one way or another to give up on the aspiration to absolute freedom or will be obliged to cloak it in literary artifice. That is why the day of accusers, of literary illuminati, conscientious objectors, flamboyant rebels, and nonconformist suicides seems to be over in our societies, or at least adjourned *sine die*. That is why our martyrs are more and more often martyrs of political conflict rather than martyrs of the

struggle of ideas and subversive action. The killings that occur from time to time make that abundantly clear. Tahar Djaout, for instance, was assassinated as a political adversary, not for the audaciousness of his work, which his killers had in any case never read. The young man who stabbed Naguib Mahfouz in the back of the neck believed he was eliminating an unbeliever, an enemy of God. In other circumstances, he might have been in a crowd of the writer's admirers asking for his autograph.

Thus the question of the responsibility of intellectuals, which has been debated for decades, must for us be posed otherwise than in terms of such ideas as commitment or the organic intellectual. Formerly, responsibility meant the moral and physical enlistment in those struggles defined as decisive against oppression, exploitation, and injustice. Intellectuals belonged in the camp of the disadvantaged and abused and their aspirations were based on an identification with that camp. The barbarism they indicted could only be that of the dominant ideology, that of the crimes and turpitude of the ruling classes, the greedy and servile executives of imperialism.

My word, how simple things were then, how clear the tasks, how fine the hopes and vast the dreams! What spurred intellectuals forward even more vigorously in those days was their sense that in espousing the cause they could guide the fight in the direction of their own demands. Their goals were not just political. They wanted to see the old world collapse. Their freedom of speech was not as limited as one might

suppose. They were not afraid to attack taboos or engage in near-heretical actions, for their reputation as fighters for justice lent them credibility. The veneration that surrounded them on occasion even let them attribute a cosmic, even messianic meaning to their political tasks. Such strayings were sometimes denounced by the watchdogs of ideological orthodoxy, sometimes viewed with indulgence and put down to the caprices and fantasies of intellectuals and poets – deemed in any case hopelessly bizarre.

What has now become of this "responsibility"? I believe that it has moved from outside to inside. The poet – epitome of the intellectual – has been chased from the city and now follows a wandering path apart from the caravan. The intellectuals' ties to their fraternal tribe – their people – have been attenuated. They observe with great alarm that the masses who were supposed to storm the heavens and bring about the rebirth of the world and of mankind have submitted here and there to the song of bearded sirens promising them expedited justice and paradises more conventional and more certain. The sphere of ideas has shrunk dramatically, giving way to a new trade, that of ready-to-wear notions. When a community wrestles with problems of survival, it focuses on its immediate needs, especially those related to the alimentary canal, and becomes deaf to the nuances of speeches and blind to projected visions.

This shrinkage and suspension of thought results almost mechanically in the rejection of rational debate, of what is contemptuously

dismissed as mere rumination. It quite naturally gives rise to intolerance, moral conformism, and the refusal of pluralism and difference. It is open season on heresies, and all weapons are authorized.

In this way, but almost imperceptibly (what hyper-gifted observer could have foreseen present developments?), the intellectuals find themselves trapped. Should they not give up their attachment to solidarity and justice, their drama turns into tragedy. They discover that their marginality does not have the form it had in more normal times, when it enabled them to do honor to their function and preserve their critical spirit and independence of thought. It is now different in nature and clearly reflects an internal exile. The point is no longer for them to fight for their role to be recognized as of social utility: more brutally, it is for them to determine whether or not they still have any place in their own society.

The place I mean is less physical than ethical. Intellectuals can find a comfortable place so long as their thinking conforms to the order of the day and respects the newly defined boundaries that must not be crossed. In the event, however, that they refuse to abandon the entirety of their ideas, to submit to the consensus judged reasonable for social equilibrium, they will find themselves in an unprecedented situation, one where they are an actual part of a minority deprived of its basic rights. And this is particularly paradoxical at a time when recognition of the rights of all minorities – ethnic, cultural, religious and so on – are just beginning, despite everything, to be acknowledged. We are thus

confronted, in this particular case, by the only minority unable to exercise its rights and freely express its opinions when these run counter to the conventional wisdom and the established balance of forces.

What is new in this situation is the fact that the asphyxiation of freedom does not derive solely, as in the past, from the tyrannies in place. If these have had to relax their grip in some measure, there is no denying that the baton has been passed to fringe social elements and to movements within society that have appointed themselves guardians of morals and beliefs and have reconfigured the codes of behavior governing every aspect of life according to their own lights.

The anxiety I evoked above thus transcends the individual and takes on a historical dimension. It overtook me, as I now know for sure, with the Gulf War of 1990-1991. It was at that moment that I realized (and immediately voiced my conviction in several texts) that the conflict inaugurated less a new world order than a new world disorder. I forcast as one consequence of this upheaval, among others, a catastrophe that would truly set the human, social, economic and cultural continents adrift. The Gulf War put an end to faith, developed over the centuries, and especially since the Renaissance and the Enlightenment, in the unity of the human spirit and the human condition. It likewise put an end to the belief that this planet was a boat upon which we were all embarked, a boat that was the scene of an unfolding shared human adventure. All of a sudden, that war exposed an enormous rift between two humanities, two planets.

In consequence, all thinking about progress, or about simple historical delay, or about unequal exchange became instantly almost laughable. History had instituted an objective form of apartheid between the North and the South, backed up by law and police measures.

In saying this it is not my intention to incriminate the West alone, nor to designate it as solely responsible for this rupture and for the unleashing of political, social, and cultural crisis in the countries of the South. I believe that we shall need nothing less than a new understanding of universal history if we are to retrieve the thread of human evolution and grasp the exact dimensions of the present situation.

Pointing the finger is a simplistic approach, notably where one of two antagonists washes their hands of all blame. I have always said, apropos of the Arab world, that there will be no relief so long as that world remains pathologically obsessed with the West, so long as it continues to stew in its sense of victimhood, so long as it fails to rid itself of the notion of a permanent conspiracy that undermines all its attempts at liberation and growth. For I believe that the liberating consciousness is in the first place a consciousness that attacks the internal causes of moral and intellectual poverty and paralysis. Critical thought has neither legitimacy nor relevance save inasmuch as it is global and inasmuch as it proceeds from within to without. While the critique of the other is a right, that right is far better founded when it starts from a critique of the self.

My uncompromising attitude on this point must not of course be taken as indulgence with regard to the West. I have had occasion there too to condemn the moral and intellectual poverty of a certain part of the West whose basic error, as I see it, is to have renounced the main principles of its contribution to the adventure of human thought: the indivisibility of the law, the universality of justice, an equal concern for all human conditions. The same portion of the West has also suffered a narrowing of thought thanks to which it has lost sight of the fundamental stake of all thought, namely the apprehension of the human condition and the world as a unity.

The apocalyptic picture I paint here is one I have been contemplating continually for years. But the dread it fills me with goes beyond the individual. When all is said and done, I have still had the strength to paint it without losing my reason, notably the reason that attaches me to writing, and hence to the perpetual quest for meaning and light. Despair sometimes reveals unsuspected energies. Even though the life instinct may be shaken on the individual level, there is another plane that reminds us that any particular life is part, after all, of life per se, the life of all others, and in view of that life we cannot lay down our arms, for it is the only sacred thing we can still believe in. Sacred, because it is outside good and evil. Because at some time it revealed the caress to us, and the language of love, and the transfiguration of being, and awe. At which one can only say: these things are too precious; they are gifts from humanity to itself that should be common property, a right owed us because we have been placed here without having been consulted.

So here the soft music of hope begins to make itself heard, creeping out as though from beneath the ruins of the devastated landscape.

I look about me, in one of those countries of the South drifting in the deviant current, and ask myself these new questions, so much more pressing than those I could ask in my earlier stocktakings. So how do I answer? By yourself you cannot change the world, alter the course of the drift, and indeed no one asks that of you. This is the way things are. But you can do more than bear witness, more than keep open that eye of the heart which cannot deceive you. The world is collapsing, yes, but it is not the first time, and it will not be the last. Others before have seen this and not remained silent. Their voices were raised to call for help, which eventually arrived, even if the wait lasted a century and several generations. Make sure, therefore, that you too raise your voice so that it may relay that of your predecessors and so that one day in the future other voices denouncing horror and the slumber of consciousness will rejoin yours in order to perpetuate the humble message.

Your writing is your only asset, the one that you have never sold and that no one has ever been able to buy. And do not imagine that you are its owner. This asset is yours only so long as you share it every day, every night, and especially when you are crossing perilous territory. Remember the actions familiar to you from your traditional milieu in the city of Fez. When there was a death to mourn in your family, or simply a difficult time, your father would prepare a great quantity of loaves that he would then distribute to the poor in every corner of the town.

Does not your writing resemble that simple and unostentatious gesture?

So write, for as long as you have the strength. What leaves your fingers will not feed the hungry, nor give back life to a child fooled by a bomb that he took for a toy, nor convert the predators of this world to virtue. Your writing will not repair the planet, nor reduce inequality, nor put a halt to wars or to ethnic, moral, and cultural cleansing. But you can be sure of one thing: it will never be a lie piled on other lies, a spark of hate feeding the firestorm of hate, a sprinkle of intolerance spicing up the chill smorgasbord of intolerance, or a speculator's share placed in the stockmarket of corruption.

If you write, it is to honor the pact made with yourself as soon as you became fully conscious. The greatest failure would be to lose face some day – your *human* face. And in the end, why in the world ask yourself all these questions, why torture yourself with all this accounting? For you writing is a sort of prayer begging life to keep visiting you. So if you write it is because you are still alive. Who could hold that against you?

—Abdellatif Laâbi, 1995

archipelago books
is a not-for-profit literary press devoted to
promoting cross-cultural exchange through innovative
classic and contemporary international literature
www.archipelagobooks.org